BONHOEFFER'S ETHICS

Guy Carter, René van Eyden,
Hans-Dirk van Hoogstraten, Jurjen Wiersma (eds.)

BONHOEFFER'S ETHICS

Old Europe and New Frontiers

Kok Pharos Publishing House
Kampen – The Netherlands

CIP-GEGEVENS KONINKLIJKE BIBLIOTHEEK, DEN HAAG

Bonhoeffer

Bonhoeffer's ethics : old Europe and new frontiers / Guy Chr. Carter ... [et al.] (eds.). —
Kampen : Kok. Papers of the 5th International Bonhoeffer Society Conference, Amsterdam,
1988.
ISBN 90-242-5020-X
SISO 251.8   UDC 17.000.2   NUGI 632
Trefw.: Bonhoeffer. Dietrich / christelijke ethiek.

© 1991 Kok Pharos Publishing House, Kampen, The Netherlands
Cover Design: Henk Blekkenhorst
ISBN Kok: 90 242 5020 X
NUGI 632

In memoriam Gerard Rothuizen
1926-1988

Editorial Note

Guy Carter

The work of the Fifth International Bonhoeffer Society Conference has been a labor of partnership and international collaboration from beginning to end. We of the Bonhoeffer Society are especially pleased that the publishing house Kok Pharos (Kampen, The Netherlands) has undertaken to see the written results of the Amsterdam Conference through to a useful conclusion. Though the Editorial Committee of the Amsterdam Conference accepts final responsibility for the published form of the papers, we wish to acknowledge with gratitude the work of the various contributors themselves and that of the several translators who have worked diligently to produce a readable English text.

An attempt has been made to avoid the use of language which would in any way exclude the reader on the basis of sexuality. The editorial committee regrets the limitations of language and thought which still make this a difficult goal to accomplish.

Material limitations have precluded printing of all papers presented at Amsterdam. Those contributions not printed in full are listed under 'Additional Papers'. Requests for copies of these papers should be addressed directly to the contributors. It is one of the cardinal purposes of the International Bonhoeffer Society to foster contact and exchange among those interested in the enduring contribution of Dietrich Bonhoeffer to theology, church and society.

The activity of the International Bonhoeffer Society as such represents only a small fraction of scholarly work being done in the area of Bonhoeffer studies or work essentially inspired by, or in critical dialogue with Bonhoefferian theology. May this volume serve as a bridge between the smaller and wider circle of those who continue to be guided, perplexed and informed by this twentieth-century witness of Jesus Christ, without whom theology, church and Christian engagement with society and culture today would be unthinkable.

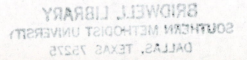

Preface

Jurjen Wiersma

This volume is the outgrowth of the Fifth International Bonhoeffer Society Conference held in The New Church in Amsterdam from 13 to 19 June 1988. The conference was devoted to the theme, 'Bonhoeffer and Europe' and gave an in-depth evaluation of Bonhoeffer's ethics, which the author himself considered the foremost task of his life. The contents of this volume have been arranged in three sections. The first part focuses mainly on Bonhoeffer's ethics in general and on a number of textual problems in particular, problems that have intrigued recent Bonhoeffer scholarship. The second part is comprised of a series of essays that embark upon a heretofore rather neglected facet of the Bonhoeffer legacy, i.e. Europe as a heritage for contemporary and future generations. The third part again endeavors to move the research beyond the impressive results that have been reaped by the International Bonhoeffer Society for Archive and Research during the first two decades of its existence. Here, the contributions included frankly explore new frontiers, picking up the broken thread of an ethics of resistance of which Dietrich Bonhoeffer was unmistakably a great representative. Therefore, one may hope that this book is not only an outgrowth of a particular conference, but that, in honour of Bonhoeffer the German and European theologian, it also becomes an 'ingrowth' of a particular theological way of life that suits the politico-historical exigencies of the actual moment and the time to come, inside and outside Europe.

On Saturday 18 June 1988, when the formal proceedings came to a close, Eberhard Bethge, the *auctor intellectualis* of all Bonhoeffer scholarship, pointed to the necessity for us to understand reality and to see our position in it. In his final analysis of the Amsterdam Conference, Bethge affirmed that in his opinion it had been a wonderful experience to come together as a scientific brotherhood and sisterhood in Amsterdam, 'in this Nineveh.' Commenting in that way, Bethge by implication made the attendants from the various continents mindful of the critical stance the minor prophet Jonah once assumed towards the givens and tokens of the wider society of his day, 'his Nineveh.'

Dietrich Bonhoeffer was not born for failure. Quite the contrary; whereas half a century ago the entire world seemed to be headed for a complete and devastating catastrophe, the young and energetic theologian gave the alarm, making a serious attempt to prevent the world and Europe in particular from being totally shipwrecked. In so doing, he sided with the victims of Nazism, violence and warmongering. He thus became deeply involved with the predicament of the dumb on whose behalf he opened his mouth, taking part in the resistance against the Führer unto his own death. This Bonhoeffer is of exemplary significance to any ethico-theological praxis by means of which people, be they theologians or be they laypersons, seek to face the multifaced challenges of the current world. In this world in the period following World War II we may have recovered ground under our feet, but as far as Bonhoeffer's engagement is concerned we may still have much ground to make up.

Therefore we enjoyed the fortuitous presence of a great number of young men and women in Amsterdam. If there is a Bonhoeffer legacy, there is an inherent need of heirs who may be entrusted with the enormous task not only of preserving its sealed and unsealed treasures but also of further developing the issues, so that a large audience will resort to it, cherishing it as a major tool of spiritual inspiration and social renewal. The Bonhoeffer fire must be kept burning because that renewal itself is at stake.

This volume could not have been completed without the highly appreciated co-operation of the contributors. For this we are greatly indebted to them. We also wish to express our indebtedness to The National New Church Foundation in Amsterdam which provided us with a fine opportunity to further Bonhoeffer scholarship as a communal enterprise.

No formal acknowledgements can adequately convey our gratitude to the large group of private persons and public institutions that accorded us a grant, generously enabling us to accomplish our initiative. By far, we are unable to list all those that granted a subsidy. Here, with the usual exception to the rule, we thank The European Cultural Foundation and The Royal Netherlands Academy of Sciences in Amsterdam. We are grateful besides to the Lutheran Seminary of the University of Amsterdam because of its support of our project. Not only did Prof. Sonny Hof favourably intercede on our behalf, but also the students Beate Jansen van Raay and Sietse van Kammen manifested themselves in *optima forma,* carrying on their shoulders the heavy burden of the practical work of the conference. In this respect, thanks are also due to our Dutch Bonhoeffer Society friends, Irene Meijer, Henk Janssen and René van Eyden; they helped the progress and the administration of our work in many different ways. Very important was the backing we received from Guy Carter, whose scientific coordination turned out to be a great help to us. His solid and substantial assistance was an enormous relief.

Now, after the *'hineni'* moment of all those who gave *acte de présence* during the Fifth International Bonhoeffer Society Conference, the volume is here. Hopefully it will arouse a *'eureka'* experience among all those who are sympathetic to the late Dietrich Bonhoeffer and his concern with a just, peace-filled and united world.

Jurjen Wiersma
Conference Secretary

SPECIAL ACKNOWLEDGEMENT

The International Bonhoeffer Society for Archive and Research wishes to express its sincere thanks to the American composer Tom Johnson (Paris) for his contribution to the Amsterdam Conference. Portions of Mr. Johnson's 'Bonhoeffer Oratorio' were rehearsed and performed by conference participants and Amsterdam musicians under the composer's direction in a public concert in the Evangelical Lutheran Church of Amsterdam on June 18, 1988.

The Society also expresses thanks to the congregation of the Parkkerk at Amsterdam for hosting the closing service of worship on Sunday, 19th June 1988, and to the congregation's minister, the Reverend Coosje Verkerk, for her assistance in planning and conducting this service.

11

Introduction

Hans-Dirk van Hoogstraten

One of the main problems of modern Western Christianity is its ambiguity in many fields. Western history shows Christ and the Antichrist at the same time. Capitalism and colonialism have brought many blessings for privileged people, but also a sea of suffering for others. In Christian tradition, Christ is being handed down *and* betrayed (the two meanings of the Latin *tradere*). The historical shape of Christ in the world is one of triumph *and* of suffering. Power has been legitimated and criticized by church and faith at different times in history and sometimes these two aspects can be observed simultaneously.

Bonhoeffer lived at a time of the latter situation; in Nazi-Germany, theologians, church leaders and other people involved in the church struggle totally disagreed on whether they should support or criticize the dominant ideology and politics. He himself was one of the main originators of the church struggle. From the beginning he did not hesitate to take a radical position. Others, on the contrary, saw fascism as *the* solution for Christian Europe at that time. Fifty years later, Bonhoeffer still has much influence. How is that possible, after such a long time in which the Western world has changed so radically?

Globally speaking, an answer can be given which contains three different aspects. In the first place, the main problems did not change as much as one might superficially think. Latin-American theologians, e.g., consider our capitalistic world-system as an ideology and practice of death, while 'economic theologians' from the U.S. praise the same system as a blessing of God. Secondly, Bonhoeffer testifies to a theoretical and existential wrestling to gain a correct, nonreligious interpretation of Christian faith. This theological transformation has become more urgent than ever. Thirdly, he recognizes secularisation with its complex consequences. All these elements surely *are* recognizable to modern Western humanity.

During the Amsterdam Bonhoeffer Conference, these different aspects were discussed. In this introduction, I will try to list the main topics and to indicate very briefly how the different lecturers dealt with these themes. What I will do is to show how each dealt with one of these aspects and with what has become the continuous thread which runs through the book. The point of departure was Bonhoeffer's *Ethics*, a collection of essays he wrote *before* his famous radical statements in *Letters and Papers from Prison*. *Ethics* shows a period of wrestling with all the contradictions in Christian culture, the dominating values and the atavism of fascist ideology. The book presents us with a brilliant image of the difficulties arising in a time in which traditional values are still alive but either are no longer working in the given situation or are working in the wrong way.

In *Ethics,* Bonhoeffer finds himself in a state of tension which can be approached as a social, cultural, ethical and theological antagonism containing several aspects of one and the same fundamental pattern. In this conference volume, Bonhoeffer's writings as well as their consequences in different situations are considered — against the background of ethical dilemmas in our time and thinking. Old European values play quite a part in these considerations — not in the last instance in relation to, and compared with the unifying activities concerning Europe in the near future.

Allan Boesak is living and working in a dualistic situation which calls for very difficult decisions comparable to the dilemmas with which Bonhoeffer was faced. He testifies to the great significance Bonhoeffer has had for him since the years of his studies in Kampen (Holland). Thus the setting of the conference *and* the book is the life of divided humanity in a divided context. At the same time it is a testimony of the courage to fight and trust in the ultimate victory. However, as the Czechoslovakian theologian *Ján Liguš* points out in his contribution, the ultimate and the penultimate cannot be identified as long as our history continues. The dialectical tension between these two elements provokes ethical consciousness without their separation in a dualistic antagonistic scheme or their identification in a dangerous actualisation of the realm of God in human history in a human institute — be it state or church! In his essay on conscience, *Heinz Eduard Tödt* makes clear that there surely *is* a gap between ethical practice and theory and that this has to do with the new terrible situation for which most Germans were not prepared and for which the old European values were not relevant. Nevertheless, this state of affairs was only a motivation for Bonhoeffer's effort toward some clarity in ethico-theological matters. *Gabriele Phieler,* living and working as a pastor in East Germany, relativises the impact of *Ethics*. She does so by stating that living in evangelical responsibility in the difficult situation of an atheist state is the first 'mandate' one in her context has to fulfill. Ethical reflexion means a second step. This sequence was as important for Bonhoeffer in his situation as it is for people living in a socialist country. In the contributions concerning textual research for the 'New Edition of Ethics', *Clifford Green* informs us of the findings which demand a rearrangement of the chronological sequence of the texts to be presented in the new edition. *Ilse Tödt* explains the difficulties she had in reconstructing the handwritten texts and she refers to the laborious work of systematizing the loose notes in the order of origin. *William Peck* and the other contributors to *New Studies in Bonhoeffer's Ethics* presented their studies on text, context and method of Bonhoeffer's *Ethics* and their views on themes in his ethical theology.

In the second part of the volume, the dualities have been given a wider scope with respect to Europe. *Frits de Lange's* essay on particularity and universality, a fundamental problem of religions from many times and contexts indeed, connects the two poles with Europe and faith. Mediator for this is the humanism of Bonhoeffer's ethics, in which the Christian and the 'Bildungsbürger' (educated bourgeoisie) find their identity. *Hans-Dirk van Hoogstraten* shows how a postulated Christian unity of Europe *('Das Christliche Abendland')* obscures the actual division. The problem is establishing what aspect is dominant in Bonhoeffer's thought about Europe: the past or the future. The division cannot be immediately undone by proclaiming the unity in Christ. Rabbi *Albert Friedlander* writes about Israel and Europe and the love-hate relation between the two. He turns around the wellknown European notion of the sad, wandering Jew. The European citizen becomes the problematic figure, and perhaps the

Jew as his companion in misfortune could be his mirror and his standby! Like Friedlander, *Edwin Robertson* pays attention to Bonhoeffer's univocal choice for the Jews, made from the first hour. Much less clear are Bonhoeffer's remarks on the French Revolution. *Raymond Mengus* shows how German conservatism in European affairs holds Bonhoeffer back from a positive attitude towards the great European revolution. *Ernst Feil* studies in depth the tension between restorative and revolutionary tendencies in Bonhoeffer's ecumenical ethic.

The third part deals with the problem of new frontiers. After having concluded that there really are many antagonisms in the field of (social) ethics and theology, and that old frontiers are passed in different ways, we will need to look for new ones. This concerns ethics as well as, e.g., Europe as Christian Occident and the institutional church within its frontiers. Bonhoeffer himself already makes proposals for the shifting of certain frontiers, but much work remains to be done in our days! *Keith Clements*, who lives and works in the Free (Baptist) Church context, shows the position Bonhoeffer could be given in the Free Church Tradition. *John de Gruchy* applies Bonhoeffer's thoughts on the Free Church to the 'Confessing Church' of South Africa. He clearly points out that freedom of the church cannot be loosened from the liberation of society. Thus church and society must understand that they don't exist as two separated realms which have nothing in common. *Martin Kuske,* from the G.D.R., underlines this unifying statement for the socialist context when he opposes godlessness full of promise to godlessness without hope, following and applying Bonhoeffer's remarks on that antagonism. And then there is the question of Bonhoeffer's view on women. About this fundamental antagonism Bonhoeffer's thought and everyday life *Renate Bethge* writes, being personally involved in the Bonhoeffer family and acquainted with Dietrich himself and his direct context of life. *René van Eyden,* a Dutch (male) scholar in feminist-theological theory, writes more detachedly about Bonhoeffer's understanding of male and female — as far as the available texts bear witness to this. *Jurjen Wiersma* shows the background of Bonhoeffer's longing for a trip to India and the influence of Gandhi on Bonhoeffer's development from pacifist to member of the resistance movement, even though the India plan was never realized. The openness of Bonhoeffer to India and contrarily, breaking through cultural antagonism, is envisaged by the Indian Nestorian bishop *Poulose Mar Poulose. Hiroshi Murakami* did the same concerning Japan. However, the common war experience makes the Japanse a special case. In the Japanese opinion, a confession of guilt is a real problem. The text on this matter, produced by the Japanese Bonhoeffer Society, which did provoke a shock in Japanese society, is quite impressive. The contribution of *Clarke Chapman* about Bonhoeffer and today's Christian peacemakers integrates all these testimonies on Bonhoeffer's great influence as a champion for peace in many differing ways. The book ends with an article by *Eberhard Bethge* which served as a sermon on the last day of the conference. Europe is calling Paul to come and preach the Gospel: the beginning of Europe's historical challenge as the Christian Occident — which turned out to be so ambiguous.

One contribution was painfully missing during the Amsterdam Conference and it is not published in this volume either: *Gerard Rothuizen* on Bonhoeffer and Nietzsche.

During the spring of 1988 Rothuizen fell terribly ill so that he was not able to prepare his challenging paper. A short time after the conference, he died. This may be the place to honour him as a faithful member of the International Bonhoeffer Society. Many of the ideas for the conference were his. This book is dedicated to his memory. May the way his ideas have been worked out in this volume be a dignified sign of our thanks and regard.

The Bonhoeffer task is not yet finished. The impact of ethics in modern times, the problems with respect to the above mentioned antagonism, the past unity of Europe in Christ and the question marks when we consider present and future — all these themes ask for continuation. That is why the next conference will probably deal with Bon-hoeffer's hermeneutics in relation to 'a world come of age.' This sequence too, is a reflection of modern ethical reflection. First, the ethical dilemma in our time, in our part of the world, in our history, must become clear. Then the hermeneutical question can be raised *and* answered. This time we were occupied with the unsealed treasures Bonhoeffer's ethical thinking held in reserve for us, as Jurjen Wiersma puts it in the Preface. This method of studying ethics makes dialectical theology once again quite fruitful. At each particular time and place it renders rigorous critical-ethical commentary upon both wrong social and personal relations and everything depending on them.

Contents

CONTENTS

PART I

BONHOEFFER'S ETHICS

What Dietrich Bonhoeffer Has Meant to Me*

Allan A. Boesak

Mr. Chairman, Ladies and Gentlemen,

Thank you very, very much for this wonderful opportunity to be with you at least at the beginning of this Fifth International Bonhoeffer Conference. I was surprised and deeply honoured by your invitation when Gerard Rothuizen told me that I was going to be asked to speak here and that I should share with the conference what has intrigued him for many years. He has always asked the question of me: 'I always wonder what it is in a white European theologian, so obviously from a very different time and a different background, that has fascinated you to the extent that now, so many years later, you say quite publicly that you have learned much from Dietrich Bonhoeffer.'

I am still not fully able to answer that question myself. I discover new themes every time I attempt to think about this. And so tonight will be what he had asked of me, to give a personal reflection on a topic that I love dearly.

I must begin, however, Mr. Chairman, Ladies and Gentlemen, by expressing to you quite publicly my gratitude to three people through whom I got to know Dietrich Bonhoeffer.

First of all, of course, Eberhard Bethge, who has brought all of this material together and out of which we have learned so much. But, more particularly, Gerard Rothuizen himself, who was my teacher in Kampen for six years and through whom I met Bonhoeffer and learned to respect this theologian of Germany who died far too early, much too soon, and yet has left a legacy not simply for Germany, certainly not only for Western Europe, but for all of us in the world. The other person that I must mention is Paul Lehmann, whom I met for the first time in 1973, when I was visiting Union Seminary in New York.

I remember all of the discussion that we had and still have whenever the two of us can meet, and what a great pleasure to learn from someone who has known Bonhoeffer personally. In 1976, when I was writing my dissertation, or finishing it rather, I wanted a motto to go with the book. The book was about black theology and black power, a black ethic and the search for something that would be unique to us in South Africa in the situation in which we found ourselves then. I looked for something that would say very clearly that we can affirm blackness as a gift of God and that we must use blackness as a gift of God to express ourselves politically as well as theologically. I was looking for something that could express very clearly what we did want and what we did not want. And so I found those words from Dietrich Bonhoeffer about God's 'no' and God's 'yes.' While God's 'no' is a 'no' resounding against injustice, suffering and inhumanity, at the same time he [Bonhoeffer] says we must also hear God's 'yes', because the 'no' does not exclude, but includes God's 'yes' to the affirmation of life, of humanity and of the essential meaning of life. I knew then that that is exactly what we wanted to say.

It was what was needed at that time, I thought. Almost ten years later, I had a deep desire to go quite specifically back to Bonhoeffer. This time, however, I was not in Kampen writing a dissertation. I was not involved with my professor in academic discussions. I was not in a climate where other students and I sat up until three o'clock in the morning, talking about Dietrich Bonhoeffer. I was in Pretoria Maximum Central Prison. And I was not allowed anything to read, except the Bible. When in the end I was given permission to ask for books, I asked my wife to make sure that she would also send Bethge's biography of Dietrich Bonhoeffer.

It was quite a revelation to me personally to realize how the years since had changed the way I read and understood Dietrich Bonhoeffer. How different it was then for me to sit with him and almost to let him speak to me, no longer in the academic background in Kampen, but in the silence of my cell for the one day that I was allowed to read. As I read, I found other words that spoke to me then more than they did when I read that book for the first time. He says: 'There are things which are worth fighting for'. He begins by saying in this letter: 'I cannot understand that you think me foolish. Because there are things which are worth fighting for without any compromise whatsoever. And I think that peace and social justice, in other words Christ, are just such things.' Of course I was drawn to that 'without any compromise whatsoever.' And I was drawn to the fact that Bonhoeffer found peace and social justice things worth fighting for, things worth suffering for, because I sat in that jail, asking myself the question: 'Is it really worth it? Why are you doing this? Is it not safer to leave these things behind and to engage in theology in a way that would not be so risky?' When you have almost a month of solitary confinement and you ask yourself these questions, Ladies and Gentlemen, then they are not mere academic questions. They were questions that, at that particular time, quite decided for me which direction my life and my doing theology in South Africa should take.

And so it was an existential challenge. I felt it a threat to my faith and reason for being to go through what I had in the last ten years, finally finding myself in solitary confinement and yet and with no conviction that it was worthwhile.

So, of course, that was what attracted me in those words. But even more fascinating is Bonhoeffer's identification of Christ with the causes for social justice and peace. It was Barth who, very long ago, in 1911 I think, said: *'Jesus Christus ist die soziale Bewegung.'* I began to see Bonhoeffer saying that social justice and peace, which are Christ in essence, which really are Christ, that are just such things worth fighting for. And that there is no compromise possible.

I must say another thing. Just today, as I was preparing myself for tonight, the Sharpeville Six, so the radio said, the Sharpeville Six were condemned to death and they are now basically waiting to see whether they can count upon the mercy of President P. W. Botha. Whether the man even understands the meaning of that word for black people is no longer an issue for debate. And so already we are beginning to prepare for a new kind of mourning. You cannot prepare yourself for a conference like this, knowing that six young people will hang in thirty-five days, and not think of Dietrich Bonhoeffer, what he would have said and what he would have done, not think of the words that he repeated so often:

'Open your mouth for the voiceless,
speak for those who have no voice,
speak for those whose voice cannot be heard.'

'Make these choices now!' seem to me to be the words that we in this conference should hear again. This is the context out of which I speak to you tonight and I ask myself again the question that I have asked so often, thinking about Bonhoeffer's contribution, thinking about Bonhoeffer's challenge to all of us in the world. One must ask: 'Can one be a theologian in South Africa or for that matter anywhere else, and not speak up for and not fight alongside the victims of oppression and tyranny?'

Can one be a theologian and not find oneself compelled to be involved in the struggle for justice and for peace? Can one be a theologian and not be willing to place at risk all that one has, indeed, also one's life if necessary, in order to authenticate one's doing theology in the world?

When I think of Bonhoeffer, I think of a theologian who has made it impossible since his life and death for anyone to do theology without understanding from the inside the meaning of struggle, the meaning of identification with those who are voiceless, the meaning of participating in the battles in this world that seek to establish justice and peace and humanity. Can one be a theologian and not do this? I think that Bonhoeffer suggests that one cannot, as he says when he quotes Luther: 'It is by living, even by dying and being damned, that one becomes a theologian, not by understanding, reading and speculation.'

Of course, after hearing words like that, we should quite properly close this conference and go home.

But we still need to face the challenge even as we meet here. There is one thing that I would like to leave with this conference. It is this particular challenge. I have always found it very, very difficult to understand, to put it very mildly, how one can study Bonhoeffer, talk about him, even love him as a theologian, be fascinated by his words, without being as involved as he has been. Can there, I ask myself, be any real understanding of the man and of what he has written, if there is no understanding and if there is no sharing of the commitment that he so obviously had? I ask this because this is what Bonhoeffer means to us and to me.

There are other things that you know already, that you hear from us from time to time and in countries like South Africa, which are almost exclusively tied to the name of Dietrich Bonhoeffer. The parallels between Nazi Germany then and South Africa now, the question that I raised about blatant oppression, injustice and war, the church at a time like that, the meaning of confession, and the meaning of a confessional church in a situation like that, and the debate in my country around the question of confession and the confessing church is evidence enough of how seriously we take this. We are, of course, fascinated by Bonhoeffer's choice to return to Germany from the United States even while being pressed so sorely by his friend Paul Lehmann to stay. And we asked ourselves again facing a similar dilemma: 'What does that mean for us in a situation like ours?' Finally, of course, there is Bonhoeffer and his role in the conspiracy; Bonhoeffer, who in this single act, even today quite mercilessly, I think, unmasks the hypocrisy of so much theology and of so much church politics, especially with regard to the debate on violence and nonviolence. And if South Africans run out of all other arguments, we grapple with Bonhoeffer, and then we think the argument is really over. It is not over, but it does present us with some realities that we do believe, I think rightly, that much of theology as it has evolved in this last forty years since the Second World War has not been able to face honestly.

Beyond what we have said, I personally continue to be haunted by Bonhoeffer's commitment to the church, by his discovery of the power of the Bible, his appreciation of discipline both as the practice of piety and what one must call, for lack of a better term, the revolutionary ethic. By that, I mean his conduct in the conspiracy which he also talks about. I am haunted by his faith in the ecumenical movement and, at last, also by the discovery that he had made in the end, that they from Germany will have to take the responsibility upon themselves to change this situation. But again, all of this is well known. What I would like to simply touch upon tonight is something else that I for myself have discovered to be profoundly meaningful.

This is the fact that, in Bonhoeffer, much of his work and his life were pervaded by the question of church without privileges and what that means. It means that the church, he says, is to be found mostly in privileged places, which for him is the wrong place for the church to be. He thinks that the proper place for the church is where there are no privileges, and that is the place that God chooses within history for the church at a particular time. And in that context he discovers that the place for this church without privileges is with the Jewish question in Germany, as Ulrich Duchrow, I think, correctly points out. I hear in this the same kind of understanding which is echoed by the Confession of Belhare of my own church, which we adopted in 1986. Let me try to say that God is in a special way the God of the poor and of the oppressed and of the unprivileged. Therefore the church has no choice but to stand where God stands, namely with the oppressed and the poor and the *un*privileged. The context in which Bonhoeffer speaks, of course, again, is the context of the church in Germany: the desire to be safe rather than the willingness to take risks; the temptation to remain quiet and the temptation to see this acquiescence as necessary for the survival of the church in those difficult times.

The whole question is one of the place and the role of the German Christians in the church and the question of the extent of compromise with the powers that be, how far we can really go. In quite another way, but I think also belonging here, is the temptation to create for ourselves the privilege of cheap grace, about which Dietrich Bonhoeffer spoke so movingly and so eloquently. But I still think it is a privilege that is not given the church; it is a privilege that the church creates for itself in order to justify something else. But there is something else that strikes me here and this is that, if I understand Bonhoeffer correctly, he places a very, very high premium on the community within the Christian church. And all of what he has said, I think, testifies to his own rootedness in the community. For me, I think, it means also that a church without privileges is simply not, for Bonhoeffer, a kind of institution which is removed from himself. He does not speak of the church as if he is not part of it. He does not speak of the church as if it is an organism of which he forms no part and in which he does not belong. He is within the church, he belongs within the church and so when he speaks of a church without privileges, he is also speaking of himself in the choices that he has to make.

I think he had some privileges that he had given up.

He could have, I think, simply remained in the way in which he grew up. He could have remained aloof from the struggles and the battles of those who were decidedly the underprivileged in his society. He could have chosen the career of a theologian who did not see the need to become so clearly and so practically involved in the political situation and to seek also a political solution to the problems that were facing his country and the world at that time. He also understood, and I think that this perhaps was for him a great sacrifice, that when he finally had to make the decision, that he would participate in such an overtly political act, in such an overtly rebellious act, that he would make his own the whole question of tyrannicide and participate in that deed, that he had to stand before God alone, without the privilege of feeling at that particular moment the communion of the saints. He had to do that without the privilege of being supported by the church. He had to do that as a person in his own right.

If what I believe is true, that Bonhoeffer placed so high a value on the community of the church, on the being together of the people of God, after having tried for all of his life to make the church, as a church, understand its responsibility in Germany at that time, and that he had then in the end to make this decision alone, this decision may have been an even greater deed than the participation in the conspiracy itself.

It is an enormously difficult thing to make a decision you believe you are compelled to make on the basis of the Gospel, to make a decision which puts you at risk, and then to know that, when you make this decision and when you set about to execute the decision, not for your own sake, but, in a sense, also for the sake of the church and for the sake of the witness of the church, that at that point you do not have the support and the solidarity and the community of the church to help you through that difficult time. I have never been called, Ladies and Gentlemen, to make this decision that Bonhoeffer had to make. I have been called to make easier decisions, and even in those easier decisions, I have found it to be extremely painful that, when the moment of truth arrives, one must say you cannot really count on the continuing solidarity of the community of the church, so that you must be carried by a sense of prayer and witness and solidarity that, if all else fails, will be there with you. It never, so we heard, occurred to Bonhoeffer that he could claim not to be responsible for the deeds of Hitler or that he could avoid guilt by not sharing in the plot, which suggested to me that his readiness to accept responsibility for what was happening in Germany, his readiness to accept the guilt for what was happening and to take the steps that were necessary to bring about the change that he believed must come, that that decision and that responsibility alone places this man in a category of theologians that almost does not exist today. I am tremendously impressed by that alone, living in a country where, for many theologians the chief occupation is to evolve a theology of pseudo-innocence even now, in terms of what is happening to people in South Africa. The first thing they do is say: 'We know that what is happening is wrong', and the second thing they do is to say to you is: 'I am not part of it.'

And so, please, do not blame me. It is this desire to be proclaimed innocent that makes them the more guilty, even in the eyes of those who suffer, and that makes it impossible for them to make any responsible decision to bring about the changes that are necessary, even though they may understand themselves to be compelled by the Gospel to do so.

In reading the other day, I almost accidentally came upon this line, where Eberhard Bethge reminds us that at almost the same time that Dietrich Bonhoeffer made the decision to become part of the conspiracy, he also wrote a confession of guilt. I think that is so revealing for this man, which brings me to another point in terms of his confession of guilt. He shares this guilt. He shares the responsibility. He confesses this guilt, but unlike so many theologians today in similar situations, it does not paralyse him. It does not take him out of his responsibility. He does not run away from the awesome deed that he must do and the awesome decision that he must make. His confession of guilt inspires him exactly to face up to the responsibility that he must take. He also knew that it was accepting this responsibility which gave him the freedom to act. And this freedom to respond, responsibility, is not easy. When a man takes guilt upon himself, he would say, in responsibility, and no responsible man can avoid this, he takes this guilt to himself and no one else. He answers for it, he accepts responsibility for it. Before other men, the man of free responsibility is justified by necessity. Before himself, he is acquitted by his conscience. But before God he hopes only for mercy. Of course, it is true that Bonhoeffer reminds us that this is a *Grenzfall*, it is an exception. But what if this exception no longer is the exception? What if this exception becomes the challenge for decisions that have to be made every day? What if the exception all of a sudden becomes normal? This, I believe, is our situation. I read Bonhoeffer and I try to understand what it is that this man is trying to teach us. I have found the whole question of responsibility and freedom to be responsible and responsible freedom a question that I must wrestle with, even if I cannot yet follow Dietrich Bonhoeffer in his decision to kill Hitler. But that is a question for another evening that we can talk about. But as to the whole point of violence and nonviolence and what is responsible, so easily we are told, yes, it is the nonviolent decision, the nonviolent choice, which is the responsible choice for the church in South Africa today. But is it? I have great doubt about that.

For the last ten years of my life I have done nothing else but engage in a ministry which included nonviolent strategies of resistance to the South African government. I knew that I had no choice. Politically it was a necessity; theologically it is a necessity for me. At this point in my life, nonviolence and the choice for nonviolence is not simply a strategy that I think I must employ because it works so well. I think, for me, it is the demand of the Gospel not only for South Africa, but for Christians in all times. That is what I believe. But is it responsible to ask people to engage in strategies of nonviolence when you know that not only will there be no change because of those strategies of nonviolent resistance, but you are bringing people to a situation in which they will suffer or go to prison or be tortured or die, or all of that, subsequently. When I take young people on the streets as I did in the early 1980s, whether it is to march nonviolently and peacefully to demonstrate a point or to emphasize a demand, or whether it is to ask them to participate in a consumer boycott or whether it is to ask them simply to stand visibly in front of a police station, and I must look on and see, as I had to, time after time after time, how they then were charged by the police and teargassed and taken off to jail and beaten up and tortured and how many of them were simply shot dead in the streets, where does my responsibility begin and end?

You can say yes, but if, even after all of that, there is a perception that something must change because a country cannot afford to kill its people on the streets, because something must break, if there is that consequence, one can argue, and not necessarily cynically, then there is a price that we must pay and the price must be paid. But if there is no change, if there is no response and if the world looks on, but does not even blink an eye, and if there is no support, what then is responsible? Can I, quite responsibly, continue to say to people in South Africa: 'Lay your life on the line for the sake of nonviolent change, because it is the right thing to do?' And when the question arises, 'Is it not time for us to come to the decision that Dietrich Bonhoeffer had to take?' what then is responsible?

And so you see, within the very situation in which I live, I am troubled by this man, as I am troubled by the situation which we have to face. And the theology that I do must find its expression not only in what I say from the pulpit but, more importantly, in what I do on the streets, when I am not any longer guided by the whole of my church. And I can only be authentic in my faith, I can only be authentic as a theologian in South Africa, if I am willing to take my belief from the pulpit or out of my study where I theorize about those things onto the streets where the witness for the Lordship of Jesus Christ must be seen.

And I must do that, because this very saying in Bonhoeffer reminds me that if I am not willing to take up my cross and be a disciple of Jesus Christ and pay the price, then I might as well forget to be a theologian or to be a Christian. I have no formulated or clear answers to these questions. I do not always know what to say to those who confront me with the realities of the South African situation. Bonhoeffer is one who said that we must remember that we must deal with the realities of this world, that we must stop dreaming. And so, when we deal with the realities of this world, this is what we come up against: an emergency that leaves us no room whatsoever in which to manoeuvre; new laws compounded upon other laws. Again, only less than a week ago, that makes our actions in terms of nonviolent resistance criminal acts and almost — not almost, indeed — impossible. What is my responsibility? How much freedom do I have to act responsibly in that situation? Again, let me say, I raise the question. I do not know the answer. It may very well be that the answer will be taken out of my hands before I have time to formulate it. I marvel that this man could become what he had become. I marvel that he could change from what he had been. I think of what he had been taught in his home and that he, from that context, could become a person that could identify so clearly with those who were not like him. That is something for which I have great admiration. Again this is because I live in a situation where this seems precisely so hard and sometimes even impossible for people to achieve, and it raises the question: 'Can those in positions of privilege really change?' Bonhoeffer says yes, and I must continue to go back to Bonhoeffer to prevent myself from becoming totally cynical as I live in South Africa and watch the white theologians of my country in terms of their own decision. I was surprised to discover that he at some point made this distinction between the office of pastor and the office of preacher, saying that, in the situation in which the church found itself then, it was necessary to do that, because the office of pastor could be far more easily claimed by what Hitler wanted to do with the church dash, could be manipulated. The office of preacher, he said, should not be given up at all, should not give in to that temptation at all. And the preacher must do that in a situation where what Hitler really wanted from the church was not so much that the church would become another Nazi party. What he wanted from the church was not so much the nazification of the church. What he simply wanted from the church was to accept an apolitical role, to say: 'Because it is politics, we have no responsibility.' In that situation, the responsibility toward prophetic witness by the church, in terms of its preaching from the pulpit and in terms of its witness outside of the church building, becomes essential. From Bonhoeffer I learned that it is not so much the freedom of religion that matters and that should be fought for, but what really counts is the freedom of the Word of God, that freedom to speak and to act as the Gospel compels us to do. I learned from him that we must not recoil from doing what has to be done and what should be done for others. I learned from him that we should not excuse ourselves by saying nothing can be done without doing our analysis first. And, at the same time, learning from him that what we are called to do is precisely proper and right analysis so that we will not be dreamy and romantic about the realities of this world, all the ethical relevance of success, or failure. From him we learn that we should know not to deny our broken past, but to accept it and, in so doing, to respond to the demands of the present. We learn from him that we should take the risk of doing and that we should not wait until we have the certainties of complete analysis, which may never come. We must make the decision and we must take upon ourselves the consequences of that decision. It is when I read this again that I ask myself in Bonhoeffer's terms: 'Can one really be an authentic theologian in any situation in which one finds oneself?' And, as he had challenged us through his life, he challenges us with words from a poem that he wrote during his last days, which in my own translation sounds something like this:

'Step out of your anxious hesitation
into the storm of life
carried only by God's word and your faith
and freedom shall receive your spirit, with joy.'

And I look around me, Ladies and Gentlemen, and as I watch the anxiety of many in the church, as I hear over and over again also in our situation the arguments about the survival of the church, I ask, 'What can we do, what should we do, to what extent should we compromise so that the state will not totally crush us?' And now, with the continuing and intensifying struggle between the church and the state in South Africa, this question is once again on our lips: 'When is it responsible to challenge the state?' we ask.

What does it help to challenge the state if tomorrow you are put in jail or you are banned or you are killed, perhaps, and then your witness is silenced? What is responsible, in terms of making the church survive so that we can live to testify another day? And as I see the fear of so many of my white compatriots as the days of white domination in South Africa are coming to an end, and they know this, I see the lack of celebration in so much of the church in my country. If I see the fear of freedom, so that people cannot accept their responsibility to be free and the joy of knowing and acting out that responsibility and doing what is right within that freedom, if I see the joylessness of so many, then I think maybe we should allow ourselves to be challenged by Dietrich Bonhoeffer again. And so let me read this poem once more:

'Step out of your anxious hesitation
into the storm of life
carried only by God's word and your faith
and freedom shall receive your spirit, with joy.'

Those who understand these words and have the courage to act them out, I think, will also understand Dietrich Bonhoeffer and may even rise to become authentic theologians.

Thank you very much.

* Transcribed by Irene Meijer from the tape-recorded address.

Textual Research for the New Edition of

Bonhoeffer's Ethics

PANEL DISCUSSION

Clifford Green (ed.)

This is a composite report on the preparatory work which has been done for the new edition of Bonhoeffer's *Ethik*, Band 6 of the Dietrich Bonhoeffer Werke. This critical edition of the Bonhoeffer texts is simultaneously being published in the Federal Republic of Germany by Christian Kaiser Verlag, Munich, and in the German Democratic Republic.[1]

Work in preparation for the new edition has actually been in process since 1980 and officially since 1985. Two editorial consultations of several days have been held in Heidelberg, in October, 1986, and in Kaiserswerth, in June, 1988. Herbert Anzinger, editorial staff person for the whole edition, attended both consultations, and Eberhard Bethge attended the second. Between the consultations there has been a good deal of correspondence and a number of meetings between individuals.

The four editors are joined here by Eberhard Bethge who has served as a consultant particularly for work on the manuscripts, notes and other Nachlass materials. In section I, Eberhard Bethge reports on the two versions of the *Ethik* he edited and published in 1949 and 1963. In section II, Clifford Green summarizes preparatory research from 1980 to 1986. Ilse Tödt presents in section III the work she and Heinz Eduard Tödt have done on the manuscripts and notes. In section IV, Ernst Feil describes the goals of the new edition.

1

The first editing of the *Ethics* was my own enterprise. From 1945 to 1948 I deciphered the handwritten manuscripts and edited and arranged them without any help or advice from other scholars. My intention was that Dietrich's fragmentary manuscripts should be published to show what his planned *Ethik* might have looked like. To order the chapters, I followed so far as possible the plan Dietrich outlined in an early stage of writing, using the 'Zettel' mentioned in the Foreword to the first editions.[2] But this approach resulted in problematic consequences. It could not do justice to the way themes and topics developed and the way changes were made during the actual writing which was done after the outline was made. This attempt to systematize the manuscripts violated the chronological order in which the manuscripts came into existence in relation to the possibly correct dating or the still undiscovered dating of some manuscripts. My underlying purpose was to show the public Dietrich's *theological* ethic. But I neglected the importance of the contextual 'Zeitgeschichte' and paid very little attention to most of the Zettel.[3] As everybody now knows, the world of theology and ethics paid little attention to the book when it was first published.

About ten years later Handfried Müller wrote his thesis on Bonhoeffer and convinced me that I should attempt to order the manuscripts chronologically, according to the order in which they were written. This would show the reader, and especially the scholar, Bonhoeffer's first approach to ethics and the process by which his thought developed. So in 1963 I published the present version of the book (6. Auflage). In the Foreword to the newly ordered edition I gave evidence about chapters whose dating was obvious; and I guessed about others where the dating was not obvious to me, using for the first time the evidence of paper types and ink and, more than previously, indications in the Zettel.

Then, nearly ten years ago, some friends began to analyse critically the order of the *Ethik* in the sixth Auflage. The first were Clifford Green and, independently, Ernst Feil. Initially reacting with a mixture of mistrust and helpfulness, I observed that they were studying the evidence with the greatest care. Then the Heidelberg team, Heinz Eduard Tödt and Ilse Tödt, joined in; he focused on the possible theological sequence while she rechecked the dating evidence of the manuscripts and the Zettel. From this we came to a sequence of Bonhoeffer's work periods on the ethics manuscripts and to the present proposal of the possible chronological sequence of writing.[4] The new edition of the *Ethik* in the Dietrich Bonhoeffer Werke might be published in this order.

At this point my consolation lies partly in the thought that fifty years from now the result of my lonely work in editing Bonhoeffer's *Ethik* will have become an exhibit in the museum of the Bonhoeffer Society! But I have also tried hard to take seriously the consequences of that new sequence and to integrate them.

What convinces me most about the dating of the new Chapter I ('Christus, die Wirklichkeit und das Gute') is to see how it exemplifies Bonhoeffer's way of working and how it parallels his way of presenting a new work in other books. In *The Cost of Discipleship* he presented at the beginning the strong thesis and central message that he wanted to develop in the rest of the book: thus we find the thesis of cheap and costly grace right at the outset. He works similarly in *Creation and Fall*. Here in the *Ethics* he begins by saying, as it were: 'This is the *Ethics* I want to write, namely an ethic of reality.' Everything seems to be said with full force right at the beginning. Then he goes on to describe the historical and ecclesiological context (Ort) of *this* ethic of reality. In the next phase he shows how this ethic is really authentic Reformation theology and begins to discuss its list of particular ethical issues. After the shocking experience of his first conspiratorial journey to Switzerland in 1941 he sits down to write about the actual feature of this ethic as an ethic of responsibility. The next phase brings him to the necessity to argue and to show the inner unity or oneness of this ethic which may seem to tear to pieces the responsible Christian in the turmoil of realities. And in the last phase Bonhoeffer comes to terms with Barth's ethics, having just read the volume of *Church Dogmatics* II/2 in Switzerland in 1942.

This is an early overview – and I really mean early, before the matter has been thoroughly worked through and then published. This overview shows how the new sequence for the third ordering of the *Ethik* and its several stages of work can be

31

understood. In this way a new vision of what Bonhoeffer wrote is made possible: the writing he considered the culmination of his life work, which now attracts so much new interest.[5]

2

Beginning in 1980, as Bethge has mentioned, three independent research projects on the ethics manuscripts were begun. At the Third International Bonhoeffer Conference held at Oxford in March, 1980, I presented a preliminary paper entitled 'Bonhoeffer's *Ethics*: A Research Brief.' In November, 1981, Ernst Feil presented a lecture at Halle entitled 'Strukturen wirklichkeitsgemässen Handelns des Christen. Ein Beitrag zur Ethik Dietrich Bonhoeffers.' This combined interpretation of Bonhoeffer's texts with some discussion of textual problems, particularly the dating and ordering of manuscripts. And in April, 1982, Peter Möser (who had completed a dissertation on conscience in Bonhoeffer as a student of Heinz Eduard Tödt) was assigned to look ahead to the new editon of the *Ethik* and identify issues the editors would have to confront. His paper[6] was the first to try to identify the 'work periods' in which Bonhoeffer's manuscripts were written.

Another important development in this period was the discovery in 1982 of the correspondence between Karl Barth and Bonhoeffer during the journey to Switzerland in May 1942.[7] This proved (as Larry Rasmussen had argued already in 1968) that he had read the galleys of Barth's *Church Dogmatics* II/2 at that time, especially the ethics under the the the heading 'The Command of God.'

My own work led to the essay on 'The Text of Bonhoeffer's *Ethics*' which was completed in the summer of 1986 and published[8] the following year as part of a project that the English Language Section of the Bonhoeffer Society had undertaken some years previously. The evidence I considered includes references in Bonhoeffer's letters, his writing outlines, references in his manuscripts[9] and, inevitably, the papers of the manuscripts and notes. Here I cannot refrain from recalling how all this effort with the papers (cataloguing their watermarks, size, color, weight, etc., and correlating them where possible with dated material like letters) evoked from Renate Bethge, along with her generous hospitality, not even barely concealed skepticism about all this 'Papierologie!'

Reflecting on my work with hindsight, the chief question that animated my efforts was this: given all the available evidence, in what order do we best *read* and *interpret* Bonhoeffer's 'chapters'? Of course, Bonhoeffer left us no Table of Contents or even a final outline; further, his ideas developed as he wrote. Therefore such an order can only be proposed on the basis of various pieces of evidence and such a proposal cannot be equated with a final arrangement Bonhoeffer himself might have made.

With this in mind, I proposed that the manuscripts be arranged in three 'blocks.' By choosing the term 'block' I meant to indicate 'a chapter or group of chapters which Bonhoeffer intended to belong together in developing a set of ethical ideas.'[10] I suggested that the present Chapter I, 'Die Liebe Gottes und der Zerfall der Welt,' be considered the first block and that Chapter VII, 'Das "Ethische" und das "Christliche" als Thema,' be considered the third block. The second block would be constituted as follows:

Ethik als Gestaltung
Erbe und Verfall
Schuld, Rechtfertigung, Erneuerung
Kirche und Welt
Die letzten und die vorletzten Dinge
Das Natürliche
Christus, die Wirklichkeit und das Gute
Die Geschichte und das Gute (2. Fassung)

In part this would follow the outline Bonhoeffer sketched on Zettel 38, but the latter parts would represent a development of his thinking as he wrote. The reasons for this arrangement cannot be detailed here, but are given in my essay.

I presented my essay 'as a report in the mid-stream of ongoing research' and pointed to a 'mass of [recent, new] evidence which requires a good deal of digestion.'[11] In light of the work of my colleagues since I wrote, and the proposal below for how the new edition should be ordered according to a reconstruction of its writing sequence, I would make here three brief comments. First, I am intrigued by the suggestion that 'Die Liebe Gottes und der Zerfall der Welt' might derive from 1942 rather than 1940, and I want to scrutinize the evidence for that conclusion. Second, in my own analysis I did not sufficiently consider that the chronological order of composition might differ significantly in the case of some manuscripts from the order in which Bonhoeffer intended they be presented and read; I intend to evaluate the evidence for the proposal below on chronological ordering.

But, in my opinion, by far the most important issue is the third: given this or that ordering of the chronological sequence of writing, in what order are we to *read* and *interpret* Bonhoeffer's manuscripts? This is a question that the editorial team has not yet addressed. But in the case of 'Kirche und Welt,' and the relation of 'Christus, die Wirklichkeit und das Gute' to 'Die Geschichte und das Gute,'[12] some colleagues are of the opinion that the order of interpretation may well differ from the order of composition.

But I get ahead of the story. In the following section Ilse Tödt reports on the latest stage of work and presents the proposal for a chronological ordering of the manuscripts.

3

As we prepared for the new edition of Bonhoeffer's *Ethik*, we worked by the rule of the General Editors of the Dietrich Bonhoeffer Werke that the basis should be the original manuscripts and notes, not the edition first published in 1949. Several preparatory tasks had to be undertaken. Clifford Green had already made a detailed catalogue of the types of paper used in the manuscripts and notes. Paper types can help to determine where and when a particular piece was written. Then all the manuscripts had to be deciphered again. This was a difficult task since Bonhoeffer wrote them in his German script which he realized was nearly illegible; when writing letters to others he used Latin script. This arduous deciphering, however, yielded a considerable number of corrections to the previously printed text, many relatively minor, but a number that are more important.[13]

Another task was deciphering and transcribing all the deleted material in Bonhoeffer's manuscripts to make it available to scholars and to see if it might yield information about the work on the manuscripts. Finally, all Bonhoeffer's writing notes (Zettel), on more than one hundred scraps of paper, had to be deciphered again. Anni Lindner had made an initial attempt in the 1940s. Herbert Anzinger and I undertook the task systematically and produced a new transcription. These notes indicate Bonhoeffer's way of working and the changes in his plans. In print they would fill about eighty pages; we plan to publish them, with commentary, in a separate edition later.

Then came the issue of the order in which the manuscripts should be published. Some discussion was held on Clifford Green's proposal summarized above. But Bonhoeffer left us no final plan for arranging his ethics manuscripts. There are hints in the notes and manuscripts of 1940 and 1941, but these were superseded in later work periods. Further, the rule of the General Editors is that the texts in the DBW volumes that Bonhoeffer himself prepared for publication would, of course, follow his original order, but all other texts must be presented in the chronological order in which they were written. For some chapters of the *Ethik*, it is easy to determine when they were written from mention of the work in letters. Others are not so obvious. Various types of evidence were examined. These include paper types, already mentioned, ink colors, and even the changing thickness of writing indicating new and worn nibs on Bonhoeffer's pen.

Further, a calendar had been created of Bonhoeffer's activities and travels during the years of work on the *Ethik* and other projects (1940-1943). This was used, along with other evidence, like letters, to identify five work periods. As is well known, Bonhoeffer did not work continuously on his ethics manuscripts. He also had to undertake other tasks for the Confessing Church and for the resistance group in the military intelligence office to which he was attached and at one time his work was interrupted by illness. Five periods of continuous work can be distinguished, and so the manuscripts will be presented in five groups; this will emphasize that the *Ethik* was by no means a complete book.

During the first phase of work with the papers and notes, I reconstructed a chronological writing order of the manuscripts. This was checked twice, by comparison with dated letters in the Bonhoeffer archives at Villiprott for several days in December, 1986 and June, 1988.

A second phase of work consisted of checking this sequence in relation to content analysis of the notes and manuscripts, of which only a brief example can be given here. For instance, the theme of 'passivity' in theological understanding appears on note sheets and in both versions of 'Die Geschichte und das Gute,' and further clarification of this theme (in order to speak adequately about the good in historical action[14]) is announced. The manuscripts 'Die Liebe Gottes und der Zerfall der Welt' ends as soon as Bonhoeffer has arrived at this point of 'passivity.'[15] This converges with other observations, for example, the appearance of the term 'Erwählung' (election) in the manuscript 'Die Liebe Gottes und der Zerfall der Welt' where Bonhoeffer takes up his *Schöpfung und Fall*. In the book of 1933 the term 'Erwählung' is not yet present in this meaning. The term reminds one of Karl Barth's *Church Dogmatics* II/2. The combined evidence points to a writing time later than the journey to Switzerland in 1942.

The sequence which represents the chronological order of writing was thus reconstructed out of the far-reaching agreement between the results of the first and second phases of work. Arranged according to the five work periods, the sequence is as follows.

First Work Period: 18 March — 13 November 1940
'Christus, die Wirklichkeit und das Gute,'
    E 200-17, 225-26   August 1940?
'Ethik als Gestaltung' (1), E 68-77
    First organization phase: Zettel 1, 38, et al.   September 1940
'Ethik als Gestaltung' (2), E 77-94
'Erbe und Verfall' (1), E 94-113
    Organization phase: Zettel 16, 61, 50, 62, 82, 63-69
    on 'Das Gute' for an unwritten chapter   ca. 9 October, 1940[16]
'Erbe und Verfall' (2), E 113-16
'Schuld, Rechtfertigung, Erneuerung,' E 117-27
Insert for 'Christus, die Wirklichkeit
    und das Gute,' E 217-25   October-November 1940
    Collection phase

Second Work Period: 17 November 1940 — 22 February 1941
'Die letzten und die vorletzten Dinge,' E 128-52   up to 10 December 1940
'Das natürliche Leben,' E 152-198   up to 22 February 1940

Third Work Period: 25 March — 25 October 1941
'Die Geschichte und das Gute' (1. Fassung), GS III, 455-77
'Die Geschichte und das Gute' (2. Fassung), E 227-78   1941

Fourth Work Period: End of 1941 — Autumn 1942
['"Personal" — und "Sach" — Ethos,' E 341-52][17]
'Die Liebe Gottes und der Zerfall der Welt,' E 19-58
'Kirche und Welt I.,' E 59-67   1942
Über die Möglichkeit des Wortes der Kirche
    an die Welt,' E 376-84
['Die Lehre vom primus usus legis nach den
    lutherischen Bekenntnisschriften und ihre Kritik,' E 323-40]

Fifth Work Period: End of 1942 — 5 April 1943
['Nach zehn Jahren,' WEN 9-31]
'Das "Ethische" und das "Christliche" als Thema,' E 279-302   1942-43
'Das konkrete Gebot und die göttlichen
    Mandate,' E 303-19

Two other pieces have also been previously printed in the Appendix of the *Ethik*. 'Staat und Kirche'[18] is now dated prior to the beginning of work on the book, and 'Was heisst: die Wahrheit sagen?' is dated in Tegel after breaking off work on the *Ethik*. They will be printed in DBW volumes 16 and 8, respectively.

According to this sequence the first manuscript of the *Ethik* to be written was 'Christus, die Wirklichkeit und das Gute,' with the parallel title 'Christus, Kirche und Welt.' Here Bonhoeffer laid the theological and methodological foundation for his *Ethik*. This chapter contains the 'hermeneutical key' for his *Ethik*, which is summarized in the following sentences and their context:

> The reality of God discloses itself only by setting me entirely in the reality of the world, and when I encounter the reality of the world it is always already sustained, accepted and reconciled in the reality of God. This is the inner meaning of the revelation of God in the human being Jesus Christ. Christian ethics enquires about the realization of this divine and worldly reality, which is given in Christ, in our world.[19]

Bonhoeffer sees the Christian's life as an active and passive participation in a circular process. The human person is placed into (not detached from) the reality of the world. Living and acting in this reality, the person will experience the world as already borne by God.

Larry Rasmussen has raised the question as to whether there are two different methodological approaches in Bonhoeffer's *Ethik*, namely 'ethics as formation' and 'ethics as command.'[20] But if it can be shown that all subsequent approaches easily fit into the first, then we can speak of a homogeneous concept of ethics in Bonhoeffer's several incomplete manuscripts.

The next stage of work is to write and discuss the commentary to the manuscripts which will be printed in footnotes. This is among the matters taken up by Ernst Feil in the next section.

4

In 1949 Eberhard Bethge edited, as Bonhoeffer's bequest, the ethical fragments which his friend had conceived with a view to publishing a book on ethics. But what could have been an end was actually a beginning. After the *Letters and Papers from Prison* were published in 1951, such an interest in Bonhoeffer arose that, beginning in 1958, his *Gesammelte Schriften* began to be published. Yet soon after the publication of the first volume, the plan of these collections began to be problematic. New materials repeatedly surfaced, negating the original editorial principles for these volumes. Finally, in addition to the first four volumes, two supplementary volumes became necessary in 1972 and 1974. Now we had some pieces twice and a unified perspective was further aggravated.

A second, no less important, aspect has to be added. All of these editions had appeared in close connection to Bonhoeffer's own time; he could have been with us quite a number of years or even decades, maybe even until today. But, in fact, the historical distance between us and his own time is increasing. In particular, a direct relationship to that time is no longer possible, especially for those from other countries or continents who want to deal with Bonhoeffer.

Both aspects were decisive for a new edition of the Dietrich Bonhoeffer Werke. This was undertaken in order to guarantee a secure textual foundation for dealing with Bonhoeffer's work, aided by the sustained support and consultation of his contemporaries who were still alive. A careful reexamination of manuscripts or texts, a commentary which is modest and yet as informative as possible, an ordering of texts according to clear principles, as well as a first summary of its historical influence up to the present – such an edition is designed to reach out to the interested reader as much as it provides for scholars, particularly those of a new generation, the necessary materials for their research. Thus there was good and sufficient reason to produce a new edition at this time.

Right from the beginning we expected that the most difficult problems arise when dealing with the *Ethik*. This results both from the particular time in which the manuscripts were written and the difficult wartime circumstances. The expense and effort necessary for a new edition could only be justified by our expectation of a comparable expansion of our knowledge. This cannot and must not mean that the new edition will be the end of research. On the contrary, it is rather intended to be the foundation and hopefully the stimulus for intensive work with these fragments of Bonhoeffer. This is precisely the meaning and purpose of this edition of the *Ethik*.

To achieve these aims a complicated commentary is necessary for the manuscripts of the *Ethik*. For one thing, it is necessary to indicate literature which Bonhoeffer worked with and worked into his own text without using quotations or giving the sources, as often happens in his writings. Thus research will get a clearer picture of the way in which Bonhoeffer appropriated already formulated ideas or, respectively, how he adapted them into his own thinking.

Secondly, it is especially necessary to clarify the contemporary references and allusions as far as possible, considering the problem posed by the coded expressions which Bonhoeffer unavoidably had to use. Here we must find a balance between a commentary which is too cautious in identifying Bonhoeffer's references to contemporary events and one which goes too far by giving the wrong impression that we are able to be very sure of all these references to his own time. There is no question that Bonhoeffer did intend to refer to, and reflect on, contemporary events. It is equally clear that there were certain ethical questions he could not openly discuss, for he had to consider that his manuscripts could fall into the hands of the Gestapo, as indeed happened to the last text which lay on his desk when he was arrested.

It is also necessary to show to what degree and in what perspective Bonhoeffer attempted in these writings to give an account for himself and for his fellow conspirators of their shared actions, which they could not justify easily, though they found themselves compelled to do them, trusting in God.

Gathering up the information available at this time, and drawing upon the insights of those who knew Bonhoeffer and his times, the editors therefore hope to be able to present an edition which is as authentic as possible.

NOTES

1. An editorial board has been appointed by the English Language Section to prepare for an English edition of the whole series.
2. Cf. *Ethik* 1966[6] (Munich: Chr. Kaiser, 1966), p. 12.
3. These notes, outlines, quotations, etc. which Bonhoeffer made in preparation for writing were deciphered for me by Frau Lindner; they were also numbered at that time, but they were not thoroughly studied.
4. See section III below.
5. See *Letters and Papers from Prison* (New York: Macmillan, 1972), p. 163; cf. p. 129.
6. 'Arbeitsschritte, Entscheidungsprobleme und klärende Vorüberlegungen zur Neuarbeitung von Bon- hoeffers *Ethik* im Rahmen der geplanten Bonhoeffer-Werkausgabe.' Neither this paper, nor mine and Feil's mentioned previously, have been published.
7. Cf. Dietrich Bonhoeffer, *Schweizer Korrespondenz 1941-42. Im Gespräch mit Karl Barth* (Munich: Chr. Kaiser, 1982), ed. Eberhard Bethge; *Theologische Existenz heute* Nr. 214.
8. See *New Studies in Bonhoeffer's Ethics,* ed. William J. Peck (Lewiston, N. Y.: Edwin Mellen Press, 1987), pp. 3-66. This also contains Rasmussen's essay mentioned above.
9. See the references to 'both the following chapters,' 'the chapter on natural rights or in the next chapter about the good' (*Ethik*, pp. 152, 162) and 'what was said back in the first chapter' *(Gesammelte Schriften* III, p. 458).
10. *New Studies,* p. 12. I wanted to avoid the connotation which Bethge had given the word 'Ansatz.' Hence 'block' for me was 'a more neutral word which does not imply that a particular block is necsessarily a ''new approach'' or that it is governed bu a particular theological theme which is different from other blocks; but nor does it exclude that possibility' (p. 11f.).
11. *New Studies,* p. 4.
12. That is, the chapters presently numbered II, V and VI respectively.
13. Two samples of Bonhoeffer's handwriting were distributed during the panel presentation. The first was Zettel 19 with the title 'Verantwortung' and the outline for the second draft of 'Die Geschichte und das Gute.' The second was the first page of sheet II of 'Die Liebe Gottes und der Zerfall der Welt' showing notes for deciphering written on it about 1948. In the middle a word has been read as 'Baum' but, in fact, Bonhoeffer was alluding to Adalbert von Chamisso's tale of the *man* (not 'Baum') who sold his *shadow* (not 'Schmuck'); cf. *Ethik*, p. 22.
14. See *Ethik,* p. 265.
15. Cf. *Ethic,* p. 58.
16. Before and after the letter to Bethge of this date; cf. *Gesammelte Schriften* II, p. 375f.
17. This and the two following pieces in brackets, which were published in the Appendix of the earlier editions, will not be printed in the *Ethik*. They were written for different purposes and audiences (e.g., a church commission) and do not seem to have been intended for the ethics book.
18. The original manuscript of this piece is lost.
19. *Ethik,* p. 208; ET p. 195, translation altered. The German text reads: 'Die Wirklichkeit Gottes erschliesst sich nicht anders, als indem sie mich ganz in die Weltwirklichkeit hineinstellt, die Wel- twirklichkeit aber finde ich immer schon getragen, angenommen, versöhnt in der Wirklichkeit Gottes vor. Das ist das Geheimnis der Offenbarung Gottes in dem Menschen Jesus Christus. Die christliche Ethik fragt nun nach dem Wirklich werden dieser Gottes und Weltwirklichkeit, die in Christus gegeben ist, in unserer Welt.
20. See his 'A Question of Method,' *New Studies in Bonhoeffer's Ethics,* Chapter III.

New Studies in Bonhoeffer's Ethics

PANEL DISCUSSION

William J. Peck, et al.

1 William Peck:
Overview and The Euthanasia Text-Segment

Our volume, *New Studies in Bonhoeffer's Ethics,* began to take shape several years ago at a meeting of the American Academy of Religion. After many discussion and planning sessions, including a three-day retreat at Princeton, New Jersey, it became what it now is: an interim report from North America with a grace note by Gerard Rothuizen from Holland. We want to dedicate our panel discussion to Dr. Rothuizen in appreciation for his contributions to this conference, for his sensitive chapter on 'Bonhoeffer and Suicide' in our book, and in profound sorrow that he cannot be with us owing to his grave illness.

His letter will serve as his report:

Dear Bill, Kampen, June 9th 1988

Being seriously ill, I am often too tired to write a letter and therefore you didn't hear anything from me when you asked for a kind of summary or 'Anliegen' (that is better, I think) of my contribution to your book. I shall try to give it to you now.

My article - encyclopedically speaking and not pastorally! - opens the road to the question (and a next article): In how far is Bonhoeffer's *Ethics* dogmatics, in how far not morality, but religion and not ethics, but mysticism? And in how far is the answer important for us in teaching ethics? How much theology (let alone: Christology) are we permitted to put into the discipline of ethics? What *is* 'theological ethics'? I think Bonhoeffer a great help to us - as an intelligent friend, a very intriguing ethicist - being influenced both by Nietzsche and the Gospel (Jenseits!) - a warm and courageous adviser, *not* as a guide forever. But we desperately need a thesis on 'Theological Ethics with DB' - don't you think so?

Have wonderful days; days that make me jealous! Yours
Gerard

Our book fits the theme of this conference on 'Bonhoeffer's *Ethics,* the History of a Book,' because it came out of a similar impulse, namely, the realization that the *Ethics* is a relatively neglected area in Bonhoeffer studies. We noted that the lack of clarity in treatments of the *Ethics,* even in the major works on Bonhoeffer, can be attributed to insecurity about the chronology of its various parts. Clifford Green gave us a critical study of the text based on a thorough review of all the clues, including the great variety of types of paper which Bonhoeffer had to use owing to wartime scarcity. Then each of the authors responded to the new arrangement in terms of its impact on his particular topic.

In the case of my topic, the brief segment in *Ethics* on euthanasia, the rearrangement strongly reinforced my discovery that between the lines, or beneath the surface, there were important references to the 'good people' Bonhoeffer encountered among his fellow conspirators. I offered a 'close reading' of that text segment and found that new insights emerge when the *Ethics* is looked at from the perspective that it was writing performed in the context of persecution.

2 John D. Godsey:
'Bonhoeffer's doctrine of Love'

'Love' is a central doctrine in Dietrich Bonhoeffer's theology. This essay presents an exposition of Bonhoeffer's understanding of love as it is found throughout his writings. Some of his most striking thoughts are to be found in his sermons. Bonhoeffer insists that God defines the true meaning of love and God does this definitively in the event of salvation which is centered in the cross of Jesus Christ. The New Testament uses the word 'agapè' to describe God's self-giving, suffering love. Bonhoeffer contrasts this with 'eros', the self-seeking, dominating love that characterizes sinful human beings. Love for God and neighbour is sharply differentiated from love of self. Jesus commands his followers to love others as he has loved them.

For Bonhoeffer, Christian love is responsive love made possible by God's love of humanity in Christ. Love is an act, not an attitude. It must be *lived out* in everyday life, and it inevitably encompasses political action, where power is brought into the responsible service of others. Bonhoeffer's own sense of responsibility led him to join the resistance movement against Hitler as an act of love for those who were being oppressed by the Nazi regime.

While in prison, Bonhoeffer found a new way to relate divine love and human love by using the musical analogy of polyphony. In a fugue, the love of God corresponds to the *cantus firmus* or bass note, and where this is strong, human loves can be developed to the fullest extent as melodious counterpoints. Thus should all of life be polyphonous. In a real sense, Bonhoeffer's martyrdom at the hand of the Nazis provides the ultimate commentary of his doctrine of love.

3 Charles C. West:
'Ground Under Our Feet'

Dietrich Bonhoeffer was a secular Christian (tr.: 'ein weltlicher Christ'). To explore this paradox is the purpose of this essay. It has three theses.

First, Bonhoeffer's relation to the goodness of the world which was his home was immediate, concrete, and nourishing. He was an aristocrat of this world. Alienation was foreign to his being. It was for him, as for the mythical giant Antaeus, a scene of struggle, but also a source of strength. Its physical environment, its culture (including the religious dimension of that culture), its social order and human relationships of love, responsibility, and authority in family, school, society and state, expressed, for

Bonhoeffer, a blessed penultimacy where the meaning of life is to be found. He was, in the most positive sense of that word, a *Bürger*.

In the course of his short life, Bonhoeffer had many occasions to redefine this world–from an aristocracy of training and position to an aristocracy of character and intelligence (e.g., his concept of *Bildung* and his view of human rights). His sense of authority changed accordingly. His theology of interpersonal relations made him ever more open to the reconstruction of human community by free and responsible human interaction. Mandates replaced order of preservation. Bonhoeffer knew that his world was profoundly threatened, by more than the Nazi menace. But he still believed that it had come of age, could cope responsibly with its problems, and would emerge in new form through the witness of the church to prepare the way for the coming of Christ.

There is, in short, a quality to the penultimate world which, in his view, is a response to the blessing of creation as well as to the reality of Christ realizing itself among us. The limit of the other person and of God is a blessed limit, the place of love defining and redefining each person. From this center, life may develop joyfully to the full, in this world and in the world to come.

Second, Bonhoeffer's awareness of the fragility, the vanity, the pride of the world is not rooted in some social experience, but in a direct awarenessof the ultimate judging and transforming reality of God. The image of *der Mensch* in the middle, in *Creation and Fall,* having lost the beginning and the end but striving to conquer them for himself, is basic to this awareness. The patterns of human beings trying to establish their own center because they are cut off from life repeats itself over and over again, in ideals and ideologies, in human religion, in philosophy, in politics and in the personal virtues of human character: reason, conscience, freedom *et alia*. The brokenness of this world is clarified and accepted by God in the cross of Christ. In this brokenness it finds its true maturity.

The penultimate in this sense is cruciform. It rests totally on the forgiveness of sins and includes participation in the suffering of Christ as a way of worldly responsibility. Human works are good only as redeemed. Human responsibility does not ask about goodness but about appropriateness, about correspondence to the reality of Christ taking form in the world. Human acts involve the acceptance of guilt and confidence in forgiving grace as central to this witness. In the earthy Old Testament confidence, which calls believers to sin bravely, there is much of Luther. In the subordination of the law to sanctifying grace humanizing this world there is still more of Calvin. In the secular confidence and responsibility with which the free Christian acts there is a Christological view of reality that goes beyond both Reformation Fathers.

Third, this way of Christian living is neither egalitarian-liberal nor liberation-revolutionary. Bonhoeffer was neither a democrat nor a proletarian. He knew the limits of his experience at this point, as the Drama Fragment from his prison writings shows. But he suggests a way which is a challenge to both: a way based on the discontinuity of God's forgiving grace in human affairs, not the continuity of human struggle or planning with God's saving action. He suggests a style of action that is responsive to the other, open to reform, realistic about power in all forms, faithful in human relations rather than in long range ideals that sacrifice humans in the present, and above all witnessing to the judgement of God even on human goodness and the forgiveness of God for human failure in the search for human justice. We have here a guide to a penultimate future and a witness to the ultimate who is Christ alone.

4 Clifford Green:
'Church and World' and 'Religionless Christianity'

A by-product of my work on textual questions was a new insight on the relation of the *Ethics* and the 'religionless Christianity' project of the *Letters and Papers from Prison*. I refer specifically to Bonhoeffer's section on 'Church and World,' currently printed as Chapter II. On the basis of both manuscript and content evidence, I believe this 'chapter' belongs between 'Ethics as Formation' (III) and 'The Last Things and the Things before the Last'(IV).[1] Thus it is not to be read in what Eberhard Bethge once thought was a retrospective look back towards *Nachfolge,* but in the context of the resistance movement and a look forward towards the *Letters*. I summarized the content of the chapter as follows:

> The distinctive theme of this chapter is rooted in the humanist opposition to Nazism and in the Kirchenkampf. Humanists who support values like reason, culture, humanity, freedom, law, tolerance, autonomy and human rights find themselves allied with Christians in resisting barbarity, violence, arbitrariness and irrationality. Christ is the origin of these human values and the protector of secularized humanists who, like the Confessing Church, suffer for the cause of justice, goodness and humanity. The Christ whose church is to make an exclusive and uncompromised confession of faith gives the protection of his name, by affirming their cause, to those who work for humanity even though they themselves may not work in Christ's name. Hence the relationship of the church to the world must be presented in terms of Christ as the origin of human values, the crucified Christ who justifies humane behavior; and the church's relation to the world will be shaped by the theme that 'to know and find Christ one must first become righteous like those who strive and suffer for the sake of justice, truth and humanity.'[2] In short, the topic of 'church and world' is pursued under the rubric 'Christ and good people.'

In this section Bonhoeffer already begins to adumbrate theological themes that will predominate in the *Letters*.

> Other times could preach: unless you become a sinner like this publican and this harlot, you cannot know and find Christ. But we must rather say: unless you become righteous like these people who struggle and suffer for justice, truth and humanity, you cannot know and find Christ.[3]

Other points made here by Bonhoeffer anticipate the discussion of humanity's coming of age and the religonless Christianity project, as we see in the following summary.[4] 'The children of the church had grown *independent (selbstständig;* cf. *mündig)* of their mother. Yet Christ is the origin of the reason, justice, culture, and human rights affirmed by the secularized humanists. Resisting Hitler's onslaught on these human goods has created a new alliance between Christians and humanists as the latter seek the origin and protection of their values. In the perilous time of the Antichrist, there seems to be a 'general unconscious knowledge' (cf. unconscious Christianity) that

Christ is the source and protector of humane values. If Matthew 12:30 ('Those who are not with me are against me') represents the uncompromising claim of the Confessing Church, Mark 9:40 ('Those who are not against us are for us') points to the alliance between the Confessing Church and the humanists. When the Beatitudes bless those persecuted for righteousness sake, this does not refer to people persecuted for their witness to the name of Christ; it is a blessing on those 'who are persecuted for a just cause, and, as we may now add, for the sake of a true, good and human cause.' They are blessed, and some even come to profession of faith, because their suffering leads them to Christ (cf. sharing the suffering of God at the hands of a godless world in the *Letters*).

Limits of space prevent further discussion here. However, the evidence indicates that this little and neglected section of the *Ethics* discusses the political, existential, and theological *Sitz im Leben* of the religionless Christianity project of the *Letters and Papers from Prison*.

5 Larry Rasmussen:
'A Question of Method'

What follows is a partial summary of the chapter, 'A Question of Method.' It was included in the panel presentation of the volume edited by Wm.J. Peck.

The contention is that two methodological themes are explicitly discussed in Bonhoeffer's *Ethics,* 'conformation' and 'command'; that both can be traced throughout large portions of the Bonhoeffer *corpus;* but that 'ethics as formation' is both the more original and the more enduring theme. A subtheme is that Bonhoeffer's discussion of 'ethics as command' in *Ethics* is heavily dependent upon a reading of the galley-proofs of Barth's *Church Dogmatics,* II/2, in May of 1942, even though there was no mention of this by Bonhoeffer in *Ethics*, by Barth in later commentary on Bonhoeffer, or by Bethge in the early editions of the biography. Subsequently discovered letters from Bonhoeffer to Barth now verify Bonhoeffer's 1942 reading of the section, 'The Command of God,' in II/2.

The oral presentation in Amsterdam included a cursory view of 'conformation' and 'command' as methodological motifs in the Bonhoeffer writings. Detailed treatment is found on pages 105-135 of the Peck volume. The oral presentation gave greater attention to a summary of the similarities and differences of the methods, in answer to the question, is there one method or two, in Bonhoeffer's ethics. The summary of the comparison is as follows, as cited from pages 135-138, and as presented in Amsterdam.

In both, the overriding thrust is toward concreteness.

In both, the ethic is an ethic of reality and realization. The Gestalt Christi and the command of God both have correspondence with reality. They bring to concrete expression in this world the cosmic reality given in Christ.

In both, ethics is done contextually. The ways Christ takes from among human beings vary through time. God's concrete command can only be heard in a local and temporal context.

In both, ethics is relational.... The Christian moral life is an ongoing, dynamic relationship with its center, God-in-Christ.

In both, the relational, contextual ethic becomes increasingly 'filled.' Both methods move from an atomistic ethic to an ethic emphasizing the coherence and continuity of the Gestalt Christi, or the command of god. The outcome in both is a large place for the 'natural' and for the mandates and their innate laws.

In both, the mandates play an indispensable role. In one, they are the media of conformation; in the other, the media of obedience. In both, they compose the pre-ethical, though moral, environment, and they prevent life from an overburdening by the ethical.

In both, the ethical occupies a 'peripheral' location. It has a fixed time and place. The ethical arises when the structured flow of life in the mandates has been subjected to disruption and/or severe questioning; when 'who Christ is for us today' is in doubt, or what the command of God is concretely is itself problematic.

In both, moral action is the same. Obedience to the command of God is, for moral content, identical with conformation to Christ....

For both motifs, all the faculties of the self are employed in ethical discernment....

In both, the methodological direction is from the question and answer about the indicative to the question and answer about the imperative. From: 'how is Christ taking form among us here and now?' to: 'what action on my part conforms to his action?' From: 'what is God-in-Christ commanding here and now?' to: 'what action on my part is action in keeping with this command? In both, the weight is clearly on the indicative. It is permissive, authorizing life. [Note: the book, p. 137, reads incorrectly: 'Clearly on the imperative.']

In both, the underlying assumption for Christian ethics is reconciliation, i.e., the recovered unity of God and the world in Christ. In both, the point of departure is the body of Christ....

In both, deputyship has an ontological base and the supreme ethical deed is the deed of free responsibility. This deed is the breakthrough to reality at the particular time and place of the 'ethical.' In both, however, the final judgement of the deed lies in the hands of God. Both are ethics firmly grounded in justification by grace alone.

If these are the similarities, are there differences? There are none of great consequence. Bonhoeffer's is an ethic of reality and realization which finds methodological expression in two basic motifs, conformation and command. Yet it is worth noting that the former is the more original and more enduring. Ethics as command should be viewed as a genuine motif, but a subordinate one. *Letters and Papers from Prison* neglects it entirely. In any event, we must take Bonhoeffer seriously when he says his ideas for *Ethics* were unfinished. That holds for matters of method, as for others.

6 Robin W. Lovin:
'The Biographical Context of Bonhoeffer's Ethics'

More than most books, the text of Bonhoeffer's *Ethics* requires biographical and historical interpretation. Although the *Ethics* has been an important part of my teaching and thinking for more than a decade, I remember that when I first read it as an undergraduate, I found it incomprehensible, and I put it back on the shelf for several years. When Bill Peck invited me to write an essay on the biographical context for *New Studies in Bonhoeffer's Ethics*, I therefore had good reason to appreciate the importance of the assignment.

My essay is not a work of original historical research. It is an ethicist's reflection on the text of *Ethics* in light of what the editoral circle for the new edition in the *DBW* has learned about the circumstances of its writing. To be sure, it is difficult to trace causal connections between specific events in Bonhoeffer's life and conceptual developments in the book. Bonhoeffer was not so reactive in his writing. The coincidental discovery that he had, in fact, read part II/2 of Barth's *Church Dogmattics* before writing his own chapter on the commandment of God and Christian ethics perhaps accounts for this new emphasis in his work. The reflections on 'the natural' in Chapter IV may have been related to his closer contact with Roman Catholic thought during his stay at the monastery at Ettal in the winter of 1940-41. Even in these cases, however, the materials from other sources are thoroughly reworked, and the ideas expressed are linked to Bonhoeffer's thought as a whole. *Ethics* is the work of a man deeply involved in the events of his time, straining to find clue to meaning and guidance for action in everything he read, but *Ethics* is never an occasional work which could be exhaustively explained by specific events or intellectual encounters.

What does emerge from a rereading of *Ethics* with special attention to the biographical background is a heightened awareness of the political dimension of the text. We have become accustomed, perhaps especially in North America, to treat 'responsibility,' 'warrant,' and 'deputyship' as theological concepts that have applications to political ethics. We cannot appreciate the originality and creativity of Bonhoeffer's *Ethics* until we see that he encountered these first as political ideas. He was able to give them a broader meaning and to provide normative guidance for the dilemmas of resistance precisely by relating them to theological concepts of vicarious action and accountability before God. Political concepts which left persons trapped in a framework of loyalty and obedience to legal authority become, in Bonhoeffer's work, the authorization for a free act outside of constituted structures, an act which trusts in God's grace rather than in legal justifications. Only thus can the possibility of 'responsible action' in the more narrow, legal sense be retrieved from a distorted political reality and restored for future generations.

NOTES

1. See *New Studies in Bonhoeffer's Ethics*, pp. 22-32.
2. *Ethics*, p. 61.
3. *Ethics*, p. 61; translation altered.
4. See Clifford Green, 'Bonhoeffer's ''Non-Religious Christianity'' as Public Theology,' *Dialog* 26.4 (Fall 1987), p. 277.

Conscience in Dietrich Bonhoeffer's Ethical Theory and Practice

Heinz Eduard Tödt

Conscientia – in Luther's German translation *Gewissen* – is a well-known word whose meaning is nevertheless difficult to grasp. The concept was formed in the languages of the ancient Mediterranean world. The Latin word *conscientia,* a loan translation from the Greek, was inherited by the European and American culture and handed on to Christians all over the world. Everyone in the West or in Christendom understands what 'a bad conscience' means. It includes both an intellectual and an emotional component. To be bothered by a bad conscience means to be conscious of having done or failed to do a certain thing, and in such a way that a negative self-judgment is connected with it. The intellectual judgment is accompanied by displeasure impairing the spiritual well-being. We speak of pangs of conscience, and pangs are painful. We react to a bad conscience. It is suppressed, or we try to make good, e.g., asking the injured party for forgiveness, so that, being forgiven, conscience may calm down. We should not consider conscience to be some spiritual organ of the human being. Rather, it is a temporal sequence of events, a process, with characteristic structures.

Literature on this phenomenon shows that we enter a labyrinth when trying to define the essence, function, origin, evolution, or constitution of conscience. We find ourselves confronted with conceptual and practical pluralism. Obviously there is no universally accepted understanding of conscience. Challenged by the problems of our time and situation, we have to take it upon ourselves to develop a relevant under-standing of conscience. It will be indispensible for this endeavor to know how other times and other people experienced and interpreted conscience. With this purpose in mind we shall look into the understanding of conscience which Dietrich Bonhoeffer struggled to find as a theologian in the midst of the conflicts of resistance and conspiracy.

We must remember that the understanding of conscience is hotly debated in the following four fields.

1. In the *modern movement for civil and human rights*, conscience gained an extraordinarily public significance. Concepts such as freedom of conscience, which is a public right of the individual, were introduced into national constitutions and international conventions.

2. The *influence of humanism on culture* led to the proclamation of the autonomous person's dignity. This person is interested in its proper integrity and unity, fears damage to self-esteem and therefore listens to the voice of conscience.

3. *Psychology, psychoanalysis, and other human sciences* worked out theories about the forming of conscience in the socialization of the individual. By stating, e.g., a relationship between superego and conscience, a fundamental anthropological state-ment is made. In this view, conscience appears shaped by the father's or other person's influence.

4. For *Christian preaching and teaching,* especially in the Reformation tradition, the relation of faith and conscience is a fundamental problem. Some Lutheran theologians tended to directly identify conscience with faith.

Dietrich Bonhoeffer did not follow the Lutheran tendency of granting conscience an exceedingly central position, but assigned it another. In attempting to grasp and assess his concept of conscience, we can take advantage of an unusual opportunity. The source material, including diaries and letters, allows both a reconstruction of Bonhoeffer's theory and insight into Bonhoeffer's practice of conscience. Peter Möser, in his outstanding dissertation on this topic[1], found that Bonhoeffer's practice hardly came to expression in his theory. I will implicitly deal with Möser's conclusion in what follows, limiting myself to the period from the summer of 1939 to April 1943.

1

The Inner Call to Return from Emigration

In the spring of 1939, the occupation of the remainder of Czechoslovakia, in violation of treaty, and the aggressive agitation against Poland foreshadowed the imminent outbreak of war. For Bonhoeffer, who intended to refuse the draft and the oath of allegiance to Hitler, there seemed to be no longer any place in Germany. He stood nearly alone with his radical position. American friends feared that he would soon meet his end in a concentration camp and invited him to the United States. His partners in the German church struggle, the Brethren and the church-leading Councils of Brethren of the Confessing Church, urged him to accept the invitation. Refusing the draft was punishable by death, and such a 'Bonhoeffer affair' would have dangerously confirmed the incriminations disseminated by the National Socialists that the Confessing Church was unpatriotic, 'un-German,' or even treasonous. This was the situation in which Bonhoeffer on June 7, 1939, with conflicting feelings, boarded the ship that would bring him to New York.

Bonhoeffer's diary during the voyage mirrors the doubts which wracked him. His thoughts often revolved around the biblical words of the daily Moravian *Losung.* On June 9, he took comfort from the promise that Christ is everywhere with those who belong to him. Yet this immediately made him ask, 'Or have I, after all, avoided the place where He [Christ] is? Where He is for me? No, God says: You are my servant.'[2] Bonhoeffer struggled hard against the self-reproach of having left the place where he should be. Yet the inner accusation remained and tormented him.

Once in New York, he promptly began to counteract the emigration plan. He did not wish to commit himself to long-term obligations. Homesickness for the brethren of the Confessing Church, for Germany, tormented him. This hit him, a well-traveled man, as a surprise. But, after all, he was on a trip with perhaps no return. On June 15, he noted, 'The self-accusations because of a wrong decision return with nearly suffocating force. I have been very desperate.'[3]

It is certainly strange that pangs of conscience should overcome Bonhoeffer. As far as anyone could tell, his situation in Germany was hopeless, since he would not give up his basic convictions. Under such circumstances, the human right to emigrate, *ius emigrationis,* has been valid for centuries. But a person's conscience is not only informed by general rules. It addresses the individual life in a highly personal, vital way. On June 20, Bonhoeffer noted, 'It makes me wonder that I am never completely certain of my motives for my decisions. Is that a symptom of lack of clarity, of inner dishonesty, or is it a sign showing that we are led beyond our understanding, or is it both?'[4] In Bonhoeffer's experience, decisions in his life were not the direct result of ethical-rational argument, but were also influenced by an intangible certainty of being led.

Later on the same day, he noted, 'Today's *Losung* speaks terribly severely of God's unescapable judgment. He no doubt sees how many personal interests and how much anxiety participate in today's decisions, no matter how courageous it may appear. The reasons for an action which we present to ourselves or to others are certainly insufficient. Anything can be justified. Ultimately, our actions stem from a level which remains hidden to us.'[5]

Is conscience a voice arising from a level which lies deeper than a human being's rational arguments can reach? Bonhoeffer wrote this entry on the crucial day of June 20, 1939, after having decided to decline the offer of an occupation in the United States. His central argument for the dangerous return reads, 'We can no longer escape it. It is not that we are indispensable, as though we were needed (by God!?), but simply because our life is there and because we leave our life behind, and destroy it, in case we do not return to be there again. It is nothing pious, but nearly physical. God, however works not only through pious motives, but through such vital impulses as well.'[6]

It certainly is odd, too, that Bonhoeffer, in self-reflection, did not resort to the noble motivation that the Confessing Church in Germany needed him – which would not have been an exaggeration. Instead, he stated bluntly and disarmingly: 'I must go back because my life is there.' At his departure from Germany he had not realized so clearly that he would not be able to detach himself internally from this life with his brethren, with his Confessing Church, with his family, not even when an acute threat of death hung over that life. Now this was clear.

Was the decision of June 20, 1939, a matter of conscience? Does the warning voice of conscience remind a person of the essentials of his life?

In conversation with himself, Bonhoeffer did not appeal to the fact that he had a task to do in Germany. However, he had to explain to his disappointed and perplexed American friends, who had gone to great lengths for him, his sudden decision to return. The main reason which he gave them can be found in a letter written in early July to Reinhold Niebuhr: 'I have come to the conclusion that I made a mistake when I came to America. I must live through this difficult period of our national history with the Christians of Germany. Otherwise, if I did not share the trials of these times with my people, I would not have the right to help reconstruct Christian life in Germany after the war.'[7]

This statement is obviously not identical with the considerations in the diary, where Bonhoeffer never alludes to the spiritual authority necessary for a time after Hitler.

Can a person present to others, even to friends, reasons other than those which appear decisive in self-reflection? I think one must, in order to make it possible to be understood, provided that the reasons are true as well. Conversation with oneself is different from, and more individually related to conscience, than conversation with others. In Bonhoeffer's diary, his conversations with himself often end prayer-like. On June 20, the entry concludes, 'At the end of this day I can only pray that God will judge this day and all its decisions with mercy. It is now in his hands.'[8]

In the entry of July 7, on the voyage back to Europe, Bonhoeffer wrote, 'I am glad that I was there and I am glad that I am on my way home.' He later spoke of a 'liberated' conscience. In the diary, the doubtful, self-tormenting tone now is a matter of the past, in spite of the fact that he, by returning to Germany, ran into danger. Bonhoeffer was at one with himself.

Can we read this diary, supplemented with letters, as an unintentional account of a process of conscience? May we do so even though Bonhoeffer uses the word 'decision' frequently and the word 'conscience' hardly at all? I am convinced that this document implicitly shows his dealing with the phenomenon which we call the appeal of conscience, a summons from the depths of what, to Bonhoeffer, is life.

We now must examine whether any of this reappears when Bonhoeffer speaks of conscience in the *Ethik* manuscripts.

2

The Unsteadiness of Isolated Conscience

More than a year after the painful decision process in New York, Bonhoeffer wrote the first section of the manuscript 'Ethics as Formation.' He was now deeply involved in the subversive plans of the resistance group in the office of foreign intelligence (Admiral Canaris). The problems which he treated in the manuscript bothered him deeply. This can be gathered from the fact that two years later, at New Year 1943, he wrote a further similar text – the famous essay, 'After Ten Years.' With concern, sorrow, and anger Bonhoeffer had seen that many honorable men, of whom one would never have believed it possible, had finally 'tumbled,' i.e. had conformed, for security's sake, to the Hitler regime, or entered into active complicity with it. Subsequent generations raised and will raise the question whether these men, who had witnessed so many Nazi atrocities – such as the pogroms of November 1938 against German Jews, or the attack in Poland, camouflaged with lies, and the acts of annihilation in Poland – and who nevertheless now cooperated with that regime, had no conscience.

It is a credit to Bonhoeffer's high-mindedness that, in his manuscript, he did not speak of such disappointing behavior in a tone of contempt, but instead tried hard to understand what happened in and to those honorable people. He analyzed their fate with an intensity rarely found in other authors' texts from this period. Neither the convinced National Socialists, nor the unprincipled opportunists aroused his interest, but rather the representatives of high humanity, of considerable ethos.[10]

Bonhoeffer characterized the attitude and failure of three pairs of corresponding types of people. We will deal here only with the 'man of conscience.' To that inwardly led man corresponds, at the other pole, the outwardly led 'man of duty.' The 'man of conscience' appears as one who 'is advised and supported by nothing except his very personal conscience.'[11] Can he endure, while Hitler's totalitarian regime, with its absolute claim on the person, drags him into dilemmas demanding decisions of him, and into straining conflicts? Bonhoeffer observed that the following occurred: 'The innumerable honorable and alluring masks and costumes in which evil approaches him make his conscience anxious and uncertain, until he finally is content with a soothed rather than a clear conscience, until he finally lies to his own conscience so as not to despair; because a man whose only security is his own conscience will never be able to understand that a bad conscience can be stronger and more salutary than a deceived conscience.'[12]

How does this failure come about? The first factor is the regime's thoroughly successful disguising 'in the robes of relative historical and social justice,'[13] giving the bewildering, deceptive impression that it represents after all, in spite of evil deeds, a cause which is essentially good and in the best interests of the German people. In retrospect, with all the information we think to have as to facts not known at that time, it seems incomprehensible that persons of integrity and learning succumbed to such deception. But intellectual giants like Carl Schmitt, Martin Heidegger, Emanuel Hirsch and many renowned theologians and church leaders were among those decived, especially as long as the regime had use for them and allowed them to hold prestigious positions.

These famous men share with the 'man of conscience' the weakness of yielding to deception. The 'man of conscience' is troubled by the dilemmas which force him to make his decision. Being in a dilemma means that each of the choices of action open to me will violate my conscience. Having chosen the lesser evil, and because I forget, since I avoided the greater evil, that the chosen option is evil as well: that was the great temptation for those who stayed in their influential positions under the Hitler regime, collaborated with it against their convictions and subjectively soothed their conscience by referring to their still good intentions. Objectively, however, they became accomplices to unimaginable atrocities, to which they closed their eyes. Bonhoeffer concludes: If only these collaborators would at least remain honest and have the bad conscience which is adequate to their behavior, instead of lying to themselves! However, this is impossible for a man whose life is steadied solely by his good conscience. He cannot live without self-respect but must be honorable at all costs. Consequently he is forced to play down the evil reality in order to escape the salutary pressure of a bad conscience urging him to turn from collaboration to dangerous obstinacy.

In the text of 'After Ten Years,' Bonhoeffer declares that only he will persevere 'whose final standard is not provided by his good sense or reason, his principles, his conscience, his freedom, his virtue, but who is prepared to sacrifice all these when being called in faith and sole commitment to God to obedient and responsible action.'[14] May I actually sacrifice my good conscience in a dilemma? If I put the question in this way, I refer to an egocentric, autistic conscience, that of the person who, interested in himself and without communication with others, seeks support in his conscience exclusively. In order to be adequate to reality, rather than egocentric, conscience should stay related to others. Bonhoeffer's charge against the theorist in ethics and his conscience is that both remain abstract, detached from concrete reality.[15] How can conscience be, at the same time, both an intimate inner voice and communicative, related to others and to events challenging responsibility? Here we should recall Bonhoeffer's situation in June, 1939, in New York. His conscience warned him not to separate himself from the essentials of his life from the community with the brethren in the Confessing Church, from the fate of Germany and of the Christian civilization. But is human conscience not perhaps incurably egocentric, since it is a voice within the sinful person in a fallen world?

3

The Damage to Conscience After the Disruption of Creation

In the chapter fragment, 'The Love of God and the Decay of the World,' Bonhoeffer does not directly speak of the situation in the Third Reich, but begins with the fundamental human situation as expressed in the biblical narrative of the Fall in Genesis 3. Before the Fall, Adam lived in immediate knowledge of God as his origin. In the reality which encountered him he had no need of a knowledge of good and evil. For some inexplicable reason Adam in his freedom wanted to be in control of reality. For that purpose he needed a specific knowledge – the ability to distinguish good and evil. Access to this knowledge radically altered the human person's position in reality. In Bonhoeffer's words, 'Knowing good and evil means knowing oneself to be the origin of good and evil, the origin of an eternal choice and election.'[16] To him who 'knows' in such an egocentric way, reality is no longer revealed as it had been in the beginning, as creation. Now it is encountered merely as constructed by the person who high-handedly decides between good and evil. Human perception of reality now is anthropocentric; the human being is the one who devises and evaluates all. This inevitably results in constructions governed by a one-sided perspective.

Today we recognize this one-sidedness, e.g., in the fact that anthropocentric use of nature leads to its destruction. The original position of the human person in reality is lost to such an extant that we cannot even reconstruct it in thinking. We know ourselves only as alienated – separated from origin, from reality, from our own selves.

The reality constructed by the human being is full of contradictions, in which the person is entangled. This causes the person to be destructive. According to Genesis 4, the next step is Cain's fratricide of Abel. The human person, a murderer, proceeds on the path of destruction bringing death to the animal world, the plant world, and the environment.

What does this mean for conscience? Is it entangled, too, without alternative, in the destructiveness of a disrupted reality?

According to Bonhoeffer, shame is deeper and more comprehensive than conscience. Shame still reminds the person of the separation of the whole life from the origin – God is the origin –, from the other human beings, from reality, from the self. Because the person as alienated cannot 'bear with one's own self,'[17] cannot tolerate the self as it is, shame demands that the human being be veiled, covered, or masked. The person refuses 'to become aware of all that grows within the self,'[18] – or represses what really is in the self and pretends to be a different person, one who cannot be blamed as guilty. Yet it is the person's shameful need to hide from the other which points, in fact, to the original reality in which the human being felt no need for shame.

Conscience, according to Bonhoeffer, plays a much more limited role than shame. At first, it only 'concerns the person's relation to the self.' Then, however, it becomes arrogant enough to stylize itself as the source of religion. 'It makes the relation to God and to other human beings arise from the person's relation to the self. Conscience pretends to be the voice of God and the norm for the relationship to other human beings.' Conscience makes the person believe the self to have become like God, knowing both good and evil, and thus knowing the origin of all things. The person does not deny his or her own evil, 'but in conscience summons the self to retreat from the self that became evil and return to the better self, to the good.'[19] This call of conscience, on the one hand, testifies to the truth that the human being's goal is goodness. At the same time, however, it makes believe that the person, through the self alone, is capable of overcoming disunity and of retrieving the unity of the origin. This endeavor, although religiously and ethically glorified, nevertheless is hubris – godless glory. The person cannot break free from being *incurvatus in se ipso*, inevitably self-centered, and therefore in unending conflict with the surrounding world.

On the basis of this biblical-theological analysis of conscience, Bonhoeffer could see reasons for the disturbing failure of the 'man of conscience' in the Third Reich. In this situation, that type of person was bound to expect that, unless he himself deceived and lied to his conscience, he would be torn apart by the potentials of conflict. Nothing in reality as understood by him could ever be stronger than the dilemmas facing him under the Nazi regime.

Bonhoeffer's biblical-theological critique of conscience in his manuscript-fragment 'The Love of God and the Decay of the World' looks devastating. There is no ground left either for the Protestant or for the Catholic myth of conscience. But does this mean that Bonhoeffer eliminated conscience as an anthropological dimension from his thinking?

4

The Role of Conscience in Responsible Life

In the text 'After Ten Years,' Bonhoeffer remarks that the Germans, with their self-forgetful readiness for subordination, traditionally lack a basic wisdom – 'that of the necessity of the free responsible act, even against vocation and commanded task.'[20] Considering this deficiency which proved disastrous under Hitler, Bonhoeffer delineates, in one of his *Ethik* manuscripts, 'the structure of responsible life.' Bonhoeffer can only covertly hint at the circumstances under which he thinks and acts, since the manuscript might at any time fall into the hands of the Gestapo. Yet the topics he deals with include, maybe as the most important one, that free and responsible act planned for the overthrow of the Nazi regime. This manuscript contains a section which Bethge in the published edition entitled 'Conscience.' According to a preview by Bonhoeffer himself, this section falls under the heading, *'self-scrutiny* of life and action,'[21] to which correspond two sections in 'The Love of God and the Decay of the World' on discerning and on doing the will of God.[22]

The readiness to accept inevitable guilt is a prerequisite of responsible action. Especially with a view to the coup d' état, but not only with respect to this extreme situation, Bonhoeffer says of the person who wishes to shirk responsibility, 'He places his personal innocence above his responsibility for the others, and he is blind to the more pernicious guilt with which he thus burdens himself, blind also to the fact that innocence will prove true only in entering for the sake of the other into the community of his guilt.'[23] Bonhoeffer's thesis that acting as demanded by personal responsibility means acceptance of guilt is, naturally enough, controversial in ethics. Can a person become guilty by killing the instigators of massive genocide, in order to save the lives of millions of people? Certainly such a deed might cost the lives of many innocent people. It probably could not be carried out without civil war, or other unforeseeable consequences. And execution without trial and with no recourse to a law would remain an offense, since evil means cannot be justified by good ends. Indeed, Bonhoeffer considered tyrannicide an action which burdened those responsible for it with guilt, even though it was unavoidably demanded – which in the case of Hitler it was. He had to be killed because the oath of allegiance to 'the *Führer*' blocked to a large extent the resolution to overthrow the regime.

Against the willing acceptance of guilt 'there is a protest of incontrovertable sublimity. It comes from the high authority of conscience refusing to sacrifice its purity to any other good, refusing to become guilty for any other person's sake.'[24] In accordance with Immanuel Kant's philosophy, to which the expression 'sublimity' alludes, all of Christian ethics are agreed that it is never advisable to act against one's own conscience. What Bonhoeffer states here reminds one unmistakably of Luther's declaration to the Edict of Worms in 1521, '...and so I remain constrained by the Scripture passages I have cited, and my conscience remains bound by the Word of God. Therefore I cannot and will not recant; for to act against conscience is difficult, destructive, and dangerous.' Bonhoeffer makes clear: In the formal sense that conscience is protesting against any act which endangers a person's being in unity with the self, conscience remains a binding authority. To act against conscience 'is along the line of suicidal action against one's own life.'[25]

What is the content of that unity of the person with the self? The call of conscience has its origin and goal in the autonomy of one's own ego. It therefore follows a self-established law and is a self-justification of the fallen human being. In this way, conscience is deeply entangled in sin. Nevertheless its call must be respected even if conscience cannot bring about the unity to which it calls. Unity is won at the very point where it is apparently surrendered, namely, where conscience no longer strives for the unity of the isolated self, but rather appeals to the self in the community which Jesus Christ grants to the human being. Faith brings about 'that I can only find unity with myself when I surrender my I to God and men. The origin and goal of my conscience is not a law, but the living God and living man encountering me in Jesus Christ.'[26] This means a transformation of our relationship to the norms appropriated by conscience, including 'the Law' – a transformation which we can perceive when looking at Jesus. By breaking the Sabbath law and other laws because of the holiness of the law of love for God and man, Jesus became the liberator of conscience, liberating it for the service to God and the neighbor. The liberated conscience 'unites with responsibility grounded in Christ to bear guilt for our neighbor's sake'[27] – guilt which, in 1941, is seen in the breach of the law prohibiting high treason and assassination.

Bonhoeffer describes how a Christian, in the new freedom from the law, deals with conscience. In tradition, this was treated as the topic of the *tertius usus legis*, or the *usus in renatis*, which concerns the function of the law for the reborn, for those who believe. The autistic nature of conscience, which 'the Law' cannot dispel, is overcome where reconciliation through Christ with God dispels the *incurvatio hominis in se ipso*, and thereby opens the human being to community with God and with the surrounding world, initiating a new self which sees itself as a gift of grace. This renewal of the human being causes his conscience to change. The concrete need of one whose neighbor I am becomes more important than the supposedly guiltless self-identity of an isolated ego. In the situation of conspiracy, the consequences of this view of a transformed conscience were considerable.

From the first plan to overthrow the Nazi regime in 1938 until the last attempt on July 20, 1944, the military commanders in high positions, whose power to command was indispensable for a coup d'état, were unable to bring themselves to give, in personal responsibility, orders that action be started. Several of them were ready to use their commanding power if they recived an authorizing command to that effect. All these persons did not wish to break the soldier's law which consists in the connection between command and obedience. They did not feel free from the oath which they had sworn, even though Hitler, the recipient of that oath, had long destroyed its foundation by many criminal deeds. To personally intervene in the course of history and to take upon themselves the guilt associated with it – that was more than their own inner authority would allow these military leaders to do. With a view to them, Bonhoeffer writes, 'Whoever sticks to his co-responsibility for the course of history, no matter what, because that person knows that it has been enjoined by God, will find, beyond unfruitful critique and likewise unfruitful opportunism, a fruitful attitude towards contemporary events. The final responsible question is not how I can heroically extricate myself from the affair, but how a coming generation might continue to live.'[28]

It was Bonhoeffer's intention to join responsible action, connected with the acceptance of guilt, to liberated conscience. A unity of the two is possible when conscience is no longer ego-centered but opened by the encounter with Christ so that it can include in its self-examination responsibility for the neighbor and for the continuing life of a coming generation. It is possible since the responsible human being does not have to carry the burden of guilt alone but stands under the promise of forgiveness.

Without diminishing the unity of liberated conscience and responsibility, there remains an irremovable tension between the two. Acceptance of guilt has its limits. The call of conscience cannot be ignored when it warns that the I which is formed in the relation to Christ will be destroyed by the intended action. Even the liberated and no longer autistic conscience calls to unity, though not to an identity within the self, but to the unity of being in Christ. We also must not repress but remain conscious of the fact that even liberated conscience will confront responsible action with 'the Law.' Law here means law of life, life's guardian and protector. As such, law must be taken very seriously. It may only be broken when a breach is unavoidable, will pass, and does not destroy life, but upholds it in its true sense. The so-called law and justice which held the unjust regime of the National Socialists in power had indeed to be broken in order to make true justice valid again. Bonhoeffer is convinced that the responsible person gains freedom from and authority over the law through that person's orientation to Christ. When conscience reminds him of the importance of the law of life, then he must listen, but he must still not hear it as the last word. The law of life is penultimate in relation to the ultimate, Christ.

Bonhoeffer's conclusion is that whoever incurs guilt in responsible action is responsible for the guilt. He will accept the concomitant guilt because he feels obliged to act in free responsibility. 'Before the others, the person of free responsibility is justified by need; before the self, the conscience acquits, but before God the responsible person hopes for grace alone.'[29] How can it be that conscience acquits one in one's own eyes, when one must admit before oneself that one is entangled in guilt? One is acquitted because the guilt incurred was inevitable, and because liberated conscience hopes for the forgiveness of guilt.

5

Innovation and Unity in Bonhoeffer's Understanding of Conscience

It was no doubt the tremendous pressure of the conspiracy situation that compelled Bonhoeffer to rethink the relation between responsibility, acceptance of guilt, and conscience. I know of no other contemporary texts in which personal conscientious decisions and theological reflection on conscience affect each other so vitally. And yet Bonhoeffer did not allow the pressure of events to dictate insights to him, but rather preserved a broad space of freedom for his theological thinking. Bonhoeffer's theology is biblically inspired and biblically bound and therefore is free to get in touch with concrete reality.

There is no question that Bonhoeffer's concept of conscience is an outright rejection of all variants of the neo-Lutheran understanding of conscience. It is characteristic of neo-Lutheranism to regard conscience as a fundamental dimension, since the law of

God, which will wreck the human being's self-sufficiency, is supposed to make itself felt in conscience. The alarm caused by the wreckage is credited with opening up access to the gospel, to faith in its fullest sense. This is emphasized by the strict sequence: first law, then gospel. Hearing the law as God's unconditional claim causes the human being to founder, acknowledge sin and depend on justification through Jesus Christ. This is acknowledged in the conscience. Conscience thus is linked especially to the *usus theologicus legis* or the *usus elenchticus*. While the realization of being a sinner makes a person's conscience anxious, the belief in justification and forgiveness comes as a liberation. Bonhoeffer, however, denies that conscience is primarily bound up with law.[30] He sees conscience primarily bound up with Christ. This makes him turn against the Lutheran principle that the sequence law-gospel is not reversible. In other words, he sides here with Karl Barth. Why?

In Luther's worldview, the law had a clear place and function. Both atheism – to which modern indifferentism belongs – and nihilism were absent from his world. For Luther, all people, even those who, from the standpoint of Christendom, were unbelievers and godless, were confronted by the law of God insofar as God's law was concrete in natural law which coincided with the Decalogue. The powerful significance of God's law for everyone had been internalized in personal as well as in collective consciousness. Accordingly, Christian proclamation had to address the human person again and again with a vivid description of the law of God, to arouse the human's conscience and lead to the acknowledgment of sin.

In the world of Barth and Bonhoeffer, natural law as the universally valid law of God, evident to all, no longer existed. Neo-Lutheranism unintentionally stressed this fact. Lutheran opinion leaders, fighting against the Barmen Theological Declaration, had to explain what God's concrete law meant in the present situation, i.e. under National Socialist government. In the Ansbach Council of June 11, 1934, they declared that the law 'points to our obligations within the structures ordained by God to which we are subject, such as family, nation, race (i.e. blood relation) ... The natural structures ... manifest to us God's claiming will' – in other words, they are the concrete law of God.[31] This explanation of the law, which referred to nation and race in the sense of modern ideologies, confirmed that this was no longer Luther's world in which God's law had been a natural law with evident validity to which conscience corresponded. In the contemporary world there was, as Bonhoeffer said, 'no more ground under one's feet,'[32] no basis for a universally binding ethic and corresponding conscience. The world had become religionless inasmuch as a universally valid law of God could no longer be discovered in it, only laws of nature and evolution. The principle of the frustrating encounter with law as the preparation for faith was without metaphysical backing. Ultimate reality had to be looked for in a different way. Neither of its own accord, nor from its relatedness to law, but only in its orientation to Christ could conscience now gain authority and specificity.

By no means does Bonhoeffer deny that conscience, as a forum of disputing inner voice in the human being, is a universal phenomenon. However 'natural conscience' is understood by him to be a 'sentinel to warn against transgressing the law of life.'[33] The laws peculiar to life and essential to its preservation are expressly dealt with in the chapter-fragment, 'The Natural Life.'[34] What is unnatural will destroy life, and life is to a certain degree capable of fending off destruction. A regime which notoriously treads underfoot all justice must in the long run destroy itself, just as the antichrist destroys the world. But the laws of natural life are difficult to recognize and contradictory in themselves, or antinomian. In order to interpret them one must place them in the perspective which was opened when Christ came into this world. Christ's promise is, 'I am the life.'[35] The mystery of true life is shown in the paradox of the saying of Jesus, 'Whoever wants to save his life will lose it, but whoever loses his life for my sake will save it.'[36] Life perceived in its naturalness and life given in Christ is not two kinds of life, but is one, and comes to clarity and unity in Christ. Similarly, it can be said of conscience that the 'liberated conscience remains what it was as natural conscience, namely, the sentinel against the transgression of the law of life.'[37] Liberated conscience does not merely warn. It also authorizes taking upon oneself free responsibility. Luther spoke of this authority, this freedom, when he said in 1535, 'If only we have Christ, we can initiate new laws, new Decalogues, which are clearer than that of Moses.'[38]

Are there connections between Bonhoeffer's experience in 1939 and his statements in the *Ethik* with respect to conscience? In both instances we find a process of self-examination. In addition to the voice of reason with its arguments pro and contra, vital emotions come into play, as represented by Bonhoeffer's tormenting homesickness in 1939. This emotion reminds him of the essence of his life – the community with his brethren in Germany, a community of discipleship. In the *Ethik*, he says that conscience warns against transgressing the law of life, the law of one's own life. During the voyage to the United States in 1939, Bonhoeffer was beset by moral doubts whether he had not in the end been dishonest with himself. He regarded it as dishonest not to accept the life which he felt to be his proper life. In the *Ethik*, he speaks of the call of conscience to unity with oneself. Already before arriving in the United States in 1939, Bonhoeffer asked himself, 'Have I [with this departure from dangerous Germany] left the place where He [Christ] ... is for me?' In the *Ethik*, he says that the liberated conscience 'calls me to unity with myself in Jesus Christ.'[39]

Peter Möser assessed the relationship between Bonhoeffer's practice and theory of conscience rather skeptically. I come to a different conclusion, since I find that the chief points of Bonhoeffer's practice in 1939 and theory in the *Ethik* are congruent. In agreement with Karl Barth's basic view, Bonhoeffer had to reject the Neo-Lutheran teaching on conscience. Yet he differs from Barth at a certain point, namely, when he speaks of the conscious acceptance of guilt in the action demanded as free responsibility. Here he enters a dimension of Christian self-examination which had never before been explored. The incurring of guilt in an act which in terms of morals is unconditionally required is usually considered to be tragic.[40] The entanglement in guilt of those involved in the conspiracy against Hitler also seems tragic. Bonhoeffer rejects this interpretation. For the one thing which in the Bible and to Luther is of ultimate importance is not a tragedy but the reconciliation of the world to God through Jesus Christ in acceptance and forgiveness of guilt. What is important is single-minded obedient living by the power of reconciliation which authorizes one to take upon oneself free responsibility. Such living is the goal of Christian self-examination, and thus of liberated conscience.

NOTES

1. Peter Möser, *Gewissenspraxis und Gewissenstheorie bei Dietrich Bonhoeffer* (Heidelberg, 1983).
2. Isaiah 41:9. Bonhoeffer, *Gesammelte Schriften*, ed. E. Bethge, vol. I, (Munich, 1958), p. 294.
3. Ibid., p. 298.
4. Ibid., p. 303.
5. Ibid., pp. 303f
6. Ibid., p. 309.
7. Ibid., p. 320.
8. Ibid., p. 304.
9. Ibid., p. 315.
10. Bonhoeffer, *Ethik als Gestaltung,* in *Ethik,* ed. E. Bethge, (1949), re-ordered edition (Munich, 1963), p. 72. The latter edition is cited below.
11. Ibid., p. 70.
12. Ibid., p. 70.
13. Bonhoeffer, *Gesammelte Schriften* vol. I, p. 357.
14. Bonhoeffer, *Widerstand und Ergebung*, ed. E. Bethge, new edition (Munich, 1970), p. 14.
15. Bonhoeffer, *Ethik*, p. 69.
16. Ibid., p. 21.
17. Ibid., p. 23.
18. Ibid., p. 24.
19. Ibid., p. 27.
20. Bonhoeffer, *Widerstand und Ergebung*, p. 15.
21. Bonhoeffer, *Ethik,* p. 238.
22. Ibid., pp. 41ff., 47-58.
23. Ibid., p. 256.
24. Ibid., p. 257.
25. Ibid., p. 257.
26. Ibid., p. 259.
27. Ibid., p. 260.
28. Bonhoeffer, *Widerstand und Ergebung*, p. 16.
29. Bonhoeffer, *Ethik*, p. 263.
30. Ibid., p. 259.
31. See K.D. Schmidt, *Die Bekenntnisse des Jahres 1934* (Göttingen, 1935). p. 103.
32. Bonhoeffer, *Widerstand und Ergebung*, p. 12.
33. Bonhoeffer, *Ethik,* p. 263.
34. Ibid., pp. 154-158.
35. John 14:6; 11:25; cf, *Ethik*, pp. 230ff.
36. Luke 9:24.
37. Bonhoeffer, *Ethik*, p. 263.
38. Luther, *Disputationsthesen für Hieronymus Weller*, Weimar edition 391, 47; cf. Bonhoeffer, *Ethik*, p. 268.
39. Bonhoeffer, *Gesammelte Schriften* vol. I, p. 294; Bonhoeffer, *Ethik*, p. 259.
40. Bonhoeffer, *Ethik*, p. 245f.

Dietrich Bonhoeffer: Ultimate, Penultimate and Their Impact

THE ORIGIN AND ESSENCE OF ETHICS

Ján Liguš

1

A Brief Survey of the Ultimate and Penultimate

The theological concept of 'the Ultimate and the Penultimate' occurs in several of Bonhoeffer's earlier works. The first evidence is found in a letter dated 1926, which was written to a fellow student named Widmann. In the letter, Bonhoeffer reproached him for making the penultimate the decisive criterion. Although we possess Widmann's response, Bonhoeffer's letter is no longer available. As a result we are unable to reconstruct an essential part of that discussion.[1]

Two years later Bonhoeffer again raised the question of the ultimate and the penultimate in one of his Barcelona sermons on 1 John 2:17, delivered on August 26, 1928, in which he held this world and everything that happens in it to be penultimate. It becomes such in light of 'the ultimate,' which means 'death.'[2] Even death, however, becomes the thing before the last, over against eternity.[3]

In the lecture, 'Problems of Theological Anthropology II: Belief and Believing' (1932), Bonhoeffer dealt with the expressions *habitus* and esse. We may assume, based on the content of the lecture, that they refer respectively to the last thing and the thing before the last. We quote: 'The *habitus* is aware it is penultimate in light of the definitiveness of the esse and does not take itself too seriously.'[4] Although he did not say *expresso verbo* that being is the ultimate, he does explicitly state that the *habitus* is aware of its own penultimate character.

In discussing Karl Heim's book, *Belief and Thinking,* Bonhoeffer again raised the question of the ultimate in connection with 'the radical question', which is identical with 'the question of God.'[5] In the year 1935 he returned once more to the theme of the last things in his sermon on Acts 1:1-11, in which he held the outpouring of the Holy Spirit to be the ultimate. In this vein he explained the words of Jesus, 'Do not leave Jerusalem, but wait for the gift my Father promised.'[6]

According to *Letters and Papers from Prison,* the first chapter of *The Cost of Discipleship* also deals with the relation of the ulimate to the penultimate.[7]

Later, in *Ethics,* Bonhoeffer devoted a separate chapter to the abovementioned topic, entitled 'The Last Things and the Things Before the Last.'[8] The chapter was written while Bonhoeffer was staying at the Benedictine monastery of Ettal (1940-1941). Here he also wrote several other chapters of *Ethics.* Originally he intended to title his *Ethics, Wegbereitung und Einzug,* an idea which he later abandoned.[9] The individual chapters of the book were written gradually. Some are no longer extant, and even those we do have are fragmentary.[10] If Bonhoeffer had lived longer he would

59

certainly have come back to some of the theological questions raised in the *Ethics*. He might even have arranged several things differently. In the *Ethics,* however, he could only formulate the more pregnant and systematic theological problems and their relevance to the concepts of the ultimate and the penultimate. Here he also tried to express their mutual theological relation.

Finally, Bonhoeffer returned to the penultimate and ultimate while in prison. In two of his letters, dated December 5 and 18, 1943, he elaborated the things before the last and the last things. We quote from the former.

> It is only when one knows the ineffability of the Name of God that once can utter the name of Jesus Christ. It is only when one loves life and the earth so much that without them everything would be gone that one can believe in the resurrection and a new world. It is only when one submits to the law that one can speak of Grace, and only when one sees the anger and wrath of God hanging like grim realities over the head of one's enemies that one can know something of what it means to love them and forgive them... You cannot and must not speak the last word before you have spoken the next to the last. We live on the next to the last word, and believe on the last... In my *Cost of Discipleship* I just hinted at this (in Chap. I.), but did not carry it any further. I must do so someday.[11]

We add a second quote from the letter dated December 18:

> Once a man has found God in his earthly bliss and has thanked him for it, there will be plenty of opportunities for him to remind himself that these earthly pleasures are only transitory, and that it is good for him to accustom himself to the idea of eternity... The last words mean that God gathers up again with us our past, which belongs to us.[12]

According to the two letters quoted, the penultimate and the ultimate are respectively 'the ineffability of the name of God' and 'the name of Jesus Christ'; 'love of life and the earth' and 'the resurrrection and a new world'; submission 'to the law' and 'grace'; 'the anger and wrath of God' and 'to love to forgive'; 'earthly bliss', 'earthly pleasures' and 'eternity.' Thus, both of the letters outline the issue's theological importance and breadth, a breadth and importance evident in *Ethics,* as well.

2

The Return to the Ultimate and the Penultimate in Ethics

Why did Bonhoeffer return to the subject of the ultimate and penultimate in *Ethics*? There were two main reasons. The first was a personal theological desire to speak a complementary word to the very important theological subject which he had already once experimentally outlined. In his *Letters and Papers from Prison*, he related this personal desire to *The Cost of Discipleship,* in which he understood the Christian's relation to the world only in negative terms. Bonhoeffer wanted to express it differently in order to avoid a non-bilblical understanding of the relation between the ultimate and penultimate. It was also, however, connected with a theological development; for the second reason seems to have been the contemporary theological situation in

'Western Christendom' as well as the theological situation which Bonhoeffer noted for its misunderstanding of 'the connection of the penultimate with the ultimate, even though their attitude to this ultimate is not in any way hostile.'[13] Bonhoeffer contributed to that theological discussion by attemping to find a theological answer to this biblically and ethically pressing question. His answer was very significant in his own time no comma, and is still important today.

Bonhoeffer seemed to characterize his theological situation at that time as having two *extreme solutions* to the problem of the relation between the ultimate and the penultimate. They are the so-called Christian *radicalism* and *compromise*. In radicalism 'the stability of the penultimate which was closely linked here with the ultimate is imperilled,'[14] whereas a compromise solution endangers the character and quality of the ultimate. Radicalism understands Christ as 'a destroyer and enemy of everything penultimate and everything penultimate is enmity towards Christ.' In the compromise solution, the role of Christ is understood in the opposite way. Christ serves as 'eternal justification for things as they are.'[15] Radicalism is one-sided in that it sees all earthly things in light of 'the approaching end.' Yet radicalism can take two forms. On the one hand, it manifests itself 'in withdrawing from the world', while on the other, it strives for 'improving the world.' This latter form of radicalism, however, 'confuses the reality of the living Jesus Christ with the realization of the Christian idea.'[16]

In contradistinction to radicalism, compromise proclaims the dignity of the penultimate. It 'retains its rights on its own account and is not threatened or imperilled by the ultimate.' But while compromise acknowledges the status quo in this world, it neither influences nor determines its form.[17] Both radicalism and compromise arise from a sort of hate. Radicalism hates 'creation', and compromise hates 'the justification of the sinner by grace alone.'[18]

By way of contrast, in searching for the resolution of the relation between the ultimate and the penultimate we must be aware that it is for the sake of 'the ultimate that we must speak of the penultimate.' And yet again, the things before the last do not exist on their own. They are not self-existent, 'as though a thing could justify itself in itself as being a thing before the last things.'[19] Things only *become* penultimate, because the penultimate is dependent on the ultimate. That also means that 'the penultimate... does not determine the ultimate. It is the ultimate which determines the penultimate.'[20]

Both of these temptations can also be found in Christian churches today, and they both appeal to Jesus Christ for support. One radical temptation, it seems to me, is for Christians to detach themselves from the problems of this world. It is demonstrated by the indifference of the churches toward social, political, economic and peace activities. They do not take part because their point of departure is the end of the world.

Compromise is also indifferent towards the strivings of the people for social justice and a better future, because Christ once for all justified the penultimate. It shares radicalism's economic, social, and political passivity, albeit for different reasons. Although their approach to reality is similar to a certain extent, they differ in their theological justification for that approach. Neither radicalism nor compromise want to bear their Christian responsibility for the penultimate as they should. To the adherents of Christian radicalism it must be said 'that Christ is not radical in their sense.' The followers of compromise must also hear 'that Christ does not make compromises.' Radical Christians do not see God's love for this world revealed in Jesus Christ (John 3:16), and compromising Christians omit the biblical relevance of the end (1 John 2:17).

The only consistent resolution of the relation between the ultimate and the penultimate is found in Christology. It lies in God's saving work, in the person and life of Jesus Christ. 'In Him alone lies the solution for the problem of the relation between the ultimate and the penultimate.'[21] In Jesus Christ God's three saving acts are implied: incarnation, crucifixion, and resurrection.

Jesus Christ incarnate means that 'God enters into created reality.' The incarnate God, Jesus Christ, does not render the human reality independent, nor does He destroy it in anticipation, 'but He allows it to remain as that which is before the last, as a penultimate which needs to be taken seriously...'[22] The event of Christ's crucifixion means 'that God pronounced His final condemnation on the fallen creation.' He attributed to His Son, Jesus, 'the iniquity of us all' (Isa. 53:5). The world may live before God because Jesus Christ died for its sins. The resurrection of Jesus witnesses to us 'that God out of His love and omnipotence sets an end to death and calls a new creation into life, imparts a new life – "Old things are passed away" (2 Cor. 5:17).' The resurrection brought us a new life of victory over death. This new life with the incarnate, crucified, and risen Lord Jesus is to be lived in this world of the penultimate.[23] He is the real connection between the ultimate and the penultimate.

3

The Ultimate and the Penultimate: What are they?

3.1. *The ultimate – time and quality*

Bonhoeffer speaks of the ultimate in two ways. On the one hand, he considers the ultimate to be the reformative disclosure of the omitted biblical message, which at that time was known as the 'event of justification of a sinner' by faith and by grace alone. On the other hand, he also views the ultimate in a wider context using the expressions: 'God's compassion on a sinner', 'God's final word', 'God's own free word', or 'the Gospel' in general.[24] Into this context are taken justification by faith (*sola fide*) and by grace (*sola gratia*) as well as God's complete saving, gracious acts as revealed in the life and work of Jesus Christ and contained in the Holy Scripture. Specifically, the ultimate is the message of justification; more generally, it encompasses the whole Gospel which is implied in Jesus Christ.

God's compassion on sinners is the last thing temporally and qualitatively. Temporally, God's mercy is the favorable time. It does not lie within our human power, and cannot be counted on; and it is truly unique time. It is his time, given to us for forgiveness of sins. 'There is a time when God permits, awaits and prepares, and there is a final time which cuts short and passes sentence upon the ultimate.'[25]

Qualitatively, God's mercy on sinners is the last word. 'The qualitatively final word excludes every kind of method once and for all.'[26] Methods represent humanity's attempt to come to God on its own. This form of religion is strictly rejected by Bonhoeffer. The quality of God's compassion is received by faith alone. Faith is not a method, however, but the gift of God.

3.2. *The penultimate – the preaching of the Gospel*

The question may be raised whether Bonhoeffer considered the preaching of the Gospel as the ultimate or the penultimate. In some parts of his *Ethics* the preaching of the Gospel is considered the ultimate, since the preaching of grace is identified with God's action of mercy. To preach means to bring God's compassion to humanity. We could, however, also consider the preaching of God's Word a human activity, which would then be regarded as the penultimate. A distinction must be made, therefore, between the preaching of the Gospel as human action and God's mercy and compassion toward man as God's own free action. Preaching the Gospel, then, becomes the penultimate, the ultimate being God's action alone — the imparting of his compassion to sinners. Therefore the preaching of the Gospel is partly human action, and partly God's action. It is considered the penultimate because in preaching the human being acts with God. However, it is only God's action that has soteriological significance.

It is possible to preach the Gospel in a variety of ways, not all of which bring the ultimate itself. The penultimate 'is everything that precedes the ultimate, everything that precedes the justification of the sinner by grace alone.' At the same time, the penultimate is everything 'which follows the ultimate and yet again precedes it.' Bonhoeffer also speaks of the penultimate as 'any action, suffering, movement, volition, defeat, uprising, entreaty or hope.'[27] All the preceding expressions point out that the penultimate is characterized by human action — and preaching is also a human action.

It has already been stated that the final word 'excludes every kind of method once for all.' This statement can also refer to non-methodical preaching. The meaning here can be seen in the following:

> It is senseless and wrong, therefore, if one preaches to a Christian congregation today that each and every one must first become like Mary Magdalene, like beggar Lazarus, like the thief on the cross, like all these dim peripheral figures, before he can become capable of hearing the final word of God.[28]

Such a method concentrates preaching on biblical characters. It thus reduces the Gospel to human problems alone.

Bonhoeffer rejected method as a way to knowledge of God already in his earlier works. In *Act and Being* he wrote, 'There is no method for the cognition of God.'[29] In *The Cost of Discipleship* he was critical of the so-called 'Lutheran method' which was applied to justification by faith and grace alone, making costly grace cheap.[30] Bonhoeffer's *Letters and Papers from Prison* are also against method in preaching. Here Bonhoeffer was critical of preaching which reduced the Gospel to 'the so-called solving of insoluble problems of human weakness or on the border of human existence.' To this same category of preaching belongs that which deals with the 'religious premise of humanity' and the 'so-called ultimate questions — death, guilt.' Along with religious method, Bonhoeffer also rejected secular methods, such as those of 'existentialist philosophy and psychotherapy', or last but not least, preaching directed toward 'the intimate life.'[31] Also belonging to this group is preaching which calls into question a person's health, vigor, or fortune 'regarded in themselves, or looked upon as evil fruits.' This was never done by Jesus. Method is always something partial, a type of religion which does not take into account the essence of the Gospel, i.e., Jesus Christ, the incarnate, crucified, and risen Lord as the only center of the Gospel.[32]

In his *Ethics*, Bonhoeffer arrived at a theological relevance for nonreligious preaching while dealing with the ultimate and penultimate, a relevance which he again strongly emphasized in his letters from prison. This nonreligious preaching is Christological in the strict sense — it interprets the Gospel as Jesus did: 'When Jesus blessed sinners, they were the real sinners, but Jesus did not make every person a sinner first. He called them out of their sin, not into their sin.'

3.3. *Preparing the way as the penultimate*

Bonhoeffer used various biblical texts to substantiate the necessity of preparing the way. They include Psalm 107:16; Micah 2:13; Psalm 9:16; Isaiah 40:4, and particularly Luke 3:4ff. which reads, 'Prepare the way for the Lord...' – the Advent message preached by John the Baptist.

He gives the following reason for this Christian activity of preparation. First, 'it is the world itself that demands it.' The way must be prepared 'for the coming of grace.' Secondly, it is the universality of God's love revealed to us in the cross of Christ 'who desires to come to all men.'[33]

What is the preparing of the way? It is a formative activity on the very greatest scale which is inseparably connected with the preaching of the Gospel. While it is not identical with preaching, it must not be separated from it. Preparing the way is a Christian activity consisting in the removal of 'whatever obstructs it and makes it difficult', i.e., the acceptance of the justification of a sinner by faith and grace alone. Among the obstructions are personal circumstances which prevent people from believing in God, such as disappointment in belief, internal lack of discipline, etc.; conditions which make it difficult to accept God's grace. It also includes social circumstances such as living in utter shame, desolation, poverty, exploitation, oppression, and hunger. Such circumstances make it nearly impossible to believe in God's justice and might. Hence preaching the Gospel means doing the penultimate as well. The Good News of the coming kingdom of God must change such social conditions as discrimination, racism, and oppression. Evangelism must go hand in hand with social outreach, with the struggle against the unjust social order.

Doing the penultimate as an inseparable part of the preaching of the Gospel is not the same as the social reform of autonomous ethics. Rather the penultimate is actions of Christian churches done in ambiguous human conditions to lend credence to the Christian faith and the Gospel in general. 'If the hungry person does not attain to faith then the guilt falls on those who refused him bread. To provide the hungry person with bread is to prepare the way for the coming of grace.' Striving for social justice is rooted in the Gospel. At the same time, however, Christians can cooperate in this struggle with those who do not believe in God. Nevertheless, the Christian contribution to the struggle always remains a doing of the penultimate, and is unthinkable without the ultimate — justification by faith alone, i.e., the Gospel. 'To give bread to the hungry person is not the same as to proclaim the grace of God and justification to him, and to have received bread is not the same as to have faith. ... It is penultimate. The coming of Grace is the ultimate.'[34]

We suggest that a connection between the preaching of the Gospel and preparing the way can also be found in Bonhoeffer's letters from prison. We refer here to Bonhoeffer's expression, Jesus as a man 'for others.' This is a real encounter with Jesus Christ 'implying a complete orientation of human beings to the experience of Jesus as one whose only concern is for others.' Jesus Christ brought the Good News of the coming kingdom of God, and at the same time helped the people. He changed their social living conditions. And yet again even the time of nonreligious interpretation must be prepared. The penultimate has here the important meaning that 'Our Christianity today will be confined to praying for and doing right by our fellow men' before 'the day will come when men will be called again to utter the word of God with such power as will change and renew the world.'[35] Doing right means to free people from oppression and racism, to give bread to the hungry, and the like.

Preparing the way is understood as an action of God as well. Although Bonhoeffer was aware of situations in which one is able to remove obstructions and even change social conditions, he also recognized that it is beyond our abilities to change the human heart. We are unable to change a person's mind. Ultimately this must be done by God's grace which 'in the end itself must prepare' the way to us, 'and grace alone must also again render the impossible.' Here Bonhoeffer quotes Micah 2:13 to emphasize that Christ alone is the breaker of all bonds, and he himself 'makes His own way, when He comes.'[36]

In his discussion of preparing the way as Christian penultimate, Bonhoeffer expressed the most pressing and acute question concerning missionary work in the present world. Christian responsibility in this world consists of two types of Christian service. The first is the preaching of the Gospel which testifies to the word and grace of Jesus Christ. The second is the social struggle against oppression, poverty, marginalization, and racism of Third World people in Africa, Asia, Latin America, and in other parts of the world. It is unthinkable to preach the Gospel while at the same time supporting social injustice and racism by pointing to the Bible. To do the penultimate means to prepare the way for the Gospel. This is to struggle on the side of the poor, oppressed, and those who are discriminated against. This is a confessional question.

Urban Rural Mission, e.g., understands its works as evangelism in conjunction with the struggle to change social conditions.

Salvation works in the struggle for economic justice against the exploitation of people by people. Salvation works in the struggle for human dignity against political oppression of human beings by their fellow men. Salvation works in the struggle for solidarity against the alienation of person from person. Salvation works in the struggle of hope against despair in personal life.[37]

3.4. *The natural as the penultimate*

While working on the chapter entitled 'The Natural,' Bonhoeffer wrote, 'The concept of the natural has fallen into discredit in Protestant ethics.' E. Bethge reminds us that some passages of Bonhoeffer's *Ethics* were written during his stay at the monastery at Ettal where Catholic influence was very strong. In spite of this influence, however, this chapter has a much stronger Christological character than was the case in most Catholic ethics of the time. Christology here plays a key role indeed.[38]

The natural is related to creation, the Fall through which 'the creature becomes nature', and to Jesus Christ. The natural is not what Protestant dogmaticians have named *corruptio naturae humanae totaliter*. This is more appropriately called the unnatural. Nor is it what Protestant orthodoxy taught about the divine image which remained in man after the Fall, even though the natural remains after the Fall. Neither can the natural in Bonhoeffer's thought be identified with the Catholic doctrine that reason retained its essential integrity after the Fall, and was thus able to grasp the formal determination of the natural. Of course, reason belongs to the natural life, yet reason is determined by the Fall. The natural ultimately had nothing to do with a restoration of *theologica naturalis,* which Bonhoeffer criticized. The natural is not any religious profundity of the human soul. From the human soul and heart come totally unnatural things such as 'evil thoughts, sexual immorality, theft, murder, adultery', etc. (Mk. 7:21). The natural is not identified with things that are considered to be natural. The natural is the created reality of man given him by God. It shows its character and the created reality in all forms of his family relations and his national and cultural heritage. The natural is the facts given by God which make man what he is — they make substantial characters of humanity. The whole variety of the natural is expressed in Bonhoeffer's *Ethics*, especially in his chapters on 'Natural Life', 'Suum cuique', 'The Right to Bodily Life', 'The Freedom of Bodily Life', and 'The Natural Rights of the Life of the Mind.'[39]

It is of crucial importance to understand that the natural can never be something which is determined by any single part or any single authority within the fallen world. Men are to live in the natural, to shape natural facts by their lives. People shape the natural according to their attitude to God and their understanding ot the relation between the ultimate and the penultimate.

The natural, like all created things, does not exist in itself. It does not have its own autonomous existence. Rather, it exists in its relation to the Mediator. 'It is only from Christ Himself that it receives its validation.' The natural is related to the Fall, but as directed towards Christ. In him alone lies its existence. He is, as John says, 'the true light that gives light to every man [who] was coming into the world' (Jn. 1:9).

'It is through the incarnation of Christ that the natural life becomes the penultimate which is directed toward the ultimate.' And again, through Christ alone the unnatural can be exposed 'once and for all as the destruction of the penultimate.'[40] The relation of the natural to Christ does not disqualify a relative freedom of the natural life. After the Fall 'the direct dependence of the creature on God is replaced by a relative freedom of natural life.'[41] In other words, the natural is relatively free in its dependence on Christ.

The natural is determined with respect to both its form and content. Formally, it is established by God's will to preserve life within the fallen world. 'The natural is the form of life preserved by God for the fallen world and directed toward justification, redemption, and renewal through Christ.'[42] God's will for the preservation of natural life in the fallen world was realized in Jesus Christ. For Christ's sake God preserves this world. As to its contents, everything is implied in God's will, including all nations. 'The natural is the form of the preserved life itself, the form which embraces the entire human race.'[43] This will is demonstrated by God's divine mandates. Bonhoeffer speaks of 'the mandate of labor, of marriage, of the Church and the divine mandate of goverment.'[44] In his letters from prison he discusses 'friendship', 'culture and education.'[45] Divine mandates are not autonomous spheres of man's life, but also exist for Christ's sake. Their validation is through him alone. All mandates 'are directed towards Christ, and in Christ.'[46]

The natural, as facts given by God, is constantly imperilled by the unnatural in history. While the natural is directed towards Christ, 'the unnatural is that which after the Fall closes its doors against the coming of Christ.'[47] The natural is dependent on Christ alone, whereas the unnatural 'posits itself as an absolute, declares itself to be the source of the natural, and thereby disintegrates the natural life.' The natural is 'established and decided in advance.' The unnatural 'consists essentially in organization and the natural cannot be organized, but it is simply here.'[48] Bonhoeffer uses the respect children have for their parents as an example. Such respect cannot be organized – it is given – but the undermining of that respect must be organized. Finally, the natural 'is the safe-guarding of life against the unnatural.' In contradistinction to this, the unnatural 'is a destroyer of life,' the enemy of life.[49]

This tension or struggle between the unnatural and the natural has been present throughout history, and it will continue as long as life itself. However, Bonhoeffer views the struggle optimistically in anticipation of the victory of the natural. He speaks of immanent optimism 'rooted in the natural.' This is not in the sense of a gradual overcoming of sin, but rather optimism rooted in the substance of the natural. 'But so long as life continues, the natural will always reassert itself.'[50] The constant threat of a total destruction of the natural, however, 'sets a limit to the immanent optimism', and this is an eschatological end. 'You will be betrayed by parents, brothers, relatives and friends, and they will put some of you to death' (Lk. 21:16). This, of course, means the utter destruction of the natural.[51]

3.5. *The Christian life and the penultimate*

People have two alternatives by which to live their natural lives. Either they live 'to their own condemnation if they despise it', or they live to 'their own salvation if they give it its due.'[52] Which alternative they choose depends on their attitude towards the ultimate, i.e., to God's compassion on sinners. Without faith in God's justification, people live their natural lives in 'disunity with God and men.'[53] Their conscience gives witness to their disunity within themselves. The natural life, even though it is related to Christ, is not the same as the Christian life, which is 'neither a destruction nor a sanctioning of the penultimate.'[54] The Christian life presupposes receiving justification by grace and by faith alone. God's grace is an essential part of Christian ethics. It is the ultimate itself. The point of departure of the Christian life is, once again, Christology.

'Christian life is life with the incarnate, crucified and risen Christ, whose word confronts us in its entirety in the message of the justification of the sinner by grace alone.' Men begin to live in it when they come to believe in their justification. Not only that, but after the dawning of the ultimate in me, it is 'the life of Jesus Christ in me.'[55] No autonomous philosophical or religious ethic can lead to this life; it cannot be achieved through any ethical program in advance. it is only God's grace and man's faith which achieve the Christian life.

The Christian life is life with Christ, or Christ's life in me. It is the life which can be expressed in the words of the apostle Paul. 'We live by faith, not by sight' (1 Cor. 5:7). It is faith directed towards the ultimate, i.e., Christ. The Christian life 'is always life in the penultimate which waits for the ultimate.'[56]

Bonhoeffer's answer to the question of what the Christian life is demonstrates a serious attempt to avoid the two theological extremes of the day: radicalism and compromise. Both of them were rejected by him. 'The question of the Christian life will not, therefore, be decided and answered either by radicalism, or by compromise, but only by reference to Jesus Christ Himself.'[57] Before writing his *Ethics,* Bonhoeffer himself leaned toward the radical perception of the Christian life. This was the case when he wrote *The Cost of Discipleship.* He admitted this in one of his letters from prison in which he wrote: 'I thought I could acquire faith by trying to live a holy life, or something like it...'[58]

Radicalism understood the Christian life as the life which struggled against this world. It is a so-called Christian struggle 'with a hostile world for the establishment of God's Kingdom on earth.'[59] In his *Ethics,* his re-evaluation is evident, and he perceives the Christian life as life with Christ in this world. It is the penultimate directed toward the ultimate, i.e., an eschatological perspective. Bonhoeffer rejected radicalism, but does not therefore accept the compromise solution. Christology helps him to avoid both extremes.

Bonhoeffer's mind was constantly occupied with the question of what the Christian life is. The answers he applied to this question were different at different times in his life. When he wrote *The Cost of Discipleship* he understood the Christian life as following Christ. This could happen only in a struggle with the world.[60] In his *Ethics,* he views the Christian life as participation 'in the encounter of Christ with this world.'[61] The Christian life is life 'in genuine worldliness.'[62] The cross of Christ sets us free for that life. It is not life with Christ against the world, but rather, with Christ in and for this world. In his *Letters and Papers from Prison*, Bonhoeffer defines the Christian life as 'living completely in this world.' It means a participation in God's suffering 'in the world and with Christ in Gethsemane.'[63] But even while in prison, Bonhoeffer could not find an answer to the question.

> But we too are being driven back to first principles. Atonement and redemption, regeneration, the Holy Ghost, the love of our enemies, the cross and resurrection, life in Christ and Christian discipleship — all these things have become so problematic and so remote that we hardly dare any more to speak of them.[64]

Because of his death, we do not have Bonhoeffer's answer to the question of what the Christian life is. Perhaps if he had lived longer we might have been able to read his answer.

3.6. *This world seen as the penultimate*

Ernst Feil notes that Bonhoeffer reached a new understanding of the world by differentiating the ultimate and the penultimate.[65] It is our opinion that it helped Bonhoeffer to give up the radical and compromise perception of the Christian relation to this world. In radicalism 'Christ is the sign that the world is ripe for burning.' Man lives in the dilemma whether to be for Christ and against the world, or to be for the world and against Christ. The compromise solution, on the other hand, presents 'the metaphysical purification from the accusation which weighs upon everything that is.'[66] Karl Barth's theology, which Bonhoeffer called 'the positivist doctrine of revelation,' takes the radical position regarding the world. 'The world is... made to depend upon itself and left to its own devices.' It can also be said of Althaus's theological reflection that it 'left the world to its own devices.'[67] In addition, the compromise solution accepted the stance of liberal theology in 'that it allowed the world the right to assign Christ his place in that world', which later resulted in capitulation.[68]

In the broadest sense, this world is the penultimate. It could also be said that the world becomes the penultimate. We are not referring here to the world in itself, nor to the world as it is or as it understands itself. The world in itself strives 'for its own deification.' The world as the penultimate is not an autonomous world. It is the world related to Jesus Christ, regardless of whether it is aware of this relation or not. The world, like all created things, is created through Christ. It is preserved by him and with him as its end, 'and consists in Christ alone.' Paul's expression's 'by him', 'for him', and 'in him' (Col. 1:16-17) are used here. Jesus Christ only reveals 'the secret of the world' and 'the secret of God.'[69]

The secret of the world is its character. The world as it is in reality is 'dark and evil', 'godless', and 'godforsaken.' The evidence is in its attitude to Jesus Christ. The crucifixion of Jesus, God's Son, happened because 'the whole world has become godless.'[70] This character of the world was hidden, but through the revelation of Christ it was made manifest. 'The secret of God', revealed in Jesus, refers to God's love for men. The world as it is did not cease to be an object of God's attention. 'It is still the world which is loved by God and reconciled with Him.'[71] Jesus gave himself up on the cross of Calvary. He is also the living, risen Lord 'to whom all power is given in heaven and on earth. All powers of the world are made subject to Him and must serve Him each in its own way.'[72]

From the incarnate Christ, the crucified, risen Lord, emerges the missionary task of the church. The Christian church is not here in order to deprive the world of some of its territory, not to provide the basis for any kind of domination over it, but to give witness to Jesus Christ, Redeemer, Reconciler, and Lord of this world. With the message of Jesus Christ as the backdrop, this world should be understood as the penultimate. This is why the Christian can understand the world better than it understands itself.

In conclusion, it is clear that both expressions, the ultimate and the penultimate, are very important in Bonhoeffer's theological reflection. Through them he draws profound conclusions regarding the Reformation message of justification by grace and by faith alone. He also takes up again his earlier thought about costly and cheap grace, which he expressed in *The Cost of Discipleship*. By dealing with the ultimate and penultimate, Bonhoeffer succeeded in formulating a new understanding of such vital theological issues as the Christian life in this world, the relation to the natural, and finally, a new attitude toward preaching the Gospel, which is most prevalent in his nonreligious interpretation as found in *Letters and Papers from Prison*.

The theological and biblical analysis of these issues is found through an understanding of Bonhoeffer's Christology, which is the reliable foundation upon which his theological conclusions have been built. Jesus Christ, the incarnate, crucified, and risen Lord, is the only Redeemer and Reconciler of the world. He is the only connection between the ultimate and the penultimate. He alone provides the answer to the meaning of preparing the way, preaching the Gospel, the natural, and the Christian life. He alone is the essence of Christian ethics.

NOTES

1. Eberhard Bethge, *Dietrich Bonhoeffer - Theologe, Christ, Zeitgenosse*, 1st ed., p. 125.
2. Dietrich Bonhoeffer, *Gesammelte Schriften*, ed. E. Bethge, 1st ed., vol. I, p. 455. 'Die Welt ist eine Welt des Sterbens und des Todes.'
3. Ibid.
4. Bethge, pp. 1092-1095, especially p. 1094.
5. Bonhoeffer, *Gesammelte Schriften*, vol. III, p. 140.
6. Bonhoeffer, *Gesammelte Schriften*, vol. IV, pp. 184-185.
7. Dietrich Bonhoeffer, *Letters and Papers from Prison* (1967), p. 50; see also Dietrich Bonhoeffer, *Nachfolge* (1966), pp. 11ff.
8. Dietrich Bonhoeffer, 'The Last Things and the Things Before the Last,' *Ethics*, ed. E. Bethge (1971), pp. 98-159.
9. Bonhoeffer, *Gesammelte Schriften* vol. II, p. 384.
10. Ibid., pp. 389-394.
11. Bonhoeffer, *Letters*, p. 50.

12. Ibid., p. 57.
13. Bonhoeffer, *Ethics,* p. 119.
14. Ibid., p. 118.
15. Ibid., p. 105.
16. Ibid., p. 107.
17. Ibid.
18. Ibid.
19. Ibid., p. 110. 'Radicalism hates time, and compromise hates eternity. Radicalism hates patience, and compromise hates decision. Radicalism hates wisdom, and compromise hates simplicity. Radicalism hates the real, and compromise hates the word.' pp. 107-108. 'Ivan Karamazov, who at the same time makes the figure of the radical Jesus in the legend of the Grand Inquisitor.' p. 107.
20. Ibid., pp. 110-111.
21. Ibid., p. 108.
22. Ibid., pp. 108-109.
23. Ibid., pp. 102, 109.
24. Ibid., pp. 100-102, 112, 116.
25. Ibid., p. 102.
26. Ibid., p. 101.
27. Ibid., p. 102. 'The qualitatively final word, therefore, forbids us from the outset to set our eyes on the way of Luther or the way of Paul as though these were ways which we had to pursue again...,' p. 101.
28. Ibid., p. 101. 'The purpose of the Christian message is not that one should become like one or another of those biblical characters, but that one shall be like Christ himself.'
29. Dietrich Bonhoeffer, *Akt und Sein* (1964), p. 70.
30. 'Gnade als Prinzip, pecca fortiter als Prinzip, billige Gnade ist zuletzt nur ein neues Gesetz, das nicht hilft und nicht befreit.' Bonhoeffer, *Nachfolge,* p. 24.
31. Bonhoeffer, *Letters,* pp. 91, 93, 107, 115.
32. Ibid., p. 115.
33. Bonhoeffer, *Ethics,* pp. 112, 113, 117.
34. Ibid., p. 114.
35. Bonhoeffer, *Letters,* p. 160.
36. Bonhoeffer, *Ethics,* p. 112, 113.
37. WCC, *Urban Rural Mission Reflections,* papers from the WCC Celebration and Challenge Conference (Manila, 1987), pp. 21-22.
38. Ernst Feil, *Die Theologie Dietrich Bonhoeffers - Hermeneutik, Christologie, Weltverständnis* (1977), pp. 297-302.
39. Bonhoeffer, *Ethics,* pp. 125-159.
40. Ibid., p. 122.
41. Ibid., p. 121.
42. Ibid., p. 123.
43. Ibid., p. 122.
44. Ibid., pp. 179-184.
45. Bonhoeffer, *Letters,* p. 64.
46. Bonhoeffer, *Ethics,* p. 179; see also pp. 261-267 and 252-259.
47. Ibid., p. 121.
48. Ibid., p. 124.
49. Ibid., p. 125.
50. Ibid., p. 124.
51. Ibid.
52. Ibid., p. 125.
53. Ibid., p. 5. 'Man's life is now alienation from God, with men, things and with himself.'
54. Ibid., p. 110.
55. Ibid., p. 118.
56. Ibid.
57. Ibid., p. 108.

58. Bonhoeffer, *Letters*, p. 125.
59. Bonhoeffer, *Ethics*, p. 168.
60. Bonhoeffer, *Nachfolge*, p. 238; see *Letters*, p. 125.
61. Bonhoeffer, *Ethics*, p. 110.
62. Ibid., p. 263.
63. Bonhoeffer, *Letters*, p. 112.
64. Ibid., pp. 159-160.
65. Feil, p. 343. '…durch die Unterscheidung vom Letzten und Vorletzten ein Weltverständnis entwickelt, in dem durch das Ja und Nein des Glaubens zur Welt überhaupt erst echte Weltlichkeit begründet und die Konzeption des Natürlichen inhaltlich umrissen wird.'
66. Bonhoeffer, *Ethics*, p. 105.
67. Bonhoeffer, *Letters*, pp. 95, 108.
68. Ibid., p. 108. Paul Tillich's theology toward the world: 'The world unseated him and went on by itself: he too sought to understand the world better than it understood itself.' p. 109.
69. Bonhoeffer, *Ethics*, p. 52.
70. Ibid., p. 262.
71. Ibid., p. 174.
72. Ibid., p. 264.

Ethics Is Not Everything

Gabriele Phieler

If one questions Bonhoeffer on this subject, one very quickly runs into the familiar path of the way he distinguished between the ethical, or principial, 'ought'-statements, and real life in all its diversity and individuality. He constantly emphasized that the reach of basic ethical statements is far too short to grasp the whole of human life. This 'whole life' is the key for him — it is the expression of his understanding of Christ as well as the 'stuff' of the responsible act. And so, Bonhoeffer reacts very critically to ethical dispositions which bring life into the question only in situations of decision or conflict, but for the rest interrupt or fail to consider the daily flow of life. Ultimately, that can result in these obligations or ought-statements paralyzing or immobilizing real life.

Can Bonhoeffer's thoughts on this subject relate to and help us in our contemporary situation? In my opinion they can, because Bonhoeffer has attempted to describe *that* faith which opens our eyes to real life and at the same time does not lose courage or responsibility for that life, but instead obtains and actualizes freedom. In what follows I will briefly emphasize that which is especially important for me here in Bonhoeffer's thought.

1

A Look at Our Reality

When I look around me in order to verify Bonhoeffer's distinction between ethical and real life expressions, I discover no specific ethical system, but I do experience people under ought- and duty-commands which are simply there — in church, profession, family, and state. We 'ought' to do so much, and manage, at best, to do far less. And characteristic of this 'ought' is that it comes in with such a high claim to authority that it apparently is no longer questioned. Politically, for example, this command appears in the demand for the 'construction of socialism,' or 'securing the peace.' Individually it might be formulated as 'do my best for the family.' One could also find many such demands in the church under such mottos as the 'glory of God,' or 'love of neighbour.' The bad aftertaste which they commonly leave comes when one is no longer personally or totally addressed in these demands, but is simply reduced to so many 'ought'-achievements or functions. Here also lies, in my opinion, the tendency to restrict and paralyze life which Bonhoeffer discerns; political and societal structures, and even ecclesiastical and personal structures, are felt as both undesirable and immovable, incapable of question or change. Why? It is because the person who is so obliged and commanded is fragmented into individual functions so that she no longer possesses the internal coherence to set in balance against the whole. I think that a person like Gorbachev also struggles with this experience on our contemporary political landscape as he attempts by means of new thinking to put an end to paralyzing and crippling phenomena.

2

The 'Command of God'

Over against the 'ethical,' or better yet, the 'confining ethical,' Bonhoeffer perceives the command of God as having a far broader horizon. It is striking that he can see so much that is positive in 'command,' which sounds very much to me like 'ought' and 'duty.' For, 'the command is the total and concrete claim of the person by the compassionate and holy God in Jesus Christ.'[1] Or perhaps, as he would later say, 'Jesus claims the whole human life with all its phenomena for himself and the kingdom of God.'[2]

This command is therefore first of all the acceptance of the whole human life, just as it is, in Jesus Christ. In this, the command already achieves, for Bonhoeffer, the quality which 'ethics' alone cannot have — it is *total and personal*. My world and even I myself have been accepted and borne by God in Jesus Christ.

Yet Bonhoeffer does not stop at this statement of acceptance, but seeks at the same time to point out the total and concrete claim on the person. For the command of God is the will of God *for* people as well as the claim *of* God and that command is definite, clear and concrete, otherwise it would not be the command of God.

I see Bonhoeffer constantly circling around this question in his desire to describe God's affirmative answer to the human being and the freedom the human being had gained through it. The two can only be expressed together: the total and personal bond to, and acceptance of this world along with free opposition to it; or the bond to this world and the freedom from it without falling into total acceptance of the world on the one hand or flight from it on the other. This is not possible through a principial, once for all decision, but only as a life-act in lived and led communion with Jesus Christ, as the creative *formative power* in this world. The point at which the bond and freedom intersect, for Bonhoeffer, is the responsible act, not as a synthesis of the two, nor as an addition to them, but as a risk — it means to form and cope with the experienced bond to this world in personal opposition, and through it to be freed to act. It is a question of having the orientation to act, according to Bonhoeffer as the 'moral philosopher'; yet the 'ought' demand is not enough for him since it can only hinder responsible action, and since therefore — in my opinion — an 'ought' can 'function' without reference to reality and without personal involvement. We often experience strong forms of this attitude in the G.D.R., the loss of a bond with reality and the loss of personality, directly caused by overpowering ought-demands in school and society. Many then avoid this 'ought' through apathy, 'minding their own business,' and outward conformity combined with inner personal emigration. A retreat to the private domain of the 'grumbler' and the 'spectator,' a retreat from responsibility, is easy to detect (for example, when no one among us really wants to hold a higher post — and that in state and church!). The lack of responsibility, in the meantime, is also even more frequently mentioned by the state — up to the present without much result in businesses and schools — and even more strongly in literature (for example, Stefan Heym and Christa Wolf).

The command of God therefore plays the decisive role in the creative life process of bond and freedom, because it affects people totally and personally; that is the short and long meaning of it. I also think, however, that with Bonhoeffer it also concerns the fact that the command can take away fear of the bond and fear of freedom. In that regard, three main headings stood out for me:

    a. Command and Commandments

    b. Command as 'Living-With-Others'

    c. Command as Personal Guide

In all three aspects it is a question, in my opinion, of *involving oneself with reality,* and of dealing with it for the purpose of learning — and, indeed, so much greater will be the freedom experienced.

a. Command and Commandments. Bonhoeffer does not consider the commandments to be, in the first place, a list of prohibitions which one can adequately fulfill by adopting an attitude of 'avoidance.' They not only point out that which endangers human life, they also point to *life's positive content,* which needs to be preserved. They want to mediate a feeling for real life, for life in all its beauty, to those who take the commandments upon themselves. Bonhoeffer states it thus:

> ... not because 'you shall not,' but because I myself affirm the givens which confront me in the midst and fullness of life — parents, marriage, life, possessions — as God's holy statutes; because I want to and do live by them I honor my parents, I preserve my marriage, I respect the life and property of others.[3]

An affirming, fulfilling bond to life — that is what the commandments want to help us to achieve. And when we find that life threatened, contaminated, and endangered? Then it is especially difficult to live by them. I detect here in Bonhoeffer's approach, which sees formulated in the commandments negative statements through which one can discover and learn to affirm positive fundamental truths, the possibility of also confronting life's negative experiences without subordinating to them the affirmation of life or allowing them to become a negation of life. For the power of change and also the dimension in which one seeks to apply it will depend on whether we are still able to discover the affirmation of life behind all the negative things which characterize our world — the arms race, pollution, exploitation, and the violation of human rights.

b. Command as 'Living-With-Others.' By means of his 'command as living-with-others,' Bonhoeffer emphasizes that the command of God treats of permitted life, of the permission to live as a real person before God. Thus,

> The command of God permits people to be people before God; it allows the flow of life to run its course; it allows people to eat, drink, sleep, work, celebrate, and play without interrupting them, without continually placing before them the question whether they also ought to sleep, eat, work, or play, whether there are not more pressing obligations for them.[4]

I gather from this that life itself provides people with freedom with respect to the decree, a freedom which is not constantly supervised. It is the 'fullness of life' which is opened up to one through the command of God in its bond to this life. And we can experience in this bond life without fear, permitted and free. Yet this fullness of life is not only positive experiences; for Bonhoeffer, this 'living-with-others' is life in all its relations. It also contains painful and depressing experiences, since they too belong to a total life. And so, the 'stuff' of freedom can arise out of this bond, through living-with as well as through suffering-with-others. Suffering-with-others can, in fact, be understood as the impulse toward responsibility by Bonhoeffer when he writes in 'Nach zehn Jahren' ('After ten Years'): 'Idle waiting and impassive spectating are not Christian dispositions. It is not experiences of self love, but of love for one's brother, for whose sake Christ suffered, which call the Christian to action and suffering-with.'[5] But how will this free responsibility be possible if one has not also personally experienced suffering?

c. Command as Personal Guide. For Bonhoeffer it was always important that the command, which binds us to this world as it is and at the same time makes demands, gives rise to an experienced bond with God. The command, which gives life and freedom, also includes a personal guide for human life. For the human being that guide is the experience in which the fear of bond and freedom becomes (not surmountable but) bearable. Here he is also speaking, in my opinion, of a great bond, which makes possible an even greater freedom — freedom in God. It is for all intents and purposes indispensable to Bonhoeffer's search for free responsibility. I find that particularly well expressed in the following quote.

> The responsible person, who stands between bond and freedom, who must dare to act as one bound in freedom, finds his justification neither in his bond nor in his freedom, but only in him who has placed him in this — humanly impossible — situation and demands from him the act. The responsible person surrenders hinself and his act to God.[6]

Does this not make it seem that responsibility is only possible for the believer?

In my work as pastor I often experience the bonds and obligations more strongly as bondage than as freedom. Yet I see in Bonhoeffer's attempt to give shape to the 'permitted life' a good approach for myself as well: not to have to orient myself to an 'ought', but to an attractive freedom as wife, as mother, or as pastor, it is still another gain for life.

I would now like to discuss here just two areas in which it is clear to me that the bond to given reality at the same time makes real freedom possible.

The one refers to my experiences in pastoral care, in dealing with people who are going through crises. In such instances the usual way of looking at things must be abandoned since it only permits a delimited view of reality. How liberating it can then be not always have to cover up the wound which a person has suffered, but to examine, question, and bear it. Many conversations are directed to bringing the whole of reality into view and also experiencing greater strength and freedom of life by breaking down one-sidedness, in order then to attempt a new 'unprogrammed' step, a step taken in a rediscovered freedom.

The second example lies on a different level; it pertains to the relation we currently are living under between our church and state. The slogan 'Church in Socialism' has for me taken a new meaning, especially of late. It has signaled the fact that we, as a church, have allowed ourselves to bind ourselves more closely to the socialist horizon of experience. Yet it took many years before there grew out of this bond a sensibility to the needs and the weaknesses in our land which cannot simply be dismissed as opposition, but which gains for itself a hearing as a result of the affirmation of this socialist country. I think, in this regard, of the conversation between the leaders of Parliament and Bishop Leich in March 1988, in which both the positive and negative experiences could be broached by the church in an objective and understanding way, experiences which appear in none of our publications in such comprehensiveness, yet which grow out of the inner bond of living-with-others. They signaled for me and many other Christians (and non-Christians) a great gain for freedom, even when many misunderstandings arose in what ensued.

In both examples I see a gain for reality, and along with it, new possibilities for freedom, and that is a way filled with hope — a part of the way of God with us today.

NOTES

1. *Ethik*, p. 294.
2. *Widerstand und Ergebung*, p. 375.
3. *Ethik*, p. 297.
4. *Ethik*, p. 300.
5. *Widerstand und Ergebung*, p. 25.
6. *Gesammelte Schriften*, p. 68.

PART II

ETHICS AND EUROPE

A Particular Europe, a Universal Faith

THE CHRISTIAN HUMANISM OF BONHOEFFER'S ETHICS IN ITS CONTEXT

Frits de Lange

Bonhoeffer, Europe, and the *Ethics* – if we take these three themes together we greatly limit our scope. Our discussion revolves around Bonhoeffer in the years 1939-1943, when he was an active member of the resistance against Hitler; it revolves around the battlefield of Europe; and it revolves around the fragments of the book which Bonhoeffer was writing during these years in that same Europe — the *Ethics,* a book which, as we shall see later, has been strongly influenced by this specific background. But I want to limit our scope gradually, and would like to begin by making a few general remarks about Bonhoeffer and Europe.

1

Bonhoeffer and Europe? The notion of 'Bonhoeffer and Germany' seems easier for us to imagine. 'He was German' was Paul Lehmann's judgment of Dietrich Bonhoeffer after they met in 1930. In saying so, Lehmann was thinking of Bonhoeffer's 'passion for perfection, whether of manners, of performance, of all that is connoted by the word *Kultur.*'[1] But is *Kultur,* apart from its being a German word, also something restricted to German culture and German culture alone?

Bonhoeffer's upbringing in the family of a German professor was by no means devoid of a whiff of nationalism. 'For what I have I thank this nation, through this nation I became what I am' — thus Keith Clements cites the twenty-two year old Bonhoeffer at the beginning of his study of Bonhoeffer's patriotism.[2] Bonhoeffer was German and, as Clements rightly said, 'he never disowned his Germanness.' But how nationalist, for example, is a patriotism that prays for the defeat of Germany (as Bonhoeffer did in 1941)?[3] In Bonhoeffer's case, did the narrow-mindedness of nationalism ever take precedence over the broad-mindedness of humanism? To Bonhoeffer, the concept 'German' never meant first and foremost the political passion for Prussian hegemony;[4] to his mind, a cultural scale of values, not so much specifically German as generally European, always came first. If Bonhoeffer spoke with a German accent, sometimes more, sometimes less pronounced, and if at times he used words peculiar to the German vocabulary, his declensions and conjugations were those of a European grammar.

Let me explain. Bonhoeffer grew up in a family that was part of the *Bildungs-bürgertum* — a word for which no adequate translation exists because it describes a social class that existed only in eighteenth- and nineteenth-century Germany and nowhere else in Europe. The bourgeoisie, which elsewhere rose to economic and political importance as a class, saw its emancipation checked by the absolutism of the

81

small German states. It then found an alternative outlet for its ambitions, that of intellectual and cultural development, of *Kultur*. A small elite, lacking in social power, invested its energy in the *Bildung* of the personality of the individual and the *Geselligkeit* within a small circle. And so Germany became the country of Goethe and Kant, not the country of Smith and Rousseau — a country of thinkers and poets, not economists and politicians.[5]

And yet, this specifically German class consciousness of the specifically German *Bildungsbürgertum* provided the generally European humanist tradition of the sixteenth century with the sanctuary which the intensive, expansive capitalism of the rest of Europe progressively denied it. Goethe takes Erasmus once again and what used to be called *humanitas* in sixteenth-century Latin now became *Bildung* in nineteenth-century German.

The *Bildungsbürgertum* was a unique sociological constellation. But in its uniqueness it contributed to the building and continuity of a general European tradition; a tradition which, though it no longer seemed to have the right of existence elsewhere, was able to develop in relative peace in Germany, in the shade of the quest for economic and political expansion which gripped the rest of Europe.

The Bonhoeffer family was part of this intellectual and cultural elite — an elite which, with its values such as liberty, responsibility, reason, and individuality, might have been associated exclusively with a particular social class, but did not limit itself to the nation of Germany.

Studying the humanities at school, absorbing the classics, travelling to Rome; in doing so, Bonhoeffer did exactly what all humanists since the sixteenth century had done. *Kultur* is the word Paul Lehmann used to label the German Bonhoeffer. But when he went on to describe that concept in English, it became 'an aristocracy of the spirit at its best.'[6]

But maybe we are turning Bonhoeffer into a European rather too quickly and identifying the *Bildungsbürger* with the *honnête homme* or *gentleman*. For the young Bonhoeffer, Europe might have meant Rome; it certainly did not mean London, Paris, or New York.

'The West' reminded him more of the German defeat in World War I in which he had lost a brother, or of the humiliation of the Treaty of Versailles, than of the civilization of which he also was part.[7] Bonhoeffer was also brought up with the contradiction between *Kultur* and *Zivilisation* — German thoroughness as opposed to Anglo-Saxon straightforwardness and French frivolity, personal *Bildung* as opposed to mechanical technical science. He too, in view of his German background, was to choose the former and reject the latter.[8]

In post-1870 Germany, where Bonhoeffer grew up, these differences in nuance were magnified into irreconcilable antagonisms. The *gebildete* class was also mobilized, in its own way, when Germany attempted to overtake the rest of Europe after its late unification under Prussian hegemony. The frustration of having missed out on the economic revolution led, after 1870, to an outburst of revolutionary capitalism and imperialism with the rest of Europe as rival — a competition which resulted in World War I. Dietrich Bonhoeffer grew up surrounded by this competitive nationalism and the hangover of 1918 formed part of his cultural heritage.

Anti-Western feelings were never exploited in the Bonhoeffer family and so the *Geiste von 1914,* which depicted the war against France as a crusade of *Kultur* against *Zivilisation* (as did Thomas Mann in his *Betrachtungen eines Unpolitischen),* left the Bonhoeffers cold. Yet this historical and nationalist-political background does explain the young Bonhoeffer's ambivalence between universal humanism on the one hand and German nationalism on the other — the ambivalence between 'the love of our country and the peace of mankind'[9], as Bonhoeffer himself called the two in one breath when discussing in New York his membership in the German youth movement.

To the young Bonhoeffer, Europe never meant only Rome; it also meant Versailles — a diffused ambivalence toward cultural tradition and political reality as yet uncrystallized.

2

All that changed in 1930/1931. Bonhoeffer's sojourn in the United States signified in many ways a drastic breach in his understanding of himself and his attitude toward European culture. The *Gebildete,* who at first did not know what he was doing in the United States (he originally wanted to go to the East rather than the West)[10], the *Kultur*-expert who crossed the Atlantic to teach rather than to learn (he lectured on dialectical theology to an American audience), returned a different man. His attitude towards European culture underwent a threefold change.

First, Bonhoeffer became acquainted with a pragmatic-technical culture which, although it existed in part of Europe, was very different from the European culture that Bonhoeffer was familiar with. The reader of Goethe, as Bonhoeffer was, studied William James and, as he did, the interrelation between thought and deed which this pragmatism displays captivated him permanently.

The classically oriented Bonhoeffer started to explore the modern culture of the West, exchanging the museums of ancient Rome and the concert halls of Berlin for the cinemas of New York. And yet, Bonhoeffer did complain about the superficiality of a mass-culture that tended to level everything, but he did so without anti-Americanism, without the feeling of superiority of an outsider. Bonhoeffer accepted the capitalist world he became acquainted with in the United States as *his* world, even if he did criticize it. Bonhoeffer became a contemporary shareholder of his culture without nationalist or elitist reservations. From then on, Rome and New York belonged together as one cultural unit in Bonhoeffer's thinking, a 'European-American civilization'[11] with a shared present and a common future.

Second, this modern Western culture did away with the former national and cultural contrasts and posed new tasks. In New York, the German Dietrich Bonhoeffer met the Frenchman Jean Lasserre — an acquaintance which was to have a profound influence on Bonhoeffer's Christian pacifism and his understanding of the Sermon on the Mount, an acquaintance which would also banish any traces of national parochialism from Bonhoeffer's thinking.

In an interview which Jean Lasserre granted F. Burton Nelson in 1977, he described a visit to the cinema in New York in the spring of 1931, when he and Bonhoeffer went to see the film based on Remarque's novel, *All Quiet on the Western Front*.

> The audience was American, and since the film had been made from the point of view of the German soldiers, the audience immediately sympathized with the German soldiers. When they killed French soldiers on the screen, the crowd laughed and applauded. On the other hand, when the German soldiers were wounded or killed, there was a great silence and sense of deep emotion.

All this time, Bonhoeffer the German, and Lasserre the Frenchman, sat side by side in silence. This experience made such an impact on Lasserre that when talking about it forty-five years later he still bursts into tears. In his opinion it made the same impact on Dietrich Bonhoeffer. 'That experience in the movie theater was a real experience, tragically real, and it must have certainly left its mark on him.'[12] Whereas Bonhoeffer's grandfather became a citizen of Europe at the sight of the forum Romanum, Bonhoeffer became a citizen of Europe watching a movie in New York.

After his years in New York, Bonhoeffer became deeply and permanently involved in the international struggle for peace within the ecumenical movement, constantly crossing frontiers which, in his opinion, no longer had a right to exist and which also again threatened the future of Europe.

Finally, in New York, Bonhoeffer became acutely aware not only of his national, but also of his social frontiers. He came face to face with the black proletariat, made friends (Frank Fisher), and without any reservations whatsoever, became involved in a world unknown to him. This availability and open-mindedness he would maintain with the same personal application once back in Berlin. Bonhoeffer saw the other side of the capitalist coin — another facet of the same Europe, a Europe which, from then on, was voiced as much in a record of Negro spirituals played for labourers' children as through harmonious chamber music in the Bonhoeffer drawing room.[13]

And so, in the eyes of the young Bonhoeffer, the appearance of Europe had drastically changed within the space of a single year. No longer determined by the academic circles of university professor, it was now defined by the conflict-ridden social and political reality of capitalism and nationalism. From then on, Bonhoeffer's attitude was one of active involvement, no longer one of distant contemplation. Bonhoeffer had said good-bye to the stable, harmonious *Persönlichkeit*, the *Gemeinschaft* of the like-minded. Human beings treated like mass products, nations denying each other the right to exist — these were the concrete realities which from then on determined the character of the one and only 'European-American civilization.'

In this single designation which he used in his discourse, 'Das Recht auf Selbstbehauptung' (1932), Bonhoeffer embraced the whole of Western culture. But precisely when he was granting Europe such a unity for the first time, Europe was conflict-ridden and destructive in character. The European (thus Bonhoeffer too) could only survive by destroying nature and his fellow man. European civilization was a civilization of factories and wars. In this, Europe distinguished itself from the civilization of the East, which preached and practiced respect for life and a passive rather than an aggressive approach.

Perhaps, Bonhoeffer speculated in front of an audience of technical students in Berlin, India and Gandhi had a survival strategy to offer to a European-American civilization which was dragging itself further and further along the road to self-destruction.[14]

It is remarkable — also with respect to his thinking in the *Ethics,* ten years later — that in 1932 Bonhoeffer refused to acknowledge qualitative differences within the one European culture, that he saw its unity precisely in its surge toward self-destruction. Within the space of a single year, his close confrontation with this twentieth-century Europe seemed to have robbed Bonhoeffer of any faith in the power of the classical humanist values with which he had been raised. To the Bonhoeffer of 1932, conflict, not unity; mechanization, not the building of the personality; anonymity, not individuality, were the factors that comprised Europe.

During these years Bonhoeffer despaired of Europe and he no longer held any hope for the future of European Christianity. Yet to his skepticism towards Europe was linked his hopes for India. The future of the West had to come from the East.[15] Meanwhile, the distinction between Europe and America had been reduced to a minimum. The only plus Bonhoeffer was prepared to grant the Germans was their ability to realize more quickly and acutely how hopeless the situation of Europe had become.[16]

Although nothing ever came of Bonhoeffer's Indian plans, Bonhoeffer gradually became a non-European. With Europe on the verge of the abyss and Christianity dying, he looked for new fertile soil for the Christian faith.[17] Bonhoeffer's attitude in the matter became more and more radical as the political situation deteriorated after Hitler's rise to power in January 1933, and as Bonhoeffer increasingly adopted the profile of a Christian and a Christian alone.

The lecture 'Das Recht auf Selbstbehauptung' can be interpreted as Bonhoeffer's final attempt to draw from the connection between European culture and Christianity a system of ethics applicable to his situation. From 'mature European thinking' Bonhoeffer derived the notion of responsibility, which would still be able to curtail the anarchism of the Western concept of liberty, if interpreted radically. In every form of community we know in the West — marriage, work, church, nation — we recognize that same responsibility as a moral motive capable of regulating our behaviour to the point of self-sacrifice.[18] To learn this truth, the European does not have to go to India — it is part of his own tradition, his Christian tradition; for according to Bonhoeffer, the radical ideal of self-surrender can only be understood if one places 'in the background of this Western idea the horizon of Christianity.'[19] It is on the sacrifice of the one man Jesus Christ that the universal bearing and validity of responsibility are founded.

In guiding Europe back to its Christian roots, Bonhoeffer offered his culture, seemingly at death's door, a last straw in vain, and 1933 saw the last of this kind of Christian Europeanness or humanist Christianity in Bonhoeffer's theology.

The Finkenwalde training college for the ministry became Bonhoeffer's India, and Europe became the stakes in the question: Germanism or Christianity? There was no alternative.[20] After 1933 Bonhoeffer's skepticism and despair of 1932 gave way to an intense Christian expectation of parousia. Bonhoeffer's theology of discipleship had strong echatological characteristics. Europe was the battlefield where God and the devil were doing battle, while the Christian took part. The Christian had to stay in the world to prepare himself all the better to carry out a 'frontal attack.'[21] Bonhoeffer was a citizen of Europe in these years, but he was one in spite of himself.

3

Bonhoeffer's hasty but well-considered return from the United States on July 7, 1939, following his carefully prepared emigration, marks yet another turn in his attitude vis-à-vis Europe. The eschatological dissociation was abandoned in favour of an unconditional solidarity. Not that his objective judgement on the condition of Europe underwent any change after his return to Germany. 'The West has come face to face with the Void', wrote Bonhoeffer in *Ethics,* but he could have written the same in *Nachfolge.*[22] And were not the grounds for saying so even stronger in 1941 than they were in 1937?

The obvious shift in Bonhoeffer's thinking, however, was connected with his increasing involvement in the civil resistance against Hitler. His motives for returning to Germany clearly indicate the changes in emphasis in his thinking. I distinguish three.

3.1. Bonhoeffer returned to resume his share of the church struggle. 'I am drawn towards my fighting brothers. The political situation is terrible, and I must be with my brothers', he confided to Paul Lehmann on 30 June 1939. And his decision was made. 'I must go back to the "trenches" (I mean of the church struggle).'[23]

3.2. Bonhoeffer returned for the sake of Germany. He refused to be an outsider during the bleak times faced by his country, now at war; he wished to 'take part in Germany's vicissitudes.'[24] Bonhoeffer became a nationalist once again, not out of pride, but out of solidarity and readiness to share his nation's guilt. That is why he wrote before leaving the United States: 'I have made a mistake in coming to America. I must live through this difficult period of our *national* history ... share the trials of this time with *my people*.'[25] The national community became a community of destiny joined in guilt. This is how Bonhoeffer once again learned to say 'we Germans.'[26]

3.3. And yet Bonhoeffer's patriotism was determined and confined at both ends of the spectrum. Bonhoeffer's solidarity was not with Germany in general; it was with 'the *Christian* people of Germany', as he wrote. And he considered it his duty to return with a view to the 'reconstruction of *Christian* life in Germany after the war.' With Christian life in mind, Bonhoeffer found himself forced once again to link Christian faith with European culture, a connection he had come to discard during the previous years. 'Christians in Germany will face the terrible alternative of either willing the defeat of their nation in order that Christian civilization will survive, or willing the victory of their nation and thereby destroying our civilization.'[27] Bonhoeffer knew what his choice would be; he opted for Christian civilization. But it was precisely in this anti-nationalism that he discovered true patriotism: choosing a Christian Europe really meant choosing for Germany.

Bonhoeffer's choice found expression in his participation in the German resistance against Hitler, in the group centred around his brother-in-law Hans von Dohnanyi — a divergent collection of splinter groups united by the fact that they were, as Bonhoeffer's friend and confidant, George Bell, Bishop of Chichester, put it in 1945, among 'the upholders of the European tradition in Germany.'[28]

From 1939 onward, Bonhoeffer was once again a citizen of Europe, and without reservation. And along with the abyss and the void arose the question of fresh opportunities for the future of Europe. Along with pessimism concerning Hitler appeared optimism concerning the success of the resistance. On August 26, 1941, Bonhoeffer reminded Bethge of their travels through Europe together in 1936 and 1939. At the centre of the battlefield of Europe, Bonhoeffer, remembering those journeys, again spoke of 'hopes and tasks for Europe' and 'the task of the church in the future,'[29] and this in spite of the fact that Hitler was victorious on all fronts.

4

In the *Ethics,* Bonhoeffer lent shape to his hopes and fears, his appraisal and criticism of European culture. Here we rediscover many elements from his earlier views on Western culture. Sometimes we seem to be looking at the German *Kulturbürger* again, the Bonhoeffer of Berlin and Barcelona, sometimes we recognize the highly critical view of his own culture which Bonhoeffer developed in New York; throughout the work we find the Christian radicalism of the Finkenwalde Bonhoeffer. But we find all of this in a new, specifically historical and biographical setting — that of the German resistance against Hitler. As research into the background and character of this resistance takes off,[30] it becomes clear how deeply Bonhoeffer's *Ethics* is marked by this context. In one sense, the *Ethics* can be defined as an ideology of this resistance.

In saying so we do not indulge in a kind of sociological reductionism; Bonhoeffer himself took as an origin for his *Ethics,* a 'living experience', 'an actual concrete experience,' a well-defined 'situation.'[31] In his *Ethics,* Bonhoeffer wanted to write more than a general Christian ethic; he practiced a kind of contextual theology of culture in that work. *Ethics* was to serve as a draft for 'the foundation and structure of a united West' (one of the subtitles Bonhoeffer considered for the book), in which he wished to rethink the relationship between Christian faith and European culture. This constituted part of his contribution to the resistance movement. For along with his services as a courier abroad and a moral sounding board (notably for Hans von Dohnanyi), Bonhoeffer was involved in the concepetual preparation of a post-war Europe, a Germany beyond Point Zero: 'The foundations and structure of a future world' was another subtitle Bonhoeffer had ready for his *Ethics* .[32]

Present-day research concerning Bonhoeffer points out with increasing clarity how closely Bonhoeffer's cultural theology in *Ethics* was linked to the prevailing situation. Let me describe four characteristics common to both the German civil resistance and the *Ethics*.

First of all, there are the specifically German accents which had already led Karl Barth to claim that *Ethics* (he was especially thinking of the doctrine of the mandates here) 'is not quite free from a slight whiff of North German patriarchalism.'[33] In the small circle of the like-minded, Bonhoeffer learned to say 'we Germans' once again. I think it is important to stress that he did not do do out of social narrowmindedness, but out of a sense of political responsibility; in order to present a true front in the negotiations with the allies about the post-war future, Bonhoeffer, like the rest of the German resistance, had to take up a position as a German, to embody the 'other' Germany. He had to be ready to bear the specifically German guilt concerning the past and to take on the specifically German responsibility for the future role of Germany in Europe.

In this context, Bonhoeffer admitted the servile obedience, the scrupulous lack of readiness to act, the excess of thought and lack of deeds of his people. Yet at the same time he upheld the German reserve vis-à-vis Anglo-Saxon thinking. He and his fellow members of the resistance with him preferred not to have post-war Germany fall victim to an unbridled and excessive liberalism, not even in its most immediate sense of democracy.[34] In the eyes of the *Bildungs* elite of which Bonhoeffer was part, the *échec* of the Weimar Republic once again strengthened the old contradiction between *Kultur* and *Zivilisation,* a contradiction which seemed to have disappeared from Bonhoeffer's thinking from 1930 onwards.[35]

In this way he also dissociated himself from the French Revolution in so far as it embodied revolutionary nationalism. He preferred Prussian absolutism of the state, as expressed in 'true Prussian cicles', endowed with common sense, to the doctrine of the sovereignty of the people.[36] The German tradition which had to continue consisted of Bismarck as well as Kant and Goethe.

But we must be careful not to make too much of a German of the Bonhoeffer in *Ethics*. For alongside Bismarck's ideas on government we find those of Gladstone;[37] alongside Goethe's dialogue we find Shakespeare's characters. Too much of Bonhoeffer's *Ethics* finds its foundations in the Norwegian Ibsen, the Spaniard Cervantes, the Russian Dostoyevski, and the Italian Dante to speak of anything more than German *accents* in *Ethics*. The work's index of names provides ample proof of its broad base.

Secondly, I would like to draw attention to the socio-political and cultural conservatism which the resistance and Bonhoeffer's *Ethics* had in common. Neither the Wilhelmine Empire (which resulted in World War I) nor the Weimar Republic (which ended in a second catastrophe) offered a viable political concept for the ordering of German society. It seemed that the German resistance had to hark back to before 1870 to find new national foundations. The result was a strong concentration of the German *Bürger* tradition of the nineteenth century, somewhere between Western individualism and Bolshevik collectivism.[38]

Although one should avoid tarring with the same ideological brush the wide mixture of groups which together made up the German resistance, it can be said that the social utopia of its members showed strong romantic characteristics, generally combining an organic concept of social government with a strongly individualistic concept of man. In additon, the moral and intellectual elite which constituted the resistance opted for an authoritarian rather than a democratic structure of government. Bonhoeffer's *Ethics* shows obvious traces of this conservatism. In his doctrine of mandates he gave a theological justification for a model of government in which *Oben und Unten* ('top and bottom') are clearly disinguished.

In the *Ethics* Bonhoeffer hardly shows himself a model of progressivism from a socio-political point of view and the same can be said of the cultural aspect of the work. His aversion to mass consumer culture, his plea for a quality-elite (which he would develop even further in the Tegel prison[39]) showed Bonhoeffer, yet again more than ever to be a *Bildungsbürger* who lived with the notion of belonging to an intellectual and cultural, albeit, unappreciated social elite. Within ten years time the New York cinemagoer Bonhoeffer, so self-evident in 1931, had become difficult to imagine.

I will not explore any further the elitist conservatism that links Bonhoeffer to the rest of the German resistance. Others have already done so (Larry L. Rasmussen in particular comes to mind[40]) and will continue to do so.

I will deal with a fourth characteristic in slightly more detail. I am here referring to the religious-Christian motives of those involved in the resistance and the related apologetic tendencies of the *Ethics*.

Without exception the German civil resistance against Hitler seemed steeped in Christian motives. Whether one takes Goerdeler, Oster, Beck, von Dohnanyi, or Moltke, all were Christians, even if in a liberal rather than in an eccelesiastical-orthodox sense.[41] Consequently, a vital role was attributed to Christianity in their vision of a post-war Europe. After the nihilism of Nazism, the reconstruction of Europe was to be based upon positive Christian principles. The Ten Commandments were to serve as a foundation for justice, the Christian value of the individual personality as a foundation for society.[42]

In the course of these years, we see a striking reorientation towards the Christian faith in the circles of the anti-fascist *Bildungsbürgertum,* a reorientation aptly illustrated by Thomas Mann. The writer, himself the perfect embodiment of the German *Bildungsbürger,* began his first novel, *Buddenbrooks,* with a catechism smothered in stammer: to the *Bürger* in the process of emancipation, the Christian faith no longer represented a living tradition. Nor does it do so in the early works of Thomas Mann. But after the rise of fascism and his forced flight from Germany in 1933 (first to Switzerland, then to the United States), the same Thomas Mann became both a passionate advocate of the old humanist values of European culture and a defender of the 'Christian foundations of Western civilization.'[43] For (and let me draw your attention to the parallel with Bonhoeffer's paragraph on 'The Church and the World' in *Ethics*): 'Liberty, truth, true reason, human dignity — whence did we create these ideas, ideas that are the mainstay and support of our lives and without which our spiritual existence would disintegrate, if not from Christianity, which made them universal law?'[44]

Starting from this suddenly rediscovered proximity of European culture and Christianity, which had grown apart over the previous two centuries, Thomas Mann, in his exile in California in 1944, reached the conclusion that a post-war Europe had to be constructed on the foundations of the Christian faith. 'What should be restored first and foremost are the commandments of Christianity, trampled under foot by a false revolution — and from them we must derive the constitution for a future society of the human race to which all must submit.'[45] In this context, secularized humanist values such as liberty and humanity once again acquire a religious connotation. Thomas Mann considered them — and again I must draw attention to the parallel to Bonhoeffer's *Ethics* — 'a most sacred good, which has its origins in the Christian faith.'[46]

Bonhoeffer, too, experienced in the resistance this 'rapprochement' between Christianity and humanist culture. Christ, on the one hand, and righteousness and the righteous on the other, suddenly seem to recognize one another as allies in the face of the nihilistic barbarism of nazism. Bonhoeffer refuses to see this surprising proximity as a mere *Zweckgemeinschaft* — a temporary and accidental alliance against a common enemy. He interpreted it as the return of the citizen, estranged from Christianity and church, to his Christian origins. In the course of two centuries of emancipation and secularization, Christian faith and European culture had grown apart; ten years of resistance brought them back together again. In his *Ethics,* Bonhoeffer extrapolated this 'living, concrete experience' to a general dimension and used it as a model for the whole of European culture.

Christian imperialism mediated by force is out of the question here; we are dealing with a kind of *Aha-Erlebnis* — a mutual recognition, a rediscovery of the origins of European culture in the concrete context of the experience of suffering in the German church struggle and the resistance. This particular Europe once again discovers the range of a universal faith. 'The more exclusively we acknowledge and confess Christ as our Lord, the more fully the wide range of his dominion will be disclosed to us.'[47]

To Bonhoeffer the question was one of temporary 'estrangement', not 'secularization.' A hesitant reorientation towards the Christian faith is promptly labelled a 'return.' 'The children of the church, who had become independent and gone their own ways, now in the hour of danger returned to their mother.'[48] In its finest representatives (the righteous), Europe, face to face with the Void, finds a way back. Europe is the runaway child that finds the way to the Paternal home again.[49]

In *Ethics,* Bonhoeffer took his starting points from a concrete, incontestable experience. And what is more, with this experience he practiced apologetics.[50] The hesitant reorientation of the *Bürger*elite was interpreted by Bonhoeffer as an 'unconscious residue of a former attachment', simply waiting for an awakening of consciousness to become 'attachment' once again. In so doing, Bonhoeffer transgressed the boundary between the factual and the normative. He wished to help the 'righteous' who no longer dared to call himself a Christian 'with much patience to the confession of Christ.'[51] In this way Bonhoeffer hoped to pull him over the threshold of the Christian faith.

The entire *Ethics* is marked by these apologetics. This is especially clear in the sections dealing with cultural history, where Bonhoeffer saw the historical unity of Europe anchored in Jesus Christ ('Inheritance and Decay') — a unity which has been lost because the West fell away from Jesus Christ and which can only be retrieved through a return to its origins and here Bonhoeffer is thinking in concrete terms of a 'new awakening of the faith.'[52] Bonhoeffer generalized his particular experience of the resistance by laying the moral foundation of a future European political and social order solely in a living Christian faith. Enmity towards Christ, on the other hand, irrevocably leads to the abyss.[53]

Bonhoeffer's concrete ethics are also apologetic in this respect: marriage, work, state, and church can only be fully effective in their specific development and their relationship to each other when founded on their Christian origins. 'It is only from above, with God as the point of departure, that it is possible to say and to understand what is meant by the church, by marriage and the family, by culture and by government,' judged Bonhoeffer in his doctrine of mandates.[54]

Finally, Bonhoeffer's apologetic intentions can be clearly distinguished in the systematic-theological argumentation of the *Ethics*. Time and again, two concepts and their relationship to one another recur in countless variations and in every part of the work: the *Anspruch* (claim, seizure)[55] of Christ on the modern Western world, on the one hand, and the *Eigengesetzlichkeit* (autonomy)[56] which European culture has acquired in the course of the history of its emancipation, on the other. Bonhoeffer, who himself grew up in this tradition of autonomous worldliness, would not retreat beyond it. 'We cannot go back to the days before Lessing and Lichtenberg.'[57] Yet Bonhoeffer wants to understand this world better than it understands itself. 'Real worldliness'[58] is only possible when all life is geared towards and seen in Christ, on whom are founded the unity and the unbreakable bond between God and man, between Christian faith and culture. 'A world which stands by itself, in isolation from the law of Christ, falls victim to the unnatural and the irrational, to presumption and self-will', wrote Bonhoeffer in his paragraph on 'Thinking in Terms of Two Spheres.'[59] But we could have come across this same pronouncement in the chapters on 'Conformation', 'The Ultimate and the Penultimate', and 'The Mandates.' During the years in which he was working on *Ethics*, Bonhoeffer's thinking developed quickly. Time and again he created new theological models.[60] Yet the basic theological intuition behind and within his intellectual flexibility remained constant — the only future for the Christian faith and European culture is a common future, in mutual recognition and influence. Separately, neither has any future in Europe at all. Thus Bonhoeffer returned to the position he had left in 1933: a kind of Christian humanism of the type he had developed in 'Das Recht auf Selbstbehauptung.' And there is one Christian dogma that continually feeds and justifies this basic intuition: the dogma of the incarnation of God in Jesus Christ.

In the *Ethics*, the incarnation is the theological paradigm through which Bonhoeffer analyzed European culture and with which he justified his Christian apologetics. The incarnation of God made Europe what it was — a historical, political, and cultural unity. A radical rethinking of the consequences of the incarnation is the sole condition for creating the possibility of a future Europe. The incarnation of God is not only the starting point of European history, it is its purpose, its substance, its aim. And now: 'Jesus Christ has made of the West an historical unity... The unity of the West is not an idea but an historical reality, of which the sole foundation is Christ.'[61]

Just like his historical-political views on Europe, Bonhoeffer's ethical humanism is grafted on to the incarnation. Being human is participation in the incarnation of God in this world, in his crucifixion and in his resurrection.[62] Because God became human, the entire creation should be focused on humanity.[63] Because this incarnation of God is a mystery, being human is also a mystery that should not be violated.[64] Jesus is not a human. He is *humanity*. Whatever happens to him happens to man. It happens to all men, and therefore it happens to us. The name Jesus contains within itself the whole of humanity and the whole of God.[65]

Bonhoeffer does not see the incarnation as a prop, a theoretical model for acquiring a deeper understanding of history; the incarnation of God is itself the historical process which has been and will be shaped in Europe — if European humanity does not betray its own Christ-based humanity.

Bonhoeffer's phenomenological description of human life in the *Ethics* is infinitely nuanced and refined. The moral and psychological sketches in his work (I am thinking, for example, of his phenomenology of shame, of conscience, and his description of the structure of the responsible life) are among the greatest Europe has produced. But in their foundation they show a dogmatic solidity — the incarnation of God in Jesus Christ is the be-all and end-all of European culture.

5

We have placed Bonhoeffer's *Ethics* and the attitude towards Europe found in his work in their own particular context. We have read the *Ethics* as a contextual, cultural theology of Europe, historically and geographically confined by the horizon of the German resistance against Hitler in the years 1939-1943. But is the significance of Bonhoeffer's views on Europe therefore limited to that particular European context? Would not a cultural theology for a different Europe (ours, for example) benefit from the *Ethics* ? I would like to close with a few remarks on that question.

5.1. As I said before, reducing the *Ethics* to a context of concrete experience is not a form of sociological reductionism. Bonhoeffer himself did it, and he made a paradoxical discovery in the process: 'The more exclusively we acknowledge and confess Christ as our Lord, the more fully the wide range of His dominion will be disclosed to us.' Precisely in the peculiarity of his European experience Bonhoeffer discovered the universality of Christ. Being faithful to this discovery is being faithful to Bonhoeffer. He commits us to our own particular concrete experience, not his. We therefore must dissociate ourselves from some of the conservative and elitist elements in the *Ethics* which were comprehensible or even justified in their context. Also, it seems to me, the historical analysis of a Western unity created by Christ can no longer be maintained as such.

5.2. Europe, according to the analysis of modern cultural historians, is neither in origin nor in character exclusively Christian. 'One could say that, in an early phase, Islam *shaped* Europe by hemming in Christendom (seventh century) and that, in a second phase, Europe shaped *itself* in relation to Islam by driving it back at Poitiers (732),' wrote the sociologist Edgar Morin in his recent work on Europe.[66] Not Christianity, but Islam made Europe what it is.[67] Only the medieval Europe that came into being afterwards could possibly be identified with Christendom. Also, one realizes that in modern times Europe and Christianity no longer totally overlap.[68]

It is a fact that the Europe of the Middle Ages was Christian — and this again leads us to dissociate ourselves from Bonhoeffer's analysis — but it is also a fact that it had been heterogeneous, divided by schism and conflict-ridden from the start. Bonhoeffer's preoccupation with unity ('an old German *Sehnsucht'*, as Jürgen Moltmann called it),[70] which is easily understood against the background of a torn Europe, has been replaced by a historical approach which stresses the complexity of the historical evolution of Europe — its antagonisms and complementarities. Europe, again according to Edgar Morin, is a bubbling whirlpool, a 'permanent euroorganizing anarchy.' All that gives shape to Europe divides it, all that divides it gives it shape. It comes into being, develops and confirms itself in a constant state of war with itself. Europe may be a unity, but only a *unitas multiplex*.[71] In a profane, decolonized, and pluralist Europe, the image of a united and Christian Europe can no longer be retained. A contextual cultural theology which reconsiders Europe half a century after Bonhoeffer will appreciate such shifts. When reconsidering the doctrine of the Trinity, for example, one pays more attention to the complexity, the complementarity, the diversity of the relations that shaped Europe than to a personalist Christology geared toward unity.[72] And in a rationalized and secularized world, the idea of the incarnation of God, it seems, must be replaced by a Christology from below, which will stand up to reason. Is not a theology of the incarnation with a God who enters the world from above a relic of a mythical era?

5.3. And yet, I think that we will do no service to theology, Bonhoeffer, or Europe by too quickly trimming our sail to the wind. Bonhoeffer's contribution to European theology in the *Ethics* seems to me to be twofold: perhaps we have become more critical in theological hermeneutics since Bonhoeffer, and distinguish more clearly the incarnation as a model of interpretation of the very reality we interpret; and perhaps philosophy has also become more critical since Bonhoeffer in its use of the word 'humanity'; and we are acquiring a deeper understanding of its linguistic complexity and hidden ideological connotations. But a theology which neither maintains the incarnation as its basic intuition nor links it to the struggle of humanity for humanity is no longer either Christian or relevant.[73] Only a theology which takes the incarnation of God as starting point will be able to make the tradition of European humanism bear fruit, the inheritance of a particular Europe, yet universal in its intentions — as is Christian faith itself.

It will have to be a critical humanism, a humanism which discloses rather than legitimizes power, a humanism in which one person fails to inherit humanity when another does not, a 'humanism of the other man.'[74] In the *Ethics,* Bonhoeffer made a start: 'My life is outside myself, outside the range of my disposal; my life is other than myself; it is Jesus Christ.' This Christ, who comes to us in the poorest of our brothers, summons us to life in 'selfless self-assertion.'[75] This is Christian humanism at its best. It is about time that we Europeans start taking it seriously — as Bonhoeffer did.

(Translated by Wendela J. Van Santen)

NOTES

1. Quoted by Eberhard Bethge in *Dietrich Bonhoeffer. Theologe, Christ, Zeitgenosse,* 5th ed. (Munich, 1983), p. 192.
2. Keith W. Clements, *A Patriotism for Today: Dialogue with Dietrich Bonhoeffer* (Bristol, 1984), p. 21; cf. Dietrich Bonhoeffer, *Gesammelte Schriften* vol. III (Munich, 1972), p. 171.
3. Bethge, p. 835.
4. Eberhard Bethge, *Dietrich Bonhoeffer - Widerstand in preussischer Tradition?* (offprint from *Kirche in Preussen,* Munich, 1983). Bethge discusses the need for independence in which the Bonhoeffers were brought up, and speaks in this context of the 'non- or altogether anti-Prussian heritage' transmitted to Dietrich Bonhoeffer.
5. Cf. Hans Weil, *Die Entstehung des deutschen Bildungsprinzips,* 2nd ed. *(Bonn, 1977); F. de Lange, Grond onder de voeten: Burgerlijkheid bij Dietrich Bonhoeffer* (Kampen, 1985), pp. 43ff.; idem., *Een burger op z'n best: Dietrich Bonhoeffer* (Baarn, 1986).
6. Bethge, *Dietrich Bonhoeffer,* p. 192; cf. G.Th. Rothuizen, *Aristocratisch Christendom. Over Dietrich Bonhoeffer* (Kampen, 1969).
7. Bethge, *Dietrich Bonhoeffer,* p. 85.
8. Regarding the contrast *Kultur-Zivilisation,* see Norbert Elias, *Über den Prozess der Zivilization: Soziogenetische und psychogenetische Untersuchungen* vol. I (Frankfurt am Main, 1980).
9. Bonhoeffer, *Gesammelte Schriften* vol. I (Munich, 1978), pp. 74ff., (italics mine). In this context, note Bonhoeffer's membership of the extreme nationalist student organization, 'Igel,' and the paramilitary organization 'Schwarze Reichswehr,' short and soon forgotten, and also his nationalist utterances in Barcelona, where he defended the German expansion. See also Bethge, *Dietrich Bonhoeffer,* pp. 55ff., 74ff., and Bonhoeffer, *Gesammelte Schriften* vol., V, p. 17.
10. Bethge, *Dietrich Bonhoeffer.* pp. 180ff.
11. Bonhoeffer, *Gesammelte Schriften* vol. III (Munich, 1966), pp. 258ff.
12. F. Burton Nelson, 'The Relationship of Jean Lasserre to Dietrich Bonhoeffer's Peace Concerns in the Struggle of Church and Culture' (unpublished ms, June 1984), p. 9.
13. Bethge, *Dietrich Bonhoeffer.* id. pp. 272ff.
14. Bonhoeffer, *Gesammelte Schriften* vol. III, pp. 261-264.
15. Bethge, *Dietrich Bonhoeffer,* id. p. 471; cf. Bonhoeffer, *Gesammelte Schriften* vol. I, id. p. 61 and vol. II (Munich, 1965), p. 158.
16. Bonhoeffer to Erwin Sutz, May 17, 1932, *Gesammelte Schriften* vol. I, p. 32. Bonhoeffer calls Europe a 'grotesquely europeanized world' in the same letter in which the situation in Germany seems to him 'so local,' Bonhoeffer to H. Rössler, October 18, 1931, ibid., p. 60.
17. Ibid., p. 61; 'the great death of Christianity.'
18. Bonhoeffer, *Gesammelte Schriften* vol. III, pp. 261-264.
19. Ibid., p. 269.
20. Bonhoeffer, *Gesammelte Schriften* vol. II, p. 79; letter dated August 20, 1933.
21. cf. Dietrich Bonhoeffer, *Nachfolge* (Munich, 1981), p. 238; 'The protest against the world must be accomplished in the world.'
22. Dietrich Bonhoeffer, *Ethik* (Munich, 1975), p. 112.
23. *Gesammelte Schriften* vol. II, p. 35.
24. Dietrich Bonhoeffer, *Widerstand und Ergebung* (Munich, 1970), p. 196.
25. Bonhoeffer, *Gesammelte Schriften* vol. I, p. 320 (italics mine).

26. Bonhoeffer, 'Nach zehn Jahren' in *Widerstand*, p. 14; cf. *Gesammelte Schriften* vol. II, p. 417, 'The future of Germany has once again become important to me.'
27. Bonhoeffer, *Gesammelte Schriften* vol. I, p. 320.
28. George Bell, 'The Background of the Hitler-plot' in *Gesammelte Schriften* vol. I, pp. 390-398.
29. Bonhoeffer, *Gesammelte Schriften* vol. II, p. 411, letter dated August 26, 1941.
30. See Heinz Eduard Tödt, 'Der Bonhoeffer-Dohnanyi-Kreis in der Opposition und im Widerstand gegen das Gewaltregime Hitlers (Zwischenbilanz eines Forschungsprojekts)' in *Die Präsenz des verdrängten Gottes; Glaube, Religionslosigkeit und Weltverantwortung nach Dietrich Bonhoeffer*, Christian Gremmels und Ilse Tödt eds. (Munich, 1987), pp. 205-263.
31. Bonhoeffer, *Ethik*, pp. 62, 65.
32. Ibid., p. 12.
33. Karl Barth, *Kirchliche Dogmatik*, III/4 (Zürich, 1951), p. 23.
34. See Bonhoeffer, 'Gedanken zu William Paton: *The Church and the New Order*' (1941), *Gesammelte Schriften* vol. I, pp. 359ff.
35. Cf. Fritz K. Ringer, *The Decline of the German Mandarins. The German Academic Community 1890-1933* (Cambridge, Mass., 1969).
36. Bonhoeffer, *Ethik*, p. 107. In the course of these years in the resistance, Bonhoeffer became closely acquainted with these Prussian circles; see Bethge, *Widerstand*, p. 120.
37. Bonhoeffer, *Ethik*, p. 255.
38. Hans Mommsen, 'Gesellschaftsbild und Verfassungspläne des deutschen Widerstandes' in *Der Deutsche Widerstand gegen Hitler*, eds. Walter Schmitthenner and Hans Buchheim (Berlin, 1966), pp. 73-167.
39. Bonhoeffer, *Ethik*, pp. 113, 149. See also idem, *Widerstand*, pp. 327-328, and *Fragmente aus Tegel* (Munich, 1978).
40. Larry L. Rasmussen, *Dietrich Bonhoeffer. Reality and Resistance* (Nashville, N.Y., 1972).
41. Cf. Mommsen, pp. 86ff., 118ff.; Bethge, *Dietrich Bonhoeffer*. p. 702; Bonhoeffer, 'Bishop Bell of Chichester' in *Gesammelte Schriften* vol. I, pp. 375, 394; Tödt, pp. 253ff.
42. Cf. Bonhoeffer, *Widerstand*, pp. 164ff. '... that now, on the basis of Christianity, a rebuilding of the life of the nations, internally and externally, is possible.' From letter dated Nov. 27, 1943.
43. Thomas Mann, 'Vom kommenden Sieg der Demokratie' (1938) in *Essays*, vol. II (Frankfurt am Main, 1977), pp. 194-221.
44. Idem, 'Der Problem der Freiheit' (1939) in *Essays*, vol. II, pp. 228-244; cf. Bonhoeffer, *Ethik*, p. 60.
45. Thomas Mann, 'Schicksal und Aufgabe' (19449 in *Essays*, vol. II, pp. 245-261.
46. Ibid., p. 247; cf. Bonhoeffer, *Ethik*, p. 53 and *Fragmente*, p. 47.
47. Bonhoeffer, *Ethik*, p. 62.
48. Ibid., p. 60.
49. cf. ibid., p. 151.
50. Apologetics taken in the sense of a theological account of, and plea for the Christian faith in relation to culture, not as the 'product of fear' Bonhoeffer hated so much; Bonhoeffer, *Gesammelte Schriften* vol. V (Munich, 1972), p. 202; cf. idem, *Widerstand*, p. 358.
51. Bonhoeffer, *Ethik*, p. 152.
52. Ibid., p. 114.
53. Ibid., p. 115; cf. also idem, *Gesammelte Schriften* vol. I, p. 358 on, 'a worldly order, which stays within the confinements of the Ten Commandments.'
54. Bonhoeffer, *Ethik*, p. 306.
55. See ibid., pp. 51, 53, 54, 90, 151ff., 270ff., 273, 294, 303ff., 316, 354, 369.
56. Ibid., pp. 59, 102, 154, 209, 210, 212, 234, 245, 247, 315, 347, 348, 384.
57. Ibid., p. 104.
58. Ibid., pp. 314ff., 338, 349.
59. Ibid., p. 213.
60. See Clifford J. Green, 'The Text of Bonhoeffer's Ethics' in *New Studies in Bonhoeffer's Ethics*, ed. William J. Peck (Lewiston/Queenston, 1987), pp. 3-66.
61. Bonhoeffer, *Ethik*, p. 98.
62. Ibid., p. 208.

63. Ibid., pp. 240ff. On Bonhoeffer's personalism, see p. 231.
64. Ibid., pp. 75, 79.
65. Ibid., p. 77.
66. Edgar Morin, *Penser l'Europe* (Paris, 1987), p. 37.
67. Morin speaks of 'Islam as a "Europeanizer,"' ibid., p. 38.
68. Ibid., p. 39.
69. Ibid., p. 40ff.
70. Jürgen Moltmann, *Politische Theologie - Politische Ethik* (Munich, 1984), p. 22.
71. Morin, pp. 27, 48.
72. Cf., e.g., Jürgen Moltmann, *Trinität und Reich Gottes: Zur Gotteslehre* (Munich, 1980) on this general reorientation towards the doctrine of the Trinity.
73. Cf. Denis de Rougemont, *Lettre Ouverte aux Européens* (Paris, 1970), p. 47. Rougemont considers the idea of the incarnation and the absolute value of the human being as fundamental options for a European culture.
74. Emmanuel Levinas, *Humanisme de l'autre homme* (Paris, 1972).
75. Bonhoeffer, *Ethik,* p. 234.

Europe as Heritage

CHRISTIAN OCCIDENT OR DIVIDED CONTINENT?

H.D. van Hoogstraten

Can modern Europe, in light of its development, be qualified as *christliches Abend-land,* in which Jewish and Christian values and norms play — at least implicitly — a leading role? I shall attempt a modest contribution to the answer to this complicated question. Bonhoeffer's view of Europe as inheritance and decay is comparable to the growing insight that the world is governed by an economic system which begins with values which are utterly different from 'the basic concepts of the Hebrew Bible, that increasingly pervade the world-culture.'[1]

Bonhoeffer's response to Europe as the Christian Occident was manifestly positive in several places in his *Ethics*. He also described it as being threatened, with particular reference to the historical context in which he found himself.

In this essay, I will first give a description of those areas where Bonhoeffer lays greatest emphasis. I especially want to discuss the cultural-historical essay 'Inheritance and Decay' ('Erbe und Verfall'), although several other parts of his *Ethics* will be discussed as well.

Second, I will attempt to analyse the significance of the divide running through Europe — the Iron Curtain — the division between two world-controlling economic systems, as well as their political influence. This analysis is directed and delimited by the ideological and religious character of these two systems which also forms a part of the inheritance of Europe as Christian Occident!

Although we live in a different age than Bonhoeffer, we ask a common question: To what extent does a 'Christian Occident' still exist in modern times? Western society has been profoundly transformed by the Enlightenment. Bonhoeffer, however, is ambivalent toward this transformation because the content of the incontrovertible reality of Christ is not easy to find in times of reversal and revolutionary change.

This is the basic problem that we have in common. As I will attempt to demonstrate, a tension also exists for us which Bonhoeffer hardly addresses, but which can be considered and dealt with through the use of Bonhoeffer's approach to faith and reality, i.e., his theological method. The tension is that which is conquering the world like a new religion ('economic religion'[2]). This tension is not at all self-evident; it is only revealed as a result of certain fundamental theological decisions. Here we can learn from Bonhoeffer: if we want to develop theological ethics, the way of decision must be chosen.

So-called 'business ethics' serves as an example of the inextricable mixing of capitalism and Christianity without engaging in the fundamental reflection which I have in mind. The increasing popularity, on a personal level, of simple and naive ethical solutions to very complicated problems of a structural nature can be seen in such business ethics. A word of warning, however, is necessary. The theological (social) ethicist must treat this topic very carefully, since it has the potential to hinder his or her view of the religious character of present-day social mandates. This can have the same effect that fascism had in the thirties.[3]

Business ethics assumes a culturally and religiously designed realm of norms and values in which everyone participates. In order to make responsible decisions, men and women in powerful, policy-making positions need to be aware of the values they are using in making such decisions. Charles McCoy, an authority in this field, writes: 'Understood in its most comprehensive dimensions, *ethics is reflection on the moral significance of human action* ... A society has comprehensive beliefs and cultural values that provide legitimation for particular purposes and ways of living.'[4] The ethicist offers a helping hand in applying these values to the processes of decision-making.

McCoy is convinced that we live in a culture in which positive values have such great influence that they significantly affect policy-making in both economic and political contexts. Contemporary Western society is able, he claims, to return to the community experiences of the time of Plato, the Jewish prophets, or the Middle Ages. What we need is:

> ... a new understanding of corporate organization and management that can mobilize the community and culture that make up the corporation, so that it can respond effectively to the challenges of the changing environment of values in society... The corporation in this perspective, is a community with a culture and value commitments. As a community it is an organizational context of persons and groups; a system of customs, expectations, values, and purposes and a system of action and interaction.[5]

It is my opinion that the problem of applying social ethics to contemporary Western society is much more complicated than business ethics (and other related types) suggest. Let us listen to Bonhoeffer while we evaluate and judge ethics in a fundamental ethical discourse. In his *Ethics* Bonhoeffer says a great deal about the Christian or anti-Christian character of European society, the environment where, as we have seen, ethics must make its contribution. Yet according to, and together with Bonhoeffer, we must first conquer the tendency of 'thinking in terms of two spheres.'[6] As we shall see, this is necessary in order to be truly critical toward the economic system as a religion.

1

Bonhoeffer and the Christian Occident

There appears to be a tension in *Ethics* between the theological and the cultural-historical approach to reality. Bonhoeffer deals with the phenomenon of European revolutions in connection with the latter and especially points out the dangers of the French Revolution. He even goes so far as to draw a direct line from the French Revolution to the reactionary fascist-Nazi revolution of his own time and context.

Before going into this any further, it is first necessary to look at Bonhoeffer's theological approach to reality. This theme resounds throughout his *Ethics*; the Christ-reality is the *essential* reality; it is the ground which brings forth all that is. Here lies the criterion by which he judges every possible penultimate, ethics, religion, the relation of the sacred and the profane, and politics. In order to demonstrate the value which Bonhoeffer attaches to the Christ-reality and to give a taste of how positively he presents his vision, I will let him speak for himself:

> The concept of historical inheritance, which is linked with the consciousness of temporality and opposed to all mythologization, is possible only when thought is consciously or unconsciously governed by the entry of God into history at a definite place and a definite point of time, that is to say, by the incarnation of God in Jesus Christ (p. 88f.).
>
> Man's apostasy from Christ is at the same time his apostasy from his own essential nature (p.110).
>
> The division of the total reality into a sacred and a profane sphere, a Christian and a secular sphere, creates the possibility of existence in a single one of these spheres, a spiritual sphere which has no part in secular existence, and a secular existence which can claim autonomy for itself and can exercise this right of autonomy in its dealing with the spiritual sphere (pp. 196f.).
>
> He [i.e., Jesus Christ] comprises together the whole reality of the world at once and reveals the ultimate basis of this reality (p. 202).
>
> The world, like all created things, is created through Christ and with Christ as its end, and consists in Christ alone (John 1:10; Col. 1:16). To speak of the world without speaking of Christ is empty and abstract. The world is relative to Christ, *no matter whether it knows it or not* (p. 207, italics added).

These quotations reveal a rejection of *Eigengesetzlichkeit* (which Max Weber called an important characteristic of bourgeois society).[7] In addition, it urges a strong relativization of the autonomous subject. In this way, theology makes its own contribution to the breakdown of too severe a subject-object distinction as well as to the paradigm shift as described by Thomas Kuhn.[8] From this perspective, certain aspects of *Widerstand und Ergebung* can be understood: the 'being there for others' and 'to be caught up into the way of Jesus Christ, into the messianic event.'[9]

It is essential to define the unity and the togetherness of our part of the world accurately. When the subject is stripped of his alleged autonomous knowledge and morality, that which determines the acting subject is necessarily made clear. Let us see how far we come with Bonhoeffer's solutions.

1.1. *Inheritance and decay*

Bonhoeffer speaks extensively about the historical and the cultural context of the acting and thinking subject in 'Inheritance and Decay.' The authenticity and the falsity of the *Christian* Occident is the central focus. He begins this essay, which was written in 1940, with the following thesis: 'It is only in the Christian West that it is possible to speak of a historical heritage' (p. 88). Other, often older, cultures share in the timelessness of their existence. Jesus Christ has turned the Occident into a historical unity. In this way the author opposes the *christliche Vergangenheit* to the *völkische Vergangenheit*. The latter is an essential part of Nazi ideology: the unity of the German *Volk* lies in the Edda (Miskotte!), in the German race. In contrast with this, Bonhoeffer makes the courageous statement (note his context!) that our origin lies in Christ; when we go back beyond him we end up at the Jewish people!

Thus the unity of the West lies in Christ, and in the testimony of our ancestors concerning him, *not* in mythological reverence. In that unity, other influences (e.g., Greek and Roman) have their place and can flourish. This unity is a condition which, until the Reformation, was guaranteed by the authority of pope and emperor. As long as there was a Roman Catholic church (rightly identified by Bonhoeffer with the papacy) there would be nostalgia for the lost Occidental empire, the *Corpus Christianum*. Luther fought for the true unity of a Europe that was starting to crack. In this context he distinguished between two realms: the *Corpus Christi* and the world. Lord of *both* realms is the God revealed in Jesus Christ.

The real problems did not arise, however, until the world became self-sufficient in technological, scientific, and political respects. This development was irreversible, even though the physicists of the seventeenth and eighteenth centuries were still God-fearing Christians.

How then should we judge modern atheism? Bonhoeffer thinks that there is both a negative and a positive side to godlessness in Europe. He is referring to a typical occidental godlessness, which is practical in nature.[10] It appears in response to the critical question: to what are politics or technology actually subservient? With regard to politics, Bonhoeffer tries to respond by evaluating the phenomenon of revolution, in particular the French Revolution and the American Revolution.

The French Revolution was a symptom which necessarily occurred in a Roman Catholic country; it was a very strong sign of the modern Occident:

> With a most astonishing concentration of forces, the ideas, demands and aspirations of many successive generations were here suddenly all at once hurled upwards with elemental violence into the daylight of history (p. 97).

> (In erstaunlicher Zusammenballung wurden hier mit elementarer Wucht die Gedanken, Forderungen, Bewegungen vieler nachfolgender Generationen auf einmal ins Tageslicht der Geschichte geschleudert.)[11]

Consequently, we must think of it as a total and destructive revolution. Everything bursts forth simultaneously: the cult of the ratio and the deification of nature, the belief in progress and the criticism of culture, the revolution of the bourgeoisie and the revolt of the masses, nationalism and hostility towards the church, human rights and dictatorial terror. Thus, this revolution signifies the emergence of the liberated human being in his terrible violence and his most terrifying terror.

In spite of these strong words, Bonhoeffer is clearly ambivalent here. On the one hand, he praises the proclamation of human rights as a result of the revolution: humanity has freed itself from paternalism, from the social and economic exercise of power. On the other hand, present-day nihilism marks the end of the road on which the French Revolution started out. This is the negative form of Western godlessness. What is meant is not theoretical atheism, but religion born of hostility toward God.

There is a fundamental distinction between this godlessness and paganism which worships gods in human form: *here humanity* is worshipped in the form of God! This leads to vitalism, a direct result of the Christian (mostly Roman Catholic) heresy of the fundamental goodness of man (p. 103). Thus the Occident loses its firm historical ground. With the loss of the unity which was created by the image of Christ, the Occident was confronted with *Nothingness*. It is a typically Western Nothingness. As the decay of all existence, it is the sublime unleashing of all anti-divine forces. Thus Nothingness is proclaimed God (p. 106; 'the void made God'). For fear of this God, everything is abandoned: individual judgment, being human, the fellow human being. Modern humanity is incapable of maintaining the spiritually necessary vigilance. The value of suffering as the formation of life by the threat of death is denied. The dominant politics are characterized by Bonhoeffer as Machiavellianism and heroism. The true Western policy is no longer understood: the struggle between the knowledge of the right thing and the necessities of the moment.

In this way Bonhoeffer tries to draw a link between the personal attitude of citizen and that of political government. The thought that lies behind this seems to be the following: the people have abandoned the values of the Christian Occident and that is why politics are now perverted.

Against this, small measures will not help. What we need is a miraculous revival of faith. Personal conversion however has to be accompanied by a power which limits evil. This power becomes active in history in light of God's *'Weltregiment.'* In the Bible this power is called 'the restrainer' ('der Aufhaltende'), the κατεχων. With these remarks, Bonhoeffer clings explicitly to the unity of the two realms: the spiritual-personal (the miraculous revival of the faith) and the worldly-political (the restraining power). In my opinion, what Bonhoeffer has in mind with the 'aufhaltende Ord-nungsmacht' are the political forces which resist the Nazi regime, within as well as beyond the borders.[12] The church (the Confessing Church!) considers these forces her allies. All the elements of order which are still available — justice, truth, science, art, education, humanity, freedom, patriotism — return to their origin after wandering afar. This origin seems to me to be the Christian Occident, in which the two realms of Christ are united; and herein lies the reason why the church and the political power which reinstates order seek — and find — each other.

1.2. *The essence of the inheritance*

After this rendering and partial interpretation of 'Erbe und Verfall', it now seems possible to gain an accurate impression of Bonhoeffer's thoughts on Europe as Christian Occident and inheritance. It will also be worthwhile to try to point out its possibilities and limitations.

Some of the values of this inheritance are: its historicity, its unity, its humanity, and all related aspects. The inheritance however is not automatic! Decay has begun everywhere and its concrete results can be seen in many places in Germany, the heart of 'Christian' civilization. Many examples of this are mentioned elsewhere in *Ethics*, like the Despiser of Men, the Successful Man, and the Idolization of Death (under

'Ethics As Formation').

In order to fight the decay, it must first be recognized. Bonhoeffer attempts to recognize it by means of a historical survey. The point of departure of this historical investigation is essential, because the starting point defines both the method and the result. It is the irrefutably established Christ-reality which embraces all of reality. In European history we see both the confirmation and the denial of this reality. Here, however, we should be alert: its confirmation may function well for a while, but it can also easily result in the opposite of its desired purpose. Personal, cultural, political and social changes can be due to this inversion. For example, we have mentioned the French Revolution which occurred in *Roman Catholic* France: a church that lingers in the unity of the Middle Ages should expect such a reaction. A different example is the American Revolution, which is described as a symptom of typically Anglo-Saxon Christian democracy. As a historical Western phenomenon, it is evaluated rather positively by Bonhoeffer in its origin, but hardly in its ultimate effects.

Bonhoeffer wants to save the inheritance of the Christian Occident by the right act *(ethics!)* in personal and political respects. This act is born out of belief (cf. *Akt und Sein!*) which in turn is socially shaped. We think first of community (*Christus als Gemeinde existierend*),[13] but certainly also of the other 'mandate-areas': culture/ labour, family/relatives, state/government and all related aspects. In each of the social institutions which comprise society, we should live according to the 'Gestalt' of Christ.

1.3. *The positive effect of the two realms doctrine*

As we said, Christian civilization is no static fact. This ought not to be viewed only negatively, however, for within the Christian West radical changes are taking place which promote the formation *(Gestaltung)* of Christ in a certain place and time. In this way, the Enlightenment and the liberal values which it generated can fulfill such a task. Unlike Barth's criticism of 'Kulturprotestantismus', Bonhoeffer wants to link the revealed Christ-reality to the values which serve humanity.

With the help of a well-interpreted two-realms doctrine (in its shortest formulation: polemical unity), Bonhoeffer feels that this can actually be done. One of the most important problems which he encounters here is the *Eigengesetzlichkeit* (autonomy) of, for instance, technology or the state. Yet this is only a real element in the process of Occidental decay when the Lordship of Christ is abandoned in the secular realm and replaced by totally different sovereignty.

That is what Bonhoeffer calls *negative godlessness*: when another religion, which is opposed to the Christian inheritance, rules. In *positive godlessness,* the concept of autonomy has a principal position (as is even clearer in *Widerstand und Ergebung*): humanity must free itself from a leader God who would employ a *Führer.* Consequently, dealing with the inheritance which is called *christliches Abendland* means resisting its self-evident and static interpretation.

If the two realms are separated, then the danger of a negative, i.e., a religious-

Christ, adorned godlessness arises leaving no hope and contrasting very sharply with the promising godlessness which speaks anti-religiously and anti-clerically. The latter preserves — albeit negatively — a real faith in God and the church. It is a question of acting within the context of a comprehensive Christ-reality, be it consciously or unconsciously. That is the form of the Occidental Christian inheritance: ethics as a realization of the Christian values which come with Christian culture. But these ethics should be formulated in such a way that they also give rise — dialectically — to resistance to negative godlessness, in which a different religion rules.

1.4. *Economics: Bonhoeffer's 'blind spot'*

One thing is very striking in all this: Bonhoeffer hardly ever deals with the role of economics. Although he seriously considers the state, democracy, and dictatorship, we cannot help but notice that issues like industrialization and the role of money and capital seem to have passed his notice. Yet these, too, are important elements and the question is to what extent they can be considered the (pseudo-) inheritance of the Christian Occident.

This question is necessary to achieve clarity on the present situation in Europe. Through the midst of Germany — the heart of the Christian Occident — runs the great borderline between the superpowers, each having their own political and economic system. How are we going to deal with the concept of the 'Christian Occident' now that the division is a fact which cannot and should not be neglected. The West is called Christian, the East atheist. The West worships the freedom of humanity and enterprise and accepts the mediating function of money to maintain social relations and positions. The East follows at a historical distance. Where can the inheritance be found? Or is it only the Antichrist which is worshipped on both sides of the Iron Curtain? This would mean that business ethics is very naive indeed and has lost all contact with its Christian background.

In order to answer these burning questions we will now pursue the problem of evaluating our economic system in light of the division of Europe.

2

Divided Europe

Violently opposed to the fundamental unity of the Christian Occident which, according to Bonhoeffer, even wars cannot disturb, stands the present dichotomy. To be able to understand its nature we must consider the historical genesis of both systems which — ironically — border in Central Europe. Without considering their historical development in *extenso,* something can at least be said about their *common origin:* '*das christliche Abendland*'!

2.1. *Communism and capitalism as European phenomena*

The Communist system can be seen as the incarnate criticism of capitalism. To put it another way: just as the *'Bekennende Kirche'* cannot be detached from the *'Deutsche Christen'*, so communism cannot exist without capitalism. Although Bonhoeffer does not mention the Russian Revolution, the same thing could be said about it as was said about the French Revolution in 'Erbe und Verfall': what had been salted away for generations, suddenly erupted.

I would like to put forward the following thesis: *the capitalist system has evoked its own criticism, and that is precisely the kind of development which typifies the Christian Occident.*

The injustice caused by the system evokes criticism — in spite of the blessing which that same system seems to bring. Blessing and curse/judgement are in a line and on one level. For criticism to have effective power, it needs to take political shape — hence revolution. The objection that this revolution did not take place in an industrial state where democracy was developing, but in a mainly agrarian country with sovereign rule, is a different matter which cannot be discussed until we have taken a closer look at capitalism.

Capitalism can be seen as a new symbol of unity in Europe as Christian Occident (including the USA, which is populated primarily by Europeans who have destroyed most of the original inhabitants). After the Middle Ages an extremely aggressive and imperialist Europe emerged. The crusades were only a foretaste. It appeared as though the unity of the 'Abendland' wanted to spread throughout the world. At the height of colonization, Europe occupied and possessed about eighty percent of the earth's surface.

To what extent was this actually caused by Christianity or Christian culture or Christian religion? Let us suppose that this expansionism was caused by the 'canine-hunger of capital' (Marx). This in turn raises the fundamental question to what extent the Christian Occident has created a fertile culture for the development of this — in every aspect expanding — social system.

2.2. *Knowing and seeing*

Let us use the same method used by Bonhoeffer: he *knew* the Christ reality and *saw* the condition of Germany. He tried to connect the two historically. The original Lutheran intention of the two-realms doctrine. The two-realm doctrine, which he says was Luther's intention helped him to judge the situation and to accept changes.

If we want to apply a similar hermeneutic, the first thing we must do is to see the European situation and what that means for world relations. We see large contrasts between poor and rich, between North and South. Furthermore, we see the military-political contrasts between West and East and an enormous arms buildup. The contrasts on earth have never been so great as in our time. We see that science and technology have been of great blessing in many areas. At the same time we see that these blessings are reserved for only a small portion of humanity. The most important cause of this is the nature of the world economic system: life is controlled by exchange-relations.

Exchange relations are combined with the unjust distribution of goods, which seems to belong to the laws of our economy (and even the so-called 'communistic' system cannot get rid of it!). The way property, labour, and money are functioning in, and in fact dominating, the system plays a central role. Money as a general equivalent for goods is generated at the exchange, on the market. This *realized* profit is actually *produced* during the production of goods which are used for exchange. The directors, controllers, and/or owners of the means of production are not the same people as the wage earners who do the actual work; the people who *produce* the profit are not the same as those who *realize* it. In our time we only have to look at the activities of multinational concerns in the Third World to realize that this is an indispensable truth.

In Holland a so-called *'economic theology'* has been developed which has chosen as its startingpoint this (briefly described here) analysis. It attempts to cast light on the origin of modern Occidental economics. Methodologically there are striking similarities with Bonhoeffer. Just as Bonhoeffer deals with the political shape of the Enlightenment (the French Revolution) and its results in 'Erbe und Verfall', so 'economic theology' deals with the economic shape of the Enlightenment, mainly in Scotland. The main spokesman for economic theology, A.T. van Leeuwen, in his study *De Nacht van het Kapitaal (Capital's Night)*, shows that in the course of his work Adam Smith evolved from a theologian into a philosopher of morals into an economist.[14]

2.3. *Bonhoeffer and Adam Smith*

In 'economic theology' Smith's work is paradigmatically treated as a way of reducing theology and ethics (moral philosophy) to a theoretical prop for existing economic practice. The hard nucleus has not really changed since the end of the eighteenth century and will not so long as the system remains intact. Like Bonhoeffer, Smith stresses the tremendous contribution of classical thinkers to European culture. However, in Smith's thought they are not corrected by God's revelation in Christ, nor does Smith pay attention to the wide gap which sparates our society from the *polis* and its philosophers.

Smith tries to combine Greek and Christian ethical thought in order to provide an ideological basis for the market-attitude of modern man. Smith has no theological problems with this: his deistic conception of God makes it possible for him to 'tame' the criticism which in our society proceeds from God's revelation in Christ, by the Greek doctrine of virtues. God is only given a place as first cause, as immovable mover, as clockmaker.

The synthesis of neighborly love and self-love becomes the 'Great Commandment.' Van Leeuwen speaks very clearly in this connection:

This moral-theological and moral-philosophical transformation has had decisive consequences for

105

economic philosophy. The sympathy-principle, through which the self-evident fundamental pattern of bourgeois society is understood, is the exact translation of the Christian commandment of love. Every man's natural tendency to 'trade, negotiate, exchange' *(Wealth of Nations* I, ii.1) accords fully with the social nature of man created by God's wisdom, which Christianity has always envisioned. The 'natural price' *(W.N.* I. vii), which fulfills the sympathy principle in society, has in economics the same constitutional function as the principle of gravity does in the physical universe.[15]

Here we have a clearly theological legitimation of modern economic practice. The values and norms of the Christian Occident have been adapted and theology has been given the character of natural theology.

All this leads me to speak of the religious character of our present-day system of production, consumption, distribution, information, and high technology. I can do so because the system avails itself of certain mandates which bear an absolute character: they are absolutely necessary for the beneficial continuation of contemporary society, including the current status of people and countries. Freedom of action and ownership, the obligation to do (wage-) labour, the protection of the national economy and the ideology of national security are but a few examples of mandates which the economy imposes on the political government. What Marx has in fact done is no more (and no less) than to bring to light the effects of the exchange-society, which I briefly described above. Marx was convinced that this economic mechanism would grow and conquer the world. He also thought that the divide between people would only grow as a result of the different positions they took in the production process. In his opinion, politics in a country where capital has a dominant position cannot help but support, to some extent, these mechanisms. If we want to change things in a truly fundamental way, then revolution is the only possible alternative.

Marx, however, underestimated the political power of capitalism in the democratic form it was developing in the nineteenth and the twentieth centuries, in spite of his keen analyses. Marxism assumed political shape in countries which were not yet ready for real industrialization and the economy of a developed exchange-society. The criticism which the Western economic and liberal system provoked never succeeded in achieving a real political influence in that Western society. As a result, I think we have to speak of a *fatal historical development:* the internal critique of the capitalist system has taken shape outside the countries concerned in a political system that does not know a constitutional democracy. That is why criticism has been literally put outside the door and is considered the enemy. And *that* is exactly the non-Jewish and non-Christian character of our society. Because the capitalistic system arose in the Christian Occident, it is easy to understand why the opposing system prescribes atheism as an obligatory philosophy of life.

There are two most striking features of the image of the 'actually existing socialism' which prevails in Western society:

1. Little or no distinction is made between the several countries where Communist rule is established; this in spite of the fact that the recent history of Eastern Europe is well-known.

2. Criticism which could be applied to our own Western development is projected beyond the frontiers of our own sphere of influence. There it can be combatted as a localized enemy. People opposing the local regime in their particular capitalistic country can be put in jail as Communists. In that way, ideologically speaking, the Christian inheritance is protected against dangerous atheistic communism.

But again, and more urgently than ever, we must ask: Does it make any sense to speak of a *Christian Occident*, now that Christianity is used so ideologically? Are the Christian values still alive, now that the exchange-economy which has had such a destructive effect on humanity and nature has broken criticism's wing? Or should we say, accepting Bonhoeffer's opinion that the two realms are a perfect unity in a *negative* way, that a *different* religion rules in the modern Occident, which can be indicated as the collective personification of the Antichrist? If so, the burning question arises: What *does* the Iron Curtain, which runs right through the heart of the Christian Occident, really mean? Is it the symbol of a real or an artificial division on the several levels of economics, politics and ideology?

2.4. *'Entzweiung'*

Throughout Bonhoeffer's theology an essential aspect is that the *Entzweiung* (fragmentation-alienation) has been put away, that death has died, that life is structured by the life, suffering, and resurrection of Jesus Christ. This way of divine revelation means that the individual and the community are interwoven; that the subject is included in an objective reality. This is why thinking in terms of two spheres is impossible and why the doctrine of two realms regains its original critical power.
Does this really apply to modern Europe? The unity Bonhoeffer clings to so compulsively has been everywhere disturbed. There seems to be a fundamental *Entzweiung* in different areas. Superiority and inferiority of position, income, power, sex, and race define the image of Western societies. And perhaps the greatest present-day problem (which unexpectedly links East and West): culture and nature seem so alienated that nature collapses under the exploitation, the *Verwertung*.

Once there was a traditional unity. There were fights between throne and altar, but the *metaphysical unity* was beyond discussion. Nowadays the only unity is the *ideological unity* necessary for the functioning of the world system of trade, economy, and technology. One of the arguments used in Western society today to keep this unity alive is the proclamation of the unity of nature and the cosmos we live in; of this organic pattern we are a part (the *holistic view*). When we disengage ourselves from that ideology, the huge dichotomy just mentioned becomes clear to us.

For Bonhoeffer, the *natural* is an important concept in the fight against nihilism. Nature *after* the Fall is dialectical in character: it holds on to freedom *and* obedience, to autonomy *and* heteronomy, to the individual *and* the community, to heaven *and* earth, to Christianity *and* Occident, to life *and* death; in short, to the Christ-reality as the foundation of all that exists.

The whole of the *Ethics* is filled with this dialectic and Bonhoeffer is deeply

107

concerned to prevent one-sidedness, the one-sidedness of vitalism and fanaticism. For vitalism has its dangerous pendant in the deification of death, even as fanaticism can lead to the similarly horrifying surrender to a charismatic leader. This attitude then would seem to lead quickly to the golden mean: the safe course between Scylla and Charybdis. In Bonhoeffer's theology, however, this is out of the question; there is no compromise between self-interest and love for the fellow man as with Adam Smith, who tried to provide people with the proper ethical attitude when they met in the marketplace. Bonhoeffer argues from a very concrete, materially determined tension. Existentially and ideologically, he experienced the power of Nothingness, that is to say, the threat of the Fall, the chaos of the Christian Occident, and he was about to be dragged into them.[16] The Christ-reality functions as 'stopper.' There *is* an alternative, but we have to be willing to analyse and to understand the religious character of the dominant political ideology by way of the consistent dialectical approach to reality as we just described it. If we do so, Christ regains power — if I interpret Bonhoeffer correctly.

2.5. *Unity and separation now*

We may now address the changed relation between politics and economy to which Bonhoeffer hardly pays attention. Politics, which has been based on dictatorial pretension in Europe for the last while, using atavistic mythologoumena, seems to be continually forced to acknowledge its superior in liberal economic relations — to which we should add that the Nazi state was ultimately, of course, a political manifestation of capitalism-in-crisis.

The gap which separates us from the pre-enlightenment era can be analysed by means of the term 'awarding of salvational value.' A healing quality was once attributed to politics. There are many examples from the ancient past: the *polis* which was well governed could participate in *eudaimonia* (final happiness), or at least the free citizens of the *polis* could, on the condition that it was governed by philosophers (Plato!). The king of Israel, if he proved faithful to his anointing — as a messianic king, mind! — could provide justice. These functions have been taken over by the proper *economic* attitude. Nowadays, western political figures can only hold and maintain power (and serve salvation in a secular way) when they *are obedient* to the free enterprise economy. As was said earlier, the curse of the system has to be accepted as an attendant phenomenon in deference of the blessing of the 'elect.' This use of a religious phrase here is no coincidence. Karl Marx and Max Weber have their *Protestantismusthese:* the Protestant religion can be considered the most fertile soil for the growth of this economic system.[17] In order to soften the harshness of the system, the *temporary nature* of the evident injustice is often stressed. A natural theology lends a helping hand here: the law of exchange belongs to the laws of God's creation as does for instance the law of gravity.[18]

I think we can speak here of *Schöpfungsordnungen,* which are comparable to the creation orders which Bonhoeffer resisted so resolutely. In fact, orders of creation cannot be considered 'natural' in Bonhoeffer's sense of the word, because they are not directed to Christ *after* the Fall (to use Bonhoeffer's own definition again). In line with Bonhoeffer's thought, we cannot choose but to condemn the *law and the prophets of the accumulation of capital* (Marx; with this he meant the law of production and exchange) as a calamity. And this because these orders of creation, as well as those in the thirties in Germany, serve as a curse for the condemned masses: the impure races, the financially weak and the dependent, the economically powerless people (for the largest part women) and countries (and also there, women first).

Bonhoeffer tells us that there is an alternative way to interpret the Bible and tradition. We simply have to connect creation and revelation — *not* in an ontological way (as if the Fall never had happened) but in a polemical unity. A Confessional Church pleads for a theology of revelation over against a natural theology. Thus the stress on the *Diesseitigkeit* of faith *(Widerstand und Ergebung)* is very important. This is a subtle but essential distinction: the unity of faith and life is stressed without deducing God's will and blessing from the established, historically developed relations.

Bonhoeffer calls his indictment of the palpable and ideological shape of the theology of creation orders *'ethics.'* He does not stop at the proclamation of the Word, but he translates *doctrine* into *ethics* (the formation of Christ!), which results in ethical mandates. As a matter of fact, I think we now have the same task with regard to the ruling economy and the political strategy subservient to it. This is not as difficult as we might think, at least theoretically. In practice we meet with massive resistance, and it is no exaggeration to say, in line with Bonhoeffer, that consistent criticism will certainly lead to suffering.

Conclusion:
Ethics and Ethics are Two

Social ethics, business ethics, medical ethics are all related to the Western social system as it has developed up to the present time. It certainly *is* a very good thing these various kinds of ethics exist. Such reflections should be made on good and evil, on alternative actions, and on the long term results of current decisions being made in the various spheres of human action. The unbridled growth of multinational concerns or manipulation of genes are examples of such a need. But ethical reflections are also necessary on short term policy decisions in corporate and political contexts.

Only one question remains: Who is the subject who pronounces the ethical judgments?[19] Bonhoeffer puts it this way: ethical judgments are only valid when pronounced by a subject who is rooted in the Christian Occident in which Jesus Christ takes shape today, even as he did in the past, through the *ethical action of true believers*. As we have seen, this means *knowing* the ultimate reality and seeing what kind of religion is in fact ruling and controlling ethical action. The ethical subject is a community, a *'Gemeinde'*, a corporate personality. In tracing Bonhoeffer's theological development we see in his early writings a strong emphasis on the church. Here in *Ethics*, however, it is Christ who reigns through the actions of groups that resist the Nazi system, whether the individuals involved in these groups know it or not. The church is summoned to join forces with all who help shape the 'restraining power.'

If the church wants to *hold on to* and *actualize* the Christian inheritance, it must lend unequivocal support to all ethics which formulates a genuine critique of the dominant system and *its* values, while simultaneously condemning sharply all ethics which helps sustain the system in its exploitation of humanity and nature. The conciliar process — which the churches inherited from Bonhoeffer – provides an excellent opportunity to do so! This condemnation includes a pre-eschatological or penultimate a priori which could be called an eschatological reservation *(eschatologisches Vorbehalt)*: humanity that believes and knows the fundamental unity in Christ, lives as divided humanity. He/she accepts living in a world which is ruled and controlled by the power which I attempted to point to and identify in economic terms. Yet this acceptance proves itself through strong criticism, which continues as long as the false religion rules, be it consciously or unconsciously. That is the *natural existence* Bonhoeffer had in mind. There can be no talk of a true 'Christian' Occident or world where nature is given a significance other than this.

At the end, I recall the beginning: How should we approach *business ethics*? The notion of divided man *and* society seems very important to me. Metaphorically speaking, an 'Iron Curtain' runs right through our own culture and our own personal existence. This is the case on both sides of the other Iron Curtain. Unity is lost and there is no alternative but to seek a false, ideological solution. Thus *business ethics* is false when it postulates a corporate reality in which a company or even a country is an organic part. Theologically educated ethicists who have understood a bit of Bonhoeffer cannot but use and apply the unity given in Christ as a critical instrument against all other concepts of unity, whether natural or economic, as well as against all ethics which finds its criterion there. This does *not* mean that all other forms of *ethics* should be abandoned by theologians. Rather, students of Bonhoeffer should *behave exactingly and critically* within the circle of ethicists. In this way they continue to write the history of a book — *Ethics,* by Dietrich Bonhoeffer.

NOTES

1. Y. Aschkenasy and W.A.C. Whitlau, 'Joodse Hermeneutiek' in *Geliefd is de mens,* ed. Y. Achkenasy (Hilversum, 1983), p. 38.
2. This expression comes from A.Th. van Leeuwen, 'Theologie als "economische godsdienst"-wetenschap' in *De burger en zijn religie,* A.Th. van Leeuwen (Best, 1988).
3. Cf. Bertram Gross, *Friendly Fascism: The New Face of Power in America* (Boston, 1980), as quoted by Ulrich Duchrow, *Weltwirtschaft heute — ein Feld für Bekennende Kirche?* (Munich, 1986), p. 147ff. He also speaks of *Zentrumfaschismus.*
4. Charles S. McCoy, *Management in Values: the Ethical Difference in Corporate Policy and Performance* (London, 1985), p. 41.
5. Ibid., pp. 63, 68.
6. Dietrich Bonhoeffer, *Ethics* (Fontana Library, 1964), pp. 196-207. Quotations in the English language are taken from this edition.
7. M. Weber, *Gesammelte Aufsätze zur Religionssozologie I* (Tübingen, 1963), p. 552; cf. also Duchrow, pp. 26-32.

8. Th. Kuhn, *The Structure of Scientific Revolutions* (Chicago, 1962).
9. Dietrich Bonhoeffer, *Letters and Papers from Prison* (New York, 1972). pp. 361ff., 381.
10. Cf. Per Frostin, who speaks of 'methodological atheism' in *Materialismus, Ideologie, Religion* (Munich, 1978).
11. German edition (Munich, 1967), p.103.
12. This I argued in a more detailed way in my thesis *Interpretatie. Een onderzoek naar de veranderingen in het denken van Dietrich Bonhoeffer en naar de consequenties daarvan voor de vertolking van de bijbel* (Assen, 1973).
13. Cf. Dietrich Bonhoeffer, *Sanctorum Communio* (Munich, 1960).
14. A. Th. van Leeuwen, *De Nacht van het Kapitaal — Door het oerwoud van de economie naar de bronnen van de burgerlijke religie* (Nijmegen, 1984). He speaks of a 'process of reduction' in Smith's thought. About production and realization of profit see pp. 569ff. and p. 587.
15. This 'key text' can be found in ibid., p. 75, in the part that deals with Smith's moral philosophy. For the application in economic theory cf. pp. 431ff.
16. F. de Lange, *Grond onder de voeten* (Kampen, 1985), pp. 180-183 and *passim*.
17. Karl Marx, *Das Kapital I* in Marx/Engels Werke, vol. 23, p. 93; Max Weber, *Die Protestantische Ethik I* (1920). The big difference between the two is that Marx makes a scrupulous analysis of capitalism and Weber only speaks in general terms.
18. This is only possible when the two realms of the Lutheran doctrine are radically opposed so that the secular realm — as God's final purpose with his creation — can be connected with evolution and progress. The believer who is successful in the worldly sphere can be convinced of God's love for him — and that is at the same time the only connection between Christ's two realms: the salvation of the individual.
19. It is the Kantian question which should not be answered in a Kantian way. The transcendental solution of the *categorical imperative* is abandoned by all who see the interwovenness of subjective and objective reality. Most ethicists do not want radical changes because they feel comfortable in the existing relations. Their position does not allow them to be too critical.

Israel and Europe

Albert H. Friedlander

1

Am I here as a historian? A theologian? A rabbi? The three are not incompatible; it is rather a question of emphasis. All three would begin with a document, a text. It is in the interpretation of the texts that they diverge. In classic fashion, we offer two texts written at about the same time. One was written on June 15, 1944 — how could we neglect this text exactly forty-four years later! It is a talk given by Leo Baeck in the concentration camp of Theresienstadt.

The second text, written by Bonhoeffer on Christmas, 1942, is entitled 'Nach zehn Jahren.' Hidden within the beams of his parents home, Dietrich Bonhoeffer described his views on the inner life of the conspiracy against Hitler. He had little time left before entering his cell.

Baeck's text deals with the writing of history. It does not separate Europe from Israel or Israel from the Western world. In the darkness of the camp, Baeck meditated on the task of historians through the ages, from Herodotus to Thucydides, Polybius, Tacitus, Caesar — to Dante, Voltaire, Ranke (I would add here that he spoke to me also of the great contemporary Dutch historians Huizinga and Pieter Geyl, who wrote his study on Napoleon in a Nazi prison). In Theresienstadt he gave the following meditation regarding the death and rebirth of a people and a nation:

> Each people can realize its task and its spirit, and thereby it becomes a historical people. Each people is given a problem which is its own, and with which it must come to terms. Only in this way does it acquire historical worth and strength. A people becomes certain of its history when it comprehends its idea, when its own spirit, part of the spirit of humanity, becomes alive within it... It becomes the tragedy of a people when it goes astray and loses itself in others, seeking itself in other people and not finding its essential individuality which the Eternal Creator has granted it...; (but) a people can be reborn...

> The historian can be the conscience of his people and so take on the prophetic task and proclamation. The great historian Ranke ... says in his *English History*, 'The greatest thing that can happen to man is probably to defend in his own cause the general cause.' And that, too, is the greatest thing that can happen to a people, to defend and represent the cause of humanity in its own cause, to fight for itself and in so doing to fight for humanity at the same time. That is what the prophets taught long ago. And today, that is still the great task of the historian. The ... rebirth of many people could be achieved, the great interrelationships of life could be discovered, nations could draw together to form one humanity.'

The Bonhoeffer text deals with the individual who is also German and who is, as Bethge notes,[2] perhaps himself, *Civil Courage*.

> Who would deny that the German always fulfilled the utmost; in obedience, in his task, in his profession? He offered his total life here, and all of his courage. Nevertheless, the German safeguarded

112

his freedom — and where in the world has there been more passionate discussion concerning freedom than in Germany, from Martin Luther to the philosophy of idealism? — safeguarded it in that he strove to liberate himself from the expression of his own will in the service of the totality. His calling and freedom were to him two sides of the same coin. But, in that he misjudged the world. He had not counted on the fact that his readiness to subjugate himself, to give all his life to the task, could be misused to evil. When this happened, when the exercise of his calling became questionable in itself, all of his moral preconceptions tumbled. It came to be seen that the German still lacked a decisive, basic understanding: that of the necessity of free responsible action even against calling and commanded task. In its place there established itself on the one hand an irresponsible lack of scruples, and on the other hand, a self-lacerating sense of scruples which never led to action. But civil courage can only grow out of free responsibility of the free man. Only today are Germans beginning to discover what free responsibility means.[3]

Here, then, are two texts, both taken out of a situation of anguish. It is central to the teachings of both that the content of such texts cannot be divorced from the existential situation out of which they were created. Both address the history of a people, but move beyond that to an appraisal of the nature of the human being. A rabbi in the midst of a concentration camp reminds his people to seek the welfare of humanity within their own cause; a Christian preacher-prophet castigates his people for losing their freedom by failing to exercise it, by permitting injustice to be done to their powerless brethren.

Do their words help us to understand the historical situation, both then and now? Can we view the Jew and the German as paradigmatic figures for the Europe of that time, forming a pattern of brothers in confrontation? Are they Cain and Abel, or Jacob and Esau; victor and victim, or fellow sufferers? And are we to examine them as figures in a secular world, or do we note the religious dimension evident in these profound figures of questing faith?

'The Jew in Europe, in Bonhoeffer's *Morgenland*.' I must say that the initial invitation to this international conference perturbed me somewhat. The topics suggested rose out of an image of the Jew in the Western world which we have all encountered: loneliness, alienation, a denial of the promises of emancipation — the Jew as outsider, as pariah (one could cite H. Heine, Max Weber, Hannah Arendt). Then came ... we know what came. But afterwards, Israel was established. And I was asked to confront the image of the lonely European Jew, still yearning to be part of the world which had rejected him. *Abendland* or *Morgenland*. Are we to remain the Wandering Jew?

Let me first approach this problem in the guise of a historian, although only in preparation for the theological task. Baeck, in that same concentration camp talk, enjoins the lovers of Clio:

> In each people, the historian could be the one who tells the people about itself ... so that it may recognize itself in recognizing its problem, its peculiarity, ...its task. Historians have often remained silent when they should have spoken ... about every kind of violence, about every historical crime ... they have concealed so much...[4]

What can we tell the Jewish people about Europe and their role here! Have we finally been expelled? Did we ever belong? A few weeks ago, at a historical conference in

Germany, Julius Schoeps talked about the failure of the Emancipation period, about the inability of the Jew to become part of European life, of the nations in which he had requested admission. His *Gesprächspartner,* Professor Ernst Nolte, supported him totally. Yes, the Emancipation had failed. And why? 'Because', said Professor Nolte, 'you opted for Zionism, for your own nationalism. Therefore, you obviously could not be part of any European nationalism.' This is a secondhand report; I was not present at the meeting. Had I been there, I would have created mischief, and would have drawn a line from the founder of the German Conservative party, Julius Stahl, to Professor H. J. Schoeps, Julius's father, the 'last of the monarchists.' I know that I am in the minority camp on this issue. Professor Gershom Scholem was only one of many Jewish thinkers who maintained that there was never a German-Jewish symbiosis. Only assimilation occurred, and it failed. But I would assert to this assembly that the Jew in Europe *did* establish a symbiotic relationship within many of the nations of Europe, particularly within Germany. Even in France, there is a history of Sephardic Jewish life which cannot easily be dismissed. I say this even with the knowledge of last week's news story — that ironic tale of the wandering statue of Alfred Dreyfus which has now found its place in the garden of the Tuileries alongside the Louvre. The Military Academy would not accept him; but then, they never did. One news story stated that the artist was TIM, not further identified. I believe he is a great Jewish cartoonist and lithographer — another irony. His drawing of 'The Last of the Just' hangs in our Leo Baeck College. But the presence of anti-Semitism does not and should not guarantee the absence of Jews within a great nation, nor their share in its history and culture.

This applies to Germany as well. Was there a symbiosis? Of course there was — a partnership between all that was great and good in that culture, and a Jewish people who searched for that greatness and found it. We are unable to see the past because of the present — it is so hard to say 'German' and 'Jew' in the same breath. Yet how can we understand Hermann Cohen (remember his 'Deutschtum und Judentum'?), Franz Rosenzweig (recall his book on Hegel), Max Brod, Martin Buber, and Leo Baeck, without understanding that dimension in their lives! The loneliness and alienation ascribed to them was often in the eyes of the beholder, and in the eyes of the persecutor. Where it did exist, does exist, and has to exist for the Jew is in our knowledge that we live in an unredeemed world, that we are lonely in our encounter with the distant God, and only exist because of our encounters with the near God. And we were not lonely and alienated in a Europe covered with a network of Jewish communities. Those Jewish communities were part of Europe, indigenous to it. They *were* Europe. We meet today in Amsterdam — *ir va-em* of Jewish life — the city was a Jewish mother. Rembrandt held his loving mirror in front of it; the citizens of Amsterdam still yearn for it. Years ago, Otto Frank was my guide to its streets and houses, showing me the memorials, the hiding places. The fact that a Dutch criminal betrayed Anne Frank, that there were many betrayals here, did not mean that the Jews ceased to love the Dutch; and the love was reciprocated. I have ordained four rabbis who serve this community. Their presence is my assurance that Jewish life in Europe will continue.

With deep respect, then, I would turn the question around. I would ask about the alienated, wandering, suffering European, and about his need to restablish a relation-ship with the Jewish people. The shadow of the Holocaust looms over all our lives. In Israel, it is an anguished and dark presence added to an intolerable situation where the majority of Jews feel the pain of the Palestinians deeply. I do not think that a realistic peace can be achieved without the help of Europe. I deplore the government of Mr. Shamir. I also feel that the attempt to see Israel totally as racist persecutors rises in part out of the unexpiated guilt feelings of the European community and of Christianity. That is another issue. I accept the fact that we cannot view the Jew in the world today without recording the injustices taking place in Israel, and the need for establishing a situation where security and peace will permit Jacob and Esau to live together and to come close again. The Western Wall and El Aqsa stand next to one another. True prayers reach towards God from both places; and the Church of the Sepulchre is part of the same mount. Perhaps ... perhaps it will be our religious faith which will provide the answer.

Meanwhile, let it be quite clear that Judaism and most Jews cry out against the moral blindness and racism we see in one segment of the Israeli community: the black bile and racism of a Meir Kahane which continues to gain support among a frightened people; the attempts to solve the problem of security with a violence which begets violence in the camps of Sharon and Shamir, of Begin and even Rabin. The dark fear of Auschwitz still lingers, and more than a moral teaching is needed from the outside. Israel must be assured that the mad prophet and the mad soldier, Khomeini and Ghadaffi, will not be let loose. The poison brewed in the witch's cauldron, that mixture of religion and nationalism, seeps into a world where Hisbollah and Jihad groups commit acts of terror, where Muslim fratricide kills hundreds every day. It will be a continuing reproach to the Arab world that they refused to give their oil money to the starving Palestinians in the UNRRA camps, but are even now giving their seed money to arm a desperate, suffering Palestinian people who have been trained to hate and not to love. Israel can and must open itself to their need — but not without the help of Europe and America. Meanwhile, that act of discipleship viewed by Bonhoeffer as God's philanthropy (Tit. 3:4) to remain with the weak while walking the path of faith — that has been the heart of Judaism from the beginning, the instruction to be *b'nai rachamim,* children of mercy reaching out for their suffering brethren.

2

The Morgenland may provide more of an answer here, partly because religion and nationalism have fused together in the Orient and both Islam and certain sections of Jewish extremism have become infected with the same malady. Here, in the context of this conference, we may well turn back to the experience of Dietrich Bonhoeffer, who saw the fusion of nationalism and the church in Germany, and who fought against it to the point of the ultimate sacrifice. Again, when we compare the teachings of Bon-hoeffer with the message of Baeck in those days, we discover that a common heritage between Judaism and Christianity dating from that time has not been explored fully.

Permit me one ancillary comment at this point. The relationship between Bonhoeffer and the Jews has been fully explored in previous sessions. As a friend of Eberhard Bethge and Berthold Klappert, having read most of their texts dealing with Bonhoeffer and the Jewish question, I can only express my deep satisfaction that this matter has been so clearly expounded and so sensitively presented. It is the foundation from which we derive our security, upon which we can build. That there were flaws in Bonhoeffer's perception of the Jews and Judaism has been noted clearly over the years. These flaws are important and helpful to us, first, because it is much harder to work with saints than with decent, imperfect human beings, and second, because we cannot advocate sainthood towards one another as the hope for resolving ancient problems. *It is the growth and development of Bonhoeffer, his acknowledgment of wrong perceptions, which is our greatest instruction.* We can change ourselves. And we can change our institutions; but that is far more difficult. Both require the courage and strength advocated by our teachers in a dark time. It is perhaps significant that institutions rarely see courage as the ideal way of survival.

We can now turn to those writings of our teachers which deal directly with the problems. They challenge our institutions by expounding the Torah.

Here, in a Bonhoeffer Congress, I would first view his *midrash* of the text from Exodus 32, the great confrontation between Moses and Aaron when the tablets of the Law were confronted by the Golden Calf. I will assume that you know the text, and only remind you of its aftermath, when Moses returns to the Lord and says:

> The people have committed a great sin, and have made themselves golden gods. And now, forgive them their sins. If not, excise *me* as well out of the book which You have written. 'What?' said Adonai to Moses. 'I will excise *him* out of My book who sins against Me. Now, go and lead the people.'...

For Bonhoeffer, this confrontation is preceded by the debate between Moses and Aaron. He shows the conflict between them in his sermon on 'The Church of Moses and the Church of Aaron,' preaching on 28 of May 1933, in the Kaiser-Wilhelm-Gedächtnis-Kirche a few days after the 'German-Christians' had named Ludwig Müller as their national, nationalist bishop. Bonhoeffer preached:

> Moses and Aaron, the two brothers, from the same seed, the same blood, out of the same history, walking side by side for part of the way — *then* torn apart. Moses, the first prophet, Aaron, the first priest. Moses, called by God, chosen without respect of person, the man with the heavy tongue, the servant of God, who lives totally in listening to the word of his Lord. Aaron, the man with the purple vestment and the holy crown, the sanctified and sacred priest, who has to preserve the divine service for the priest...[5]

In the confrontation between the brothers, Bonhoeffer sees the internal conflict of the religious institution. Moses is on the mountain, waiting for God's word — which cannot be hurried. Aaron wants to serve the needs of the moment, the impatient congregation which would reject the universal for the particular. They want to pray. They want to sacrifice — is it a bad thing to serve their limited needs? Let them have the Church of Aaron: the church without God! Does not a 'National Church' bring sacraments to the devout? And they are eager. Bonhoeffer preaches:

Humanity is ready for any sacrifice, any sacrifice in which it can celebrate itself, can worship the work of its hands. In front of the god fashioned by the work of our hands, after our own desire, humanity and the worldly church sinks to its knees, joyous, smiling. [Everything] is offered up to it ... everything is thrown into the fiery oven of the idol ... everything that has value, that is holy... all their ideals ... and then comes the intoxication.[6]

Moses can do little against this escape into the world of emotion. The Church of Moses, the vision of God, is far away — until it returns from the Holy Mountain, until the tablets are smashed, the golden calf lies shattered upon the ground, until the World Church has been judged and God rules again. The church which presumes to make God out of its priest is omnipresent in the world seen by the preacher. It has to be torn apart, so that the congregation might reassemble as the Church of Moses. And he preaches:

Out of the impatient church there comes to be the church of the silent waiting, out of the church of stormy striving for the fulfilled desire, for seeing, there comes the church of sober faith, out of the church of self-deification there arises the church which prays prays to the One God. Will that church receive the same dedication, the same sacrifices (spent for the church of Aaron)?

The *caesura* does not remain. Again, Moses climbs the mountain. This time to pray for his people. He offers himself as sacrifice. Do not reject me with my people. We are one, O Lord. I love my brethren. But God's answer remains dark, awful, and threatening. Moses could not achieve the atonement.

Who achieves atonement? None but the man who is both priest and prophet ... the man with the crown of thorns...[7]

Our paths diverge here, but not fully. Baeck's teaching of classic religion against romantic religion, his vision of the commandment which leads to the mystery, of the mystery out of which the commandment must emerge, parallels the vision of Bonhoeffer. His total insistence upon the function of the religious institution as the prophetic challenge, of Israel as the nonconformist people, of Judaism as the teaching which rejects the timely for the timeless, is an instruction for us now. As he points out in his 1928 lecture, 'Sermon and Truth':

A Judaism adjusted to the 'timely' would be a contradiction... what has not been 'timely' in the course of the centuries? Slavery and selling human beings, tortures and witches' trials, despotism and oppression, persecution of Jews, forcible baptism ... an accommodating theology has always appeared in order to justify anything current, whether in the world of the intellect, of the state, or within the social sphere. Always, religion was ready to establish any human desire and expression... so that, today, it supports a theodicy of racism.[8]

Baeck reminds us that we must argue against the world for the sake of the world, that we must often say 'No' in order to be able to say 'Yes' at the crucial time. And he closes the lecture we have cited with a Talmudic interpretation of the Exodus passage which led Bonhoeffer to the figure of Jesus. Baeck looks at the Deuteronomy passage which deals with Moses' confrontation on the holy mountain, and cites (Deut. 34:12):

The strong hand of Moses *(yad hachazakah)*... in the eyes of all Israel. In the Talmud there is an almost blasphemous sentence: 'When Israel had set up that work of sinfulness (the Golden Calf), the Holy One, Blessed be He, wanted to tear the tablets of the Covenant out of the hand of Moses; but the hand of Moses was strong, and he tore the tablets away from God!'[9]

117

According to Baeck, this is to represent the reality of Jewish hope and inner strength: 'the most serious task assigned to us is this command to struggle, to wrestle for the tables of the covenant, in order to make them our own.'[10] In the end, it led Israel into the role of the martyr — and not only in our time. In our time, too, more victims than martyrs. But great souls like Bonhoeffer stood alongside us. This mattered — for humanity as much as for us. Whether it changed the world, whether it brought it closer to Moses than to Aaron, is yet to be discovered.

3

It may appear to you that I have become involved in homiletics, that I have preached too long (why should you be different than my congregation?). Having moved from history into rabbinics, I should move onward into theology. I can only assure you that it is all interconnected, and not unrelated to my brief. Earlier this week, I met a devout student of Karl Barth, Lili Simon, one of the pioneers of the interfaith movement in Europe and in Israel. At one point she said, 'Literature is my love; theology is my faith; and politics is my hope!'

I find this a profoundly true statement for myself as well, particularly if I substitute 'Midrash' for literature. I would like to think that a study of Bonhoeffer also culminates in a world of action, in the political arena where a secular or a religious messianism becomes a vision of hope. Yet, I would not divorce hope from our theological meditations. Seeing the Hebrew Scriptures reemerge out of the profoundly Christian sermons of Bonhoeffer, we can at least begin to assert that there can be a new orientation towards the Jewish heritage which is central to Christianity. Often I am deceived by preaching to the converted. The vast majority of Christians refuse to see this heritage, ignore it, yearn for neo-Marcionite presentations, feel threatened by Vatican Council decisions which make priests of the Church of Aaron — I think particularly of Bishop Lefebvre — cry out: if one can see truth in other religions, one has overthrown our golden church built with so many sacrifices! My hope grows slowly but with certainty, and not only in the field of politics; there, it tends to be delayed. My hope rests in my faith.

We meet each other when we pray to God. We meet each other when we wait for the Word, when we acknowledge that the House of Moses, that quiet institution of our souls, is open for the Word that will come and that must come and that has already addressed us. There is nothing that we can say about God. Nothing. But in our literature, if not our theology, we express our love and our compassion for God, Who suffers with his children. Let me then take our final Jewish text out of a current best seller in France and the United States. It is called *Twilight,* and the author is Elie Wiesel, last year's Nobel Peace Prize winner who should and could achieve the same distinction in literature. In this text, in the final pages, the protagonist hears what seems to him to be God's voice addressing him out of the mouth of a mental patient (perhaps) who is a prophet (assuredly) and who speaks to him of his own suffering and the suffering of humanity:

...I am not suggesting that you should not cry when you are hurt. But if you cry only for yourself, your cry, in spite of its echo, will remain hollow. Without others, you would never know love. Without life, death would be meaningless. I repeat: What matters is not to cry for yourself. Cry for others. And for me, too.

These last four words seem not unlike a confession uttered against his will: What? Cry for Him too? Save Him too? Cry not only to God but for God? Could God need His creatures as much as they need Him? Raphael thinks of his master in Midrash, a scholar whose erudition encompassed all the classics. Raphael will never forget his commentaries on Ecclesiastes. According to him, this desperate book refers not to man but to the King of the Universe. 'For all my days are but sorrow!' That is not man howling, but God. 'We incessantly beseech God to take pity on us', said his master, 'but who will take pity on Him? We must pity God, who suffers because of man, who suffers with man. We must pity God, who must witness His creation turning into a mockery. We must pity God, who cannot help but be God, who cannot help but be...'[11]

God suffers in this world. The *Shechina* going weeping into exile with Israel is true because it is a universal truth. Elie Wiesel discovered it in the concentration camp, which was not reserved for Jews alone. Elie's commitment for suffering humanity gave him the Nobel Peace Prize because he heard the howling, suffering God in every oppressed minority and in every human being: the light was trying to break out of the shells.

Here, in this International Bonhoeffer Conference in Amsterdam, you have studied the texts of a Christian master who looked at the same words, who saw the same truth, who died for it. He understood the suffering God, as he had come to understand the suffering of Israel. This is what Eberhard Bethge teaches us. Even in my insufficient translation, I would like this to be the closing word to this assembly:

Immediately before the failed *Putsch,* Bonhoeffer, in his letter of 18 July, 1944 wrote statements which bring the messianic suffering event of Christ and of Israel, as well as the happenings of the present, into full inclusivity. Metanoia, in this place, is a 'letting oneself be pulled along into the way of Jesus Christ, into the messianic event, so that Isaiah 53 will now be fulfilled.' Isaiah 53 as 'vicarious suffering of Israel for the nations' is not fulfilled within an 'in those days *(Damals)'* but in a 'Now', in the present, as 'life participating in the *Ohnmacht Gottes,* God's weakness in this world' (WEN, 396). It is thus the Jews who keep the Christ question open.

Two days earlier, Bonhoeffer had fashioned the formula which has now become famous 'Before and with God we live without God' (WEN, 394). Interpreting, I recast it: 'Before and with the biblical God we live without the Greek God'; 'Before and with the crucified God we live without the enthroned God'; 'Before and with the suffering God we live without the omnipotent God.' The poem written in the same days, 'Christians and Heathen', belongs to this, particularly the second verse (WEN, 382):

To God in his weakness humanity goes, Find him maligned, poor, without shelter and bread. Sin, weakness, and death held him in their throes. Christians stand by God, in his pain, in his dread.

There are signposts here, pointing in the direction of a theology after Auschwitz.[12]

We shall end here, but let us look for more signposts.

NOTES

1. Leo Baeck, *The Synagogue Review,* Great Britian: RSGB (November, 1962), pp. 7-9.
2. * Eberhard Bethge, *Dietrich Bonhoeffer: Theologe, Christ, Zeitgenosse* (Munich, 1967), p. 86.
3. Dietrich Bonhoeffer, *Widerstand und Ergebung,* New edition (Munich, 1970), p. 15.
4. Baeck, op.cit.
5. Dietrich Bonhoeffer, *Predigten, Auslegungen, Meditationen,* I (1925-1935), Otto Dudzus ed. (Munich, 1984), pp. 364ff.
6. Ibid., p. 368.
7. Ibid., p. 370.
8. Leo Baeck, 'Sermon and Truth,' in *Wege im Judentum* (1933), pp. 312ff.', as cited by Berthold Klappert, 'Christus macht den Menschen stark,' unpublished ms for *Marquardt Festschrift.*
    9. Ibid., p. 321; also in Klappert text.
10. Ibid., p. 322.
11. Elie Wiesel, *Twilight,* trans. Marion Wiesel (New York, 1988), pp. 213-214.
12. Eberhard Bethge, 'Dietrich Bonhoeffer und die Juden,' in *Konsequenzen,* eds. E. Feil and I. Tödt (Munich, 1980), pp. 206-207.

* Author's note: This is a conjecture based on the original, which read: '(I only had German texts, Eberhard: forgive this translation, without dictionaries, from your paperback *Bonhoeffer*, rororo, S. 86) *CIVIL COURAGE'* [See page 2 of the original text.]. No note was given for the Bonhoeffer quote on the same page, so I supplied it (note 3).

A Study of Dietrich Bonhoeffer and the Jews

January - April 1933

Edwin H. Robertson

It was not until Eberhard Bethge published his definitive biography of Dietrich Bonhoeffer in 1967 that we knew how early Bonhoeffer had concentrated on the question of the Jews in Germany. Even Karl Barth, who knew Bonhoeffer well, expressed surprise when he read the 'biography.' He wrote to Bethge in May 1967, after reading the book:

> It was new to me above all else that Bonhoeffer was the first, yes indeed almost the only theologian who in the years after 1933 concentrated energetically on the question of the Jews and dealt with it equally energetically. For a long time now I have considered myself guilty of not having raised it with equal emphasis during the church struggle (for example in the two Barmen Declarations I composed in 1934). But then such a text would not have been acceptable to either the Reformed or General Synod, given the spiritual disposition of even the 'Confessing Christians' in 1934. But this does not excuse the fact that I (my interests lay elsewhere) did not offer at least formal resistance in this matter at that time.[1]

That was Karl Barth, who was in protest against the tendencies of the Protestant churches in Germany to welcome the coming of the Nazis. Erik Peterson, writing to Harnack in 1928, says quite bluntly:

> Sociologically and in outlook, the Protestant Church corresponds roughly with the mentality and sociological status of the German National People's Party.[2]

Even more than Dietrich's father, Karl Bonhoeffer, his neighbours with whom the family were closely associated — Hans Delbrück and Adolf von Harnack — involved themselves politically. They had both successfully resisted Stöcker's anti-Semitic activities and checked his attempt to introduce the Jewish question to the Protestant Social Congress. During the twenties, they had watched with growing concern the attempts by the Protestant Church to revive the atmosphere of pre-1918 Germany, of royalism and anti-Semitism. The Protestants wanted a new authoritarianism and they were shot through with anti-Semitism. They had little desire to defend liberal values and listened with delight to tales of 'Western decadence.' The publication of 'Action Group' by Hans Zehrer, Edgar Jung, and Ernst Jünger, was welcomed. In opposition to this tendency, Dietrich's brother Klaus and his brothers-in-law Gerhard Leibholz and Hans von Dohnanyi increasingly identified themselves with the Weimar Republic. It was not surprising therefore that the young Renate (daughter of Dietrich's sister Ursula) could remember even as a child the many political conversations in the Bonhoeffer household:

> The Jewish question was the dominant theme in family conversation and with it all other political questions were connected.[3]

121

This attention to the Jewish question at an early date was personalized because Gerhard Leibholz was of Jewish parentage, as was Franz Hildebrandt, Dietrich's closest friend.

This being his background, how could he fail to be disgusted by some of the extreme statements issuing from Protestant church leaders? In America, 1930-1931, his interest was aroused in the racial question of 'Negroes.' His elder brother, Karl-Friedrich, wrote expressing his approval of this interest which he thought was *the* problem in America. In fact, he confessed that he had refused a post in America because he could not bear to think of his children growing up with this heritage. The children were hypothetical at the time and the judgement was without any real understanding of the greater racial problem rapidly growing in Germany. The naïveté of Karl-Friedrich's comment in January 1931 shows how easily liberal-minded young Germans could be fooled:

> At all events, our Jewish question is a joke in comparison; there cannot be many people left who maintain they are oppressed here. At any rate, not in Frankfurt...[4]

Dietrich Bonhoeffer had not noticed the rise of the National Socialist Party while he was in America, but its strength was evident as soon as he returned to Berlin. The election of September 1930, when he was on his way to the U.S.A., had raised the number of Nazi seats in the Reichstag from 12 to 107; after his return, that number rose further so that on 31 July 1932, the Nazis had 230 seats. Dietrich responded, but the summer of 1932 was largely taken up with ecumenical conferences, where his main concern had been the church. *He was painfully aware that the church in Germany was not matched to the hour*. He tried to work out what the role of the church should be in the developing situation in Germany. But first he must be clear about what the church really is:

> We can only say what the Church 'is', if at once we say both what it is from the *human* side and what it is from the *divine* side... The Church is a bit of the world, a lost godless world, under the curse, a complacent evil world. And the Church is the evil world to the highest degree, because in it the name of God is misused, because in it God is made a plaything, man's idol... But the Church is also a bit of the *qualified* world, qualified by God's revealing, gracious Word which, completely surrendered and handed over to the world, secures the world for God and does not give it up. The Church is the presence of God in the world.[5]

He did not fail to apply this theology of the church to the real situation in Germany and prepared his students for the time when they would be asked to ascribe near-divine honours to Adolf Hitler.

The Führer-Prinzip

No one had any doubt about the attitude of Adolf Hitler and the Nazis toward the Jews. Many Protestant Christians agreed with him, even if they were not so extreme in their expression, nor totally approving of the violence.

Rubenstein and Roth, in their book *Approaches to Auschwitz,* maintain that Hitler's treatment of the Jews was inevitable, given the succesion from the Gospel account of Pilate's washing of his hands, through Martin Luther, to the *Führer,* who claimed that he would complete the work of Luther. Many German Protestants agreed with him, but not all. The Bonhoeffer family viewed Hitler's accession to power as disastrous from the beginning. Their first comment was: 'This means war' and, as Renate said, all political questions of this kind were tied up with the Jewish question.

Bonhoeffer's first public statement after Hitler came to power was not specifically about the treatment of the Jews, but was consciously connected with it. He attacked the whole principle of a *Führer* who could command absolute obedience. He did this in a broadcast which went out two days after Hitler came to power. His theme was, 'The Younger Generation's Changed View of the Concept of Führer.' In the course of showing the development of the 'leadership principle' in youth work, he made no secret of his contempt for what he called *'the unnatural narcissism of youth made vain by old fools.'* His broadcast was a theological talk on the structures of authority and the dangers of a growing tendency to make idols of the leader *(Führer).* The danger lay, he said, in the temptation of the leader to succumb to the wishes of those he leads, who will always seek to turn him into an idol, thus mocking God. The broadcast was interrupted at this point, but enough had been heard to recognize his reference. He had already had experience of young Germans in his confirmation class. He had shown them care and help to such an extent that they certainly idolized him. But he saw the temptation and was already aware that the wrong kind of leader could soon lead these young men in post-war Germany to do things they might well be ashamed to do on their own initiative. The broadcast was cut, but Bonhoeffer circulated the script.

When this broadcast script[6] is compared with Bonhoeffer's preaching in this early period of concern, we can see how near the Jewish question was to his thinking. When on 3 January, Bernhard Rust was appointed Prussian Minister of Cultural Affairs, Bonhoeffer feared for his brother-in-law, Gerhard Leibholz. Rust's words were unequivocal:

> First thing on Monday, the cultural invasion of the Bolsheviks will come to an end... I shall ask the churches outright whether or not they intend to help us in our fight against Bolshevism.

In Nazi propaganda, Bolshevism was early linked to certain sections of the Jewish community. Jews were also accused of profiting from the collapsing currency and making money while brave Germans died at the front in the Great War. Jews were accused of debasing the pure German culture. The accusations were contradictory but, nonetheless, Rust's references to 'our fight against Bolshevism' had an ominous ring. It was natural that the whole Bonhoeffer family should be concerned about Gerhard Leibholz and their many Jewish friends and neighbours.

The Gideon Sermon

For some weeks, Bonhoeffer's preaching had shown evidence that he was concerned with a growing fear of the future. On 6 November 1932, his Reformation Day sermon was against all forms of Protestant pride, accusing his Protestant Church of falling from its first love (Rev. 2:4-5). He called upon it to repent and return to its first convictions: 'Remember then from what you have fallen, repent, and do the works you did at first' (v. 5). If not, then God will destroy the church as once he destroyed Jerusalem. A fragment of a sermon on 1 December 1932 took Daniel 10 as the text and recalls an experience with a mixed group of German and French youth and the power of that text upon them. It was a Frenchman who read the text and as he came to the words, 'courage' and 'peace be with you', says Bonhoeffer, they were all transformed, their gloom was dispelled and together they repeated the words of Daniel: 'Now, speak Lord for you have strengthened us.' That hope and confidence in God did not nullify his fear for the church, and he frequently repeated words that he had used in that November sermon, as the clouds gathered:

> It is becoming clear that we are in the eleventh hour of our life as a Protestant church, that there is not much time left before the decision is made whether it is all over with this church, or whether a new day is to dawn. We should also know that you do not comfort a dying man with fanfares or try to call him back to life. Fanfares belong in funeral processions, there where a cold silence is overcome by an even colder noise, there where wreaths and the dead march decorate the decay. Children frightened in the dark streets, whistling in the dark and stamping their feet to make a noise and give them courage.[7]

As that Protestant church welcomed Hitler to power a few weeks later, the fanfares and the noise of the funeral could be heard.

Bonhoeffer's first sermon after Hitler's accession to power was the Gideon sermon. It was preached to a university audience in Trinity Church in Berlin, at the end of the academic term, 26 February 1933.[8]

The text was from selected verses in Judges 6, 7 and 8, and the theme was the word of the Lord to Gideon: 'The people are too many' (Judg. 7:2). The story of Gideon's army could quite easily be paralleled with the Protestant church at that time. The bands of S.A. men who were now going to the churches promised something like a revival and many clergy welcomed their larger congregations. There was some unease about the fighting that went on in the streets after the services, but there was something of a euphoria. Hitler's words had pleased too many. In his proclamation to the German people on 1 February 1933, Hitler had promised to take Christianity under his 'firm protection' and he called it 'the basis of our whole morality.' Bonhoeffer in his sermon warned against the mistaking of popularity for revival. Gideon could not win his battle with too many soldiers!

> Do not desire to be strong, powerful, honoured and respected, but let God alone be your strength, your fame and your honour... Gideon who achieved faith in fear and doubt, kneels with us here before the altar of the one and only God, and Gideon prays with us: 'Our Lord on the cross, be thou our one and only Lord. Amen.[9]

March 1933

February ended with the Reichstag fire. In England, we all assumed that this had been accomplished by Göring's henchmen to enable the Nazis to destroy their opponents. In Germany, it led to the 'Reich President's Edict for the Protection of People and State', signed by Hindenburg. That edict of 28 February was followed by an election on 5 March which gave an overwhelming victory to the National Socialists. The people had voted away their liberty for the sake of a so-called security. The terms were horrific:

Therefore, restriction of personal freedom of the right of free speech, including the freedom of the press, of the right of association and of public assembly, intervention in the privacy of the post, telegraph and telephone, authorization of search warrants and the confiscation and restriction of property, beyond the hitherto legal limits, will be admissible.[10]

The edict was to remain in force until further notice — in fact until 8 May 1945!

For the time being, only the politicians were threatened. The churches and universities did not feel threatened and made no protest. The Bonhoeffers felt reasonably safe, except when some of Dietrich's international friends came to visit. Paul Lehmann reports that when he was visiting his friend from New York days, Klaus Bonhoeffer would get up from time to time to see if someone was listening at the door!

The Bonhoeffer family was much involved in the trial after the Reichstag fire. Dietrich's brother-in-law, Hans von Dohnanyi, temporarily seconded to the Supreme Court, had to attend all stages of the trial of Van der Lubbe, who was accused of starting the fire. Dietrich's father, as the senior psychiatrist in Germany, was called upon, with his colleague, Dr. J. Zutt, for expert psychiatric opinion. They saw Van der Lubbe three times in March and for this whole month the family was much disturbed by their involvement in 'this emotionally complex and in many ways enigmatic case.' The result of their investigation disappointed everybody. There was no mention of guilt or innocence, whether Van de Lubbe could have been instigated by others or was administered drugs during his interrogation. The report, which was eventually published in a professional journal, showed some sympathy for Van der Lubbe, but it would have been out of the question for Karl Bonhoeffer to have given an expert opinion on anything other than medical matters. Nonetheless, the family felt involved and to that extent guilty. Dietrich felt this most powerfully of all and he never quite lost this awareness of guilt shared.

Bethge also points out the irony of the fact that it was the 'Reichstag Fire Edict', bearing Hindenburg's signature, that four and a half years later closed Bonhoeffer's seminary at Finkenwalde, and it was in one of the concentration camps set up by the edict that he was executed.

Bracher assesses this edict as 'the fundamental emergency law upon which the National Socialist dictatorship . . . was primarily based.'[11] Klaus Scholder describes its immediate effect upon the Jews and Marxists, both of whom Hitler had earlier threatened with extermination:

After the 5th March election victory, a wave of terror broke over Germany which lasted throughout the summer and very quickly engulfed tens of thousands of Germans. The instrument of this wave of terror was Hitler's feared young revolutionary army, the S.A. Its victims were Communists, Jews and other real or supposed opponents of the regime.[12]

The young radio producer, Jochem Klepper, gives a vivid contemporary account in his diary, subsequently published as *Under the Shadow of thy Wings: 1932-1942*. He was a Protestant recently married to a Jewish woman:

8. *March:* What is already demanded of us in the way of anti-semitism is terrible. Even Schnabel's Beethoven recitals had quite suddenly to be removed from the programme... at the very time when Oxford University was conferring an honorary degree upon him for his 'unequalled interpretation of German art'. At the radio station we can understand one another's situation, but the mutual respect has gone. Tired thirty- and forty-year-old compromisers, intimidated by the primitive struggles for existence: from whatever angle we look at it, that is what we are.
11. *March:* It is a dreadful uneasiness, a dreadful pressure, a dreadful isolation — a fearful weakness, a fearful anxiety about existence.
29. *March:* On the whole Jewish boycott affair I have only one thing to say: I grieve for the Protestant church'.[13]

There are those who excuse themselves from action during this critical time by saying that information was difficult to come by. Of course, what was happening in S.A. camps and cellars was not generally known, although suspected. There were individual cases and enough information to know about the concentration camps and the first actions against the Jews, but Klaus Scholder is probably right in his assessment so far as the church authorities were concerned:

But the undoubted difficulty and danger of getting information was only one side of the matter. The other was that ... the central authorities of the Protestant church, the Kirchenbundesamt in Berlin, did not want to have any information.[14]

Many attempts were made to collect information. Hans von Dohnanyi was compiling material for an indictment of Hitler. Elisabeth Rotten of Dresden wrote to Siegmund-Schultze, troubled by the passivity even of what she called 'the minority in Germany who think and have remained sober.' As a result Siegmund-Schultze told the Kirchenbundesamt that he was collecting material for his magazine, *Die Eiche*, to publish in the July edition 'to give foreign friends certain information about the German situation.' In it there were to be 'explicit references to the excesses.' The official church did not want this and, as a result, on 8 April, it was reported:

Professor Siegmund-Schultze was giving cause for concern with his enquiries.
He was arrested on 21 June and deported from Germany 'on the charge of helping Jews in ninety three cases.'[15]

After the Gideon sermon, there is no text for any preaching by Dietrich Bonhoeffer until the Ascension Day sermon on 'There is no church without joy,' which he preached for Gerhard Jacobi on 25 May 1933.

But Bonhoeffer was not idle. He voted on 5 March and went to the poll with his friend of Jewish origin, Franz Hildebrandt: Franz voted for the Christian People's Party; Dietrich for the Catholic Centre Party, because of its international ties. Potsdam Day, 21 March, was used by Hitler as a means of capturing the imagination of the people. The display of pomp and ceremony was to mark the end of 'the bloodless and legal revolution.' The Protestant church was expected to acclaim and Bishop Otto Dibelius complied. Bonhoeffer, invited to tea with the bishop a few days earlier, had insisted that 'acclamation was not the Church's only role.' But on Potsdam Day, something more dangerous was happening. The Treachery Law was promulgated and this gave Bonhoeffer real problems, because he was not prepared to identify his evident loyalty to Germany with acceptance of Hitler's administration.

As anti-Semitic and anti-Communist measures increased, a boycott of Jewish firms was ordered and the 'reconstruction of the professional Civil Service' gave Germany its first non-Aryan law.

Bonhoeffer's grandmother, Paula von Hase, at the age of ninety-one, calmly walked through the S.A. cordon to shop at the Kaufhaus des Westens. About the same time, his parents went to live with Gerhard Leibholz and Sabine (Bonhoeffer's twin sister) in Göttingen so as to help them in the event of demonstrations. Dietrich and Klaus stayed on in Berlin, where among other things they held a conference with Paul Lehmann about the best ways of getting information about what was really happening in Germany to America. In this way they were already committing treason.

Bonhoeffer's treatment of the Jewish Question

On 7 April, the restructuring of the Civil Service led to the Aryan Clause which debarred Jews from public office. It was clear to Bonhoeffer that this would have serious consequences for the church. He sat down at once to work out the theological implications. This action may, as Bethge suggests, have been prompted by the proposal made by a group of ministers who gathered round Jacobi, but the suggestion was resisted. It was that they should discuss the Jewish Question and ask Bonhoeffer to write a paper to stimulate the discussion. Many clergy felt much the same as the General Superintendent, later Bishop Dibelius, did when he heard of this proposal, and disapproved:

> To me it is fairly understandable (i.e. the mob violence against the Jews) because of what Jewry, by its control of the press, finance, the theatre, etc., had done to us ... that justifiable collective anger, even when the people's frame of mind is not specifically anti-semitic, should for once vent itself in violence.

Bonhoeffer's paper is all the more impressive when we realize the general tone of the church and its leaders. It dealt specifically with the attitude of the church towards the Jews. As we read it, we must recall that this young theologian was twenty-seven and that he was a Lutheran. Later his views would be modified and he would attack the German Christian support for the treatment of the Jews more directly and with more information. But already in April 1933, he saw the evil of what was happening and attempted to appeal to the Protestant Church to change the direction in which it was heading. The paper is entitled: *The Church and the Jewish Question*.[16]

The *450th* anniversary of Luther's birth fell on 10 November 1933. The Nazis at first intended to use this to rally Luther to their side. Their German Christian supporters were already preparing for a national demonstration of the role of Adolf Hitler as the Führer who would complete the Reformation which Luther had begun. There was ample text from Luther of an anti-Semitic nature to use. And later it would be used. Meanwhile, the main emphasis was on Luther as *völkisch* prophet of the German people. His reference in Latin to his destiny to serve the German people *(Germanis meis natus sum, quibus et serviam)* in a letter of 1521 was given a warm expansion when translated as: 'I was born for my beloved Germans; it is them I want to serve.'[17] Historians worked hard to show the comparison between Hitler and Luther. Five years later they would let loose the horrors of Kristallnacht on 9 November 1938. Bonhoeffer caught the atmosphere of the time when he began his paper with two quotations from Martin Luther. First a late quotation from 1546, which argues that Jews should not be treated differently from Gentiles when they become Christians:

> We would still show them the Christian doctrine and ask them to turn to accept the Lord whom they should by rights have honoured before we did... Where they repent, leave their usury and accept Christ, we would gladly regard them as our brothers.

That was, even in Luther's day, an argument for making no distinction between Jew and Gentile in the church. But he went further back to an early quotation from 1523 and added:

> If the Apostles, who were also Jews, had dealt with us Gentiles as we Gentiles deal with the Jews, there would have been no Christians among the Gentiles. But seeing that they have acted in such a brotherly way towards us, we in turn should act in a brotherly way towards the Jews in case we might convert some. For we ourselves are still not yet fully their equals, much less their superiors. But now we use force against them... What good will we do them with that? Similarly, how will we benefit them by forbidding them to live and work and have other human fellowship with us, thus driving them to practise usury.

These two quotations may not please us very much today, but they need to be read in the light of what was happening in Germany in 1933 and, of course, in context in Luther's day. They were very cleverly chosen. After this Bonhoeffer begins *his* comments on the actions being committed in April 1933. He defines them as subjecting the Jews to special laws by the state 'solely because of the race to which they belong.' This raises two question for the theologian:

a. 'What is the church's attitude toward this action by the state?', and 'What should the church do as a result of it?' — taken together as one question.

b. 'What attitude should the church take toward its members who are baptized Jews?'

Both questions, according to Bonhoeffer, can only be answered in the light of a true concept of the church.

Bonhoeffer freely recognizes, in dealing with the first of these two questions, that the church has no right to address the state politically. It is the state which makes history, not the church. The action of the state must remain free of church intervention. That is good Lutheran teaching. But when the state is failing in its duty (which is the 'creation of law and order') by too much law and order or by too little law and order, there are three possible ways in which the church can act. *Firstly* it can ask the state whether its actions are legitimate and in accordance with its character as state, i.e., it can throw the state back on its responsibilities.

Secondly, it can aid the victims of state action. 'The church has an unconditional obligation to the victims of any ordering society, even if they do not belong to the Christian community.' In these two ways, the free church serves the free state without illegitimate interference.

'The *third* possibility is not just to bandage the victims under the wheel, but to put a spoke in the wheel itself.' Such political action may be required if the state fails in its function of creating law and order.

He further defines 'too little law' as 'if any group of subjects were deprived of their rights,' 'too much law' as 'where the state intervened in the character of the church and its proclamation, e.g., in the forced exclusion of baptized Jews from our Christian congregations.' He adds that the prohibition of missions to the Jews is another example, but the exclusion of Jews from Christian congregations was the issue in hand. His assessment of the situation in April 1933 was that the first two actions — asking the state whether its actions were legitimate, and caring for the victims — were the compelling demands of the hour. Later, political action against the state may be necessary.

In attempting to deal with the 'quite special context of the church,' he writes an unfortunate paragraph based upon Luther's 'Table Talk.' He repeats the old medieval teaching of the 'curse' upon the Jews for crucifying Christ. This is indefensible, as Rubenstein and Roth have shown in their book, *Approaches to Auschwitz.*[18] But it should not lead us to disregard this remarkable document of a Lutheran theologian helping the Protestant Church to find its way out of an impasse. His theology at this point is based upon Paul's vision of the 'grafting of the vinestock back into the vine from which it was broken off' — and that is more important for him than the medieval 'curse.'[19]

Jews may rightly be offended at Paul's and Bonhoeffer's theology of the conversion of the Jews, but few can doubt the sincerity of his vision and his deep respect for 'what he would call God's ancient people,' the Jews:

> From here the Christian church sees the history of the people of Israel with trembling as God's own, free, fearful way with his people. It knows that no nation of the world can be finished with this mysterious people, because God is not yet finished with it. Each new attempt to 'solve the Jewish problem' comes to nothing on the saving-historical significance of this people.

The importance of that must not be nullified by the reintroduction of the 'curse' to explain the suffering of this people. For Bonhoeffer rejects cheap moralizing by the church which, looking at this 'rejected people, humbly recognizes itself as a church continually unfaithful to its Lord.'

Given his theology, it is inevitable that his hope lies in the conversion of Israel, and that he then tackles the second of his questions: What attitude should the church take to its members who are baptized Jews? His unequivocal answer is that

> The church cannot allow its action towards its members to be prescribed by the state.

On this issue he calls upon all Christians to say with great clarity:

> Jew and German stand together under the Word of God; here is the proof whether the church is a church or not.

A few months later, Bonhoeffer was engaged in drafting a Declaration at Bethel near Bielefeld and sent it to Karl Barth. If Bonhoeffer's clear attitude had been maintained and his Bethel Draft used at Barmen in 1934, we would not now have the shame of saying, 'Barmen was silent about the Jews.'

NOTES

1. Eberhard Bethge, *Bonhoeffer: Exile and Martyr*, pp. 65-66.
2. Quoted by Eberhard Bethge in *Dietrich Bonhoeffer*, p. 91.
3. Renate Bethge, *Bonhoeffers Familie und ihre Bedeutung für seine Theologie* (Beiträge zum Widerstand 1933-1945, No.30), p. 7.
4. Eberhard Bethge, *Dietrich Bonhoeffer*, p. 110.
5. Dietrich Bonhoeffer, *No Rusty Swords*, pp. 149-153.
6. Ibid., pp. 186-200.
7. Quoted by Edwin Robertson, *The Shame and the Sacrifice*, p. 84.
8. Dietrich Bonhoeffer, 'Predigten, Auslegungen, Meditationen,' pp. 349-358.
9. Ibid., pp. 357-358.
10. K.D. Bracher, W. Sauer & G. Schultz, *Die Nationalsocialistische Machtergreifung*, p. 87.
11. Ibid., p. 82.
12. Klaus Scholder, *The Churches and the Third Reich*, p. 254.
13. Jochen Klepper, *Unter dem Schatten deiner Flügel*, pp. 41-46.
14. Klaus Scholder, *The Churches and the Third Reich*, p. 257.
15. Klaus Scholder, *The Churches and the Third Reich*, pp. 257-258.
16. Dietrich Bonhoeffer, *No Rusty Swords*, pp. 217-225.
17. Klaus Scholder, *The Churches and the Third Reich*, p. 545.
18. R.L. Rubenstein & J.K. Roth, *Approaches to Auschwitz*, 1987.
19. Romans 11.

Bonhoeffer and the French Revolution:

Loss or Gain?

Raymond Mengus

Introduction

It is the task and objective of this modest monograph to examine what Dietrich Bonhoeffer thought of revolution, in particular of the Great French Revolution, and what to think about what he thought.

There are only a few explicit statements about the theme addressed in the title given to my paper. The most important reference to the French Revolution is found in one of the first paragraphs of his *Ethics* — a paragraph that, like all the others, could neither be completed nor revised nor changed. We can hardly expect the few pages to count among the 'great treasures' (R.G. Smith) of Bonhoeffer's uncompleted work.

We may even come across a paradox: the man who was to inspire many a revolutionary enterprise (starting with his own person) may have a frustating effect on some of his readers (mark you, as far as revolution is concerned!) owing to the rarity and scantiness of his offer in this regard. And yet: smaller and rougher stones also make their contribution to the total image of the planned mosaic — and be this only by a dialectic detour.

1. *The Problem*

For nearly 200 years, many interpretations of the French Revolution have been given — among other places, in France and especially there. It seems as if every generation, every social class, every political party, even every religious community had its own.

A. *A Wide Spectrum of Interpretations*

The first reason for this wide spectrum is to be seen in the complexity of the historical events themselves. Depending on what year to which you direct your attention, to 1789, 1792 or to the 1793/94 period, you will always get a different picture — an exciting one or an appealing one.

In this regard the parcel called 'Revolution' contains items of varying brands.

a. The first thing that might get unpacked is the **human and civil rights declaration** of August 26, 1789. In its beginnings, the French Revolution behaved and conceived itself as an uprising against absolutism and arbitrariness. Symbolic for this was and still is the storming of the Bastille: For two centuries, the 14th of July has been the National Day of fifty-five million French men and women. (Soon only a few Lefevre fans will be left who disassociate themselves from such a national consensus.)

b. Then the French Revolution set out to establish a new, promising form of the state. After dramatic events, the old, often glorious monarchy was substituted by the Republic. The decapitation of Louis XVI was perceived as a turning point in the thousand years of French history and as a rupture of national unity. The wound was deep; it had not quite scarred over at the end of the nineteenth century when the first hundred years of the Revolution were celebrated. But it was then that the Catholics, who had so long resisted the new order, decided to rally with the Republic. No really organised monarchist party exists any longer. Even the Count of Paris, the potential heir to the throne of his ancestors, now supports the president of the Fifth Republic.

In short: Many French men and women nowadays may venerate kings and queens, secretly envy neighboring monarchies and celebrate special events even publicly — but the whole national territory is exclusively governed by the Republican Marianne. She is expected to maintain and/or expand the democratic achievements.

c. The whole thing became more difficult when it came to the revolutionary principle of the *'Laïcité' of the State*, and even more so when this modern principle was first executed in a most aggressive and bloody way. The philosophers of the eighteenth century advocated the total independence of state power from all guardianship. Many revolutionaries had to see the church as an unbearable competitor who should be pushed back into closely drawn limits. Thus a clash was programmed.

Between the 'Civil Constitution of the Clergy' of 1791 and the final separation of church and state in 1905 lay bitter, uneven struggles and, at times, irreconcilable enmities. Until the last past-war period the educational issue was to play a disastrous and dividing role in the nation.

By and by, the militant and offensive concept of laicism relieved its pressure. The Catholic Church on its side finally realized that laicality does not necessarily have to be identical with a hatred of the priesthood and a privatisation of religion, but that it can secure the ground for a coexistence or 'proexistence' of citizens of all shades. Now, the deadly threat is considered a chance by most — except for a few, very noisy exceptions. The present civil peace was secured still further by the political events of this decade: changes of government that took place without any friction, the educational pact, the constitutional 'cohabitation' — we have reconciled in a degree unprecedented in our long history.

d. The parcel of the French Revolution finally also contains hardheaded ideological figures and demands; it cannot be separated from names like *Saint-Just* and *Robespierre,* from images of terror and the guillotine: these are undeniable facts. But we must not let them obscure everything else. One may conjure them up in a frightening way, so much the more as hardly any French person today appeals to them. Who would really like to justify the genocide in the Vendée or other mass executions?

132

B. *Bonhoeffer's Interpretation*

In view of such a diversified contents in a seemingly simple and unequivocal package called the French Revolution (the list of interpretations could easily be extended and refined) let us now face the question: How does Bonhoeffer approach it and how does he proceed? What line does he give preference and why?

If we concentrate on his main reference to the French Revolution in his *Ethics* (no more comprehensive statement or allusion could be quoted, anyway), his position is as clear as clear can be: Bonhoeffer *does not choose and he does not offer a choice*. Just as if he were not aware of the complexity of the subject, this subtle and experienced man starts out to look at this bundle of phenomena called Revolution from one singular angle — as if the ethicist could totally stay out of the crossfire of the historians and immediately move to the secure ground of theological evaluation.

a. *The Position*

The texts must be reread and be read thoroughly. In today's literary context, i.e., in Eberhard Bethge's arrangement of Bonhoeffer's writings on *Ethics* which has been followed since the sixth German edition, the section 'Erbe und Verfall' (pp. 94-116) appears to be in a somewhat strange place.

Some of Bonhoeffer's best writing is found under the general title 'Ethik als Gestaltung' (p. 68ff.); Bonhoeffer's theological-systematic project climbs to its first heights with peaks like 'Gleichgestaltung' (pp. 85-91) and 'Der konkrete Ort' (pp. 91-94). Further elevations ensue, but before getting there, a historical review or evaluation of the present must be taken. The precipice is almost offensive. It is what it is — a slump.

The subject matter of the twenty problematic pages: more than two millennia of occidental history. The deliberations about them connect the nostalgic with the aggressive. The author's judgement is much more cutting than that in, say 'Das Ende der Neuzeit' by Romano Guardini, Bonhoeffer's Berlin contemporary and the university colleague he never came to know.

Bonhoeffer's judgement may be all the more negative as he is well-aware of a theological counterposition at his disposal. From up there, you may just cast a few challenging, victorious glances at your cultural environment...

b. *The Contents*

A carefree view of history in a mini-Hegelian way as such certainly is neither unuseful nor unjustified. But does the first sentence (p.94) really have to start with a dissociation of Christian tradition from all the rest, so militantly that all common ground is ruled out from the very onset? This is the first blow: without a relation to the incarnation there can be no heritage, no history. Historical philosophy is a theology of salvation — or nothing.

Such a prejudice reduces the plurality of the interpretations of history to something nearly illegitimate and disqualifies every interpretation that deviates from the only authentic one. Such an approach perceives and treats Christian reality in an *ex-clusive* and not, as fortunately will be the case later, in an in-clusive way. Such a start immediately gets to the judgement of some of the more important periods of Western history: life and relevance is only ascribed to what is connected to Christianity or can after all be interpreted in its light. Take, for instance, antiquity: 'A genuine heritage of antiquity in the occident *only* exists in relation to Christ... Antiquity becomes part of our historical heritage *only* by way of Christ' (p. 97, emphasis mine).

The same is true for the national past: 'It is no historical heritage... German, but also English, French, history only (exists) since its encounter with Christ.' If one takes a closer look at such statements, isolated or in conjunction, one cannot fail but notice their apodictic tenor. Some things may be said for them — a lot against them. Who or what will really decide this?

We are here faced with a linguistic and mental structure saturated with juxtapositions, unclarified alternatives or unexaminable immediacies. It again surfaces, blown up into ideological dimensions, when the author starts dealing with European Christian history: 'The unity of the occident is *not* an idea *but* a historical reality whose *only* foundation is Christ' (p. 98, emphasis again mine).

This is soon followed by a peculiar assessment of a phenomenon terribly widespread among Christians and reiterated to this day: 'Even the occidental wars aim at the unity of the occident... They are... never total wars.' Only the last sentence of the paragraph somewhat more realistically points to the hypothesis, the possibility, that the worst could be caused by it also and especially in our latitudes: 'Only a total war could threaten the unity of the occident.'

2. *The Assessment*

In a short outline, the Reformation is appropriately mentioned in connection with the newness of a world coming of age. The confessional divides of the sixteenth century resulted in political division, he writes, but also in 'the liberation... of the world', even if under the 'misinterpreted Lutheran doctrine of the Two Kingdoms' (p. 102).

It is astonishing to read the initial judgement of the secularization process just mentioned and defined: how positive it is, nearly exaggeratedly positive. 'It is just in these (i.e. the first attempts at modern autonomy) that one finds oneself in the middle of the true divine service demanded by Reformation Christendom.' Modern times as a liturgy! Does this hint at a misinterpretation of the Reformation and of modern times? Maybe, but the short passage does not suffice.

But the stage is set for 'Catholic France' (p. 203) and its Great Revolution.

The first attempt introduces it as 'the signal of the modern occident.' 'The new' 'chaotically' breaks through, the monstrous and the terrible. Both are mentioned, 'the truly new' and 'the monstrous', both are looked at simultaneously. Whereas the first is mainly linked with promises and promises only, the latter permanently increases its negative weight and the writer's apprehensions.

a. In Bonhoeffer's judgement of the French Revolution, he first of all has something on the side of gain. Part of such gains is his use of candid reason. Pages 103 and 104 beautifully contain his *creed with the Enlightenment*. This is nothing exciting for anyone who knows him from his life or his writings as an erudite, critical intellectual; but in our context this praise of emancipated reason is not insignificant! Henceforth, let us, retain and cultivate this gain.

Such optimism however lasts but a short while. Soon reason is placed into the service of world transformation, engages in the domination of nature and finally instrumentalises itself as technological power.

A second gain is his mention of the Declaration of Human and Civil Rights (pp. 105-106). Without any other limitation than that, it could be limited to and by the citizens.

b. But quickly we move to the loss department. It is going to be longer and more depressing.

First, the national idea loses. Without further ado it is defined as the assertion of the people against the authorities or against the state. As it is so intimately linked to revolution, and can even be likened to it, that the nation will be harder to save than even technology and reason! The worst emerges when it comes to uniting the three (p. 108): an abstract juggling of three nouns cannot replace their analysis!

And now embarrassing events pursue each other: 'At the end of the way embarked upon by the French Revolution stands nihilism': an enslavement by technology, the reign of terror of the guillotine, war, human self-destruction. This was seen in 1940, when the worst was still ahead — or still unknown.

The newest evolution of the human race reaches its final summit in a banalized atheism. There is a 'new kind of godlessness' which must be understood as a 'religion of enmity to God.' The lofty humanitarianism so much hoped for by the best brains degenerates into an 'idolization of man.'

What a somber conclusion! The only lasting values of the occident, after thousands of years of history, seem to be only these two — an enmity to the church, and godlessness. However, there is hope that the latter may also have a promising side. At this thought (p.110) the 'better' Bonhoeffer steps into the limelight again.

c. The paragraph ends in an enforced juxtaposition: in the final analysis, nothing else proceeded from the French Revolution than an eschatological nothing (p. 112). Some more gain is ascribed to the American Revolution which now appears as a counter-example and which even generates a praise of Christian democracy.

In view of all this hopelessness the author still has one ace up the sleeve which he then — hopelessly too? — slips in: The church! It may very well be that together with nothingness will grow — salvation. The law of history suddenly swerves to... the Gospel!

Apparently Dietrich Bonhoeffer was able to *intellectually* absorb neither the revolutionary idea nor the ideas of the French Revolution. In addition, his rejection of them is done predominantly in a slant that, in everyone but him, would refer us in a Nietzschean way to someone filled to the brim with resentment.

Whereas in his own *practical life* he dared to take steps and utter thoughts that, in the eyes of the powerholders and the leaders of the church, should place him in dangerous proximity to revolutionaries, in these pages of his *Ethics* he remained until deep into the wartime bound to certain attitudes and conceptions that we must explain.

135

3. *Looking for Explanations*

How did Bonhoeffer arrive at such hard statements and similarly cutting and hardly original judgements? We must seriously consider this question. Answers have already been given but they do not fully satisfy. It is evident that Dietrich Bonhoeffer after all did not simply reiterate the judgement of his milieu, he who otherwise turned his back on numerous component parts of his tradition in family, culture, confession and nation.

The man certainly is not a nostalgic promotor of a feudalistic Europe; he does not have the aspects of the 1792 emigré who has neither forgotten nor learned anything since the Ancien Regime.

Insufficient, too, would be the hypothesis that Bonhoeffer, the political activist, simply tries to make his voice heard among his contemporaries, for example among the leaders of the opposition or the resistance fighters living in and by pre-modern conceptions.

Unsatisfactory, too, would be a psychological explanation of text and circumstances by some type of auto-suggestion, as if everything was nothing but the reflective reaction of one who has been cornered and who, trying to evade the immediate pressures of an annoying present, subconsciously sets out to conjure and shroud the first historical past that gets into his way.

A. *Bonhoeffer's Relations to France*

Attempting to delve deeper, one will for instance come to examine the historical ethicist's personal relations to France in general.

One thing is quite sure, and that is that he had hardly any personal ties to the French and to French matters — with one clearly certified exception: *Jean Lasserre*. This simple statement that may and must be made here in no way impairs the image of an extremely open-minded, world-travelled cultural type of man.

But the fact is that in this regard he showed hardly any curiosity at all. Let us not forget that a new literary, ecclesiastical and also theological start, which was to contribute to the shaping of the French and an even wider landscape after the Second World War, had already borne diverse fruits in the thirties. But it was the language barrier, a greater leaning towards the Anglo-Saxon sphere of culture and a life exceedingly filled with tasks that would keep Lasserre's friend from sagaciously dealing with French motifs like the sequence of events that one day in the spring of 1789 began in Versailles.

His interest in the ecumenical movement and in Catholicism could have brought the German Lutheran to the left side of the Rhine. But the latter he could better satisfy in Rome, hardly in his own country and not at all in 'French France'; the first took him to England, Scandinavia or Geneva. In short, nothing of significance developed between Bonhoeffer and France, no genuine encounter took place — thus the occasional critic of the Great Revolution could do nothing but superficially examine the subject matter abstract to him.

136

B. *Bonhoeffer's Handling of History*

A further answer to our question might be found in the way our theologian approaches history itself. His excellent sense of reality, his decided search for truth — in this field they did not get him very far. Undoubtedly, he stopped at petrified truths. He was too quick at theologizing, at *dogmatizing* without sufficiently trying methodologically to do justice to a subject. He quickly enshrined himself in a specific view, seeing the subject from way above and thus easily missing its very core.

The suspicion could be roughly expressed like this: What did Bonhoeffer really know about the historical event called 'The French Revolution'? Obviously he tried little to learn easily accessible facts about its reasons, its course, its figures and phases. He rather prefers to use a clichéd myth (better: anti-myth); he never examined any closer and, like so many others, spent a whole life with an attitude derived from his traditional roots — only that he does so with reversed premises.

Owing to the history of contrasting interpretations of the French Revolution, a black-and-white image is easy to form; but things become more difficult when it comes to acquiring a balanced picture of the historical event itself and, much more so, when trying to arrive at some balanced judgement. This requires the ability to detect nuances, ambivalences, to leave things unanswered till the answer arrives, to live with the incomplete. Did this ask too much from Bonhoeffer, the supertalent? He reduces ambiguities, he sees the complex in one color only, he presents a multi-dimensional event in a schematic way. Where the asceticism of a weighing reservedness would be needed, he goes for a linear, one-dimensional approach and then a final verdict pushed to the extreme.

C. *An Assertive Style*

In the precinct of history a more general trait of Bonhoeffer's manner of thinking becomes evident which, incidentally, also surfaces at some other places. This manner of thinking ascribes great significance to *affirmation* and simple assertion. Certainly, the author of the considered section and of the entire *Ethics* must be conceded the courage to proceed unguardedly, perusing his thoughts and uttering them without much fuss, always facing the danger of presenting unjustifiable things: for an intellectual, quite a charming way to proceed. Genuine education and culture, so it is said, truly proves itself when one has forgotten everything. Or when one takes up his pen in a Munich hotel room or in a cell in the Ettal monastery.

But this manner of writing does not guarantee a permanent capture of the pure truth. One may just as well become very *uncritical*. One may forget that everyone's opinion is tied to a certain place and related to a certain subject. 'De quel lieu parlez-vous?' nowadays has become everyone's hobby horse, but these words do not bother Bonhoeffer in the least. The question finds no room in him. Apparently it does not even occur to him to ponder the conditions of the possibility of each and every statement.

Thus a word like 'Revolution' is quickly judged, offhandedly, nearly mechanically. The theologian who, in other places, makes differentiating analyses does not even give it a chance. He only sees it as something disturbing, the chaos of Paris, the disorder; he does not go so far as to look for some other aspects, say, signs of a possible new order. He, who later was to motivate many for the irreversibly new, for the revolutionary, apparently does not consider such a thing imaginable in the realm of the political — and cannot but deny the notion that Revolution might, after all, achieve or facilitate something positive. Deny it assertively, radically, definitively. If he only had had the chance to once revise his position!

D. *Problematic Relations to Others*

The few pages we use for our deliberations however give rise to one last comment, a comment that at first may cause some astonishment: What about Bonhoeffer's relations to things and persons which were different? Was his mindset magnanimous enough to truly accept difference?

His treatment of the French Revolution may also be read as an example of how *inclined* he was *to belittle the other man or thing, to reduce the different, to fail the alien.*

Dietrich Bonhoeffer, the human, doubtless lived with intensive relations to what was different for him, to many people and things different every time. If one has become acquainted with him by the roundabout way of meeting witnesses and reading his writings, one cannot but imagine him any other way than being a man of encounter, of exchange — an artist of human relations. It is not by chance that a gripping German compilation about him is entitled 'Begegnungen,' encounters with him. How much one would have liked to belong to this circle, this network of friendships!

But Bonhoeffer, the theologian, does not always offer this. In passages like 'Erbe und Verfall' he offers little of his inclination to discuss and of his drive to discover. He adheres massively to a familiar one-sidedness and a calming like-mindedness. Some years later he was to utter the famous reproach of a 'positivism of revelation' against Karl Barth, in his magnificent letters from prison to Eberhard Bethge of April 30, 1944, and of May 5. Wouldn't there also be something like 'positivism of ethics'?

Nothing is understandable or even possible without relating it to other things, other people. Without them nothing fruitful can grow — this is a law valid from the biological sphere to the highly intellectual one. And especially ethics lives by this; it needs the air and the breath of what is different. Only then something enlightening, dynamic, something promising for the future can ensue. Part of the game however is the *processing of messages* between the I and the you, the elaboration of mediations between the we and the it, yesterday and today, the here and the there, between culture and faith, the order of creation and the order of grace. What such statements in the *Ethics* as the one about 1789 need is a manner of thinking which mediates between historical realities and Christian properties. And it would be especially in the fields of the societal and the political that a clarifying, liberated and liberating network of mediations would be of highest possible use.

Ethicists aim at general validity; if, in addition, they think in a Christian way, they make even two pledges in looking for universality. The point, however, is that one is never right in the middle of it. Thus everything depends on how one is beginning.

4. *Consequences and Questions*

The short passages containing Bonhoeffer's critical/uncritical deliberations of the French Revolution provide a narrow basis to assess him. Nonetheless, if they are read in Paris or Strasbourg and in conjunction with other statements in his works, they allow for some temporarily definitive remarks. Hopefully, if you see the first remark you will at once see that it is in no way impudent but has something to do with a differentiating reception and thankfulness.

A. *Not Everything in Bonhoeffer Is Noteworthy*

What would be missing in the *Ethics* if those pages were missing? Many French people (but this has nothing to do with nationality) would consider such a lack a gain! Some stones in the mosaic will be superfluous — if it is true that certain flaws are part of the picture. The repeated approaches of 1939/40 have to be seen in a *very differentiated* way. The author knows best who started afresh more than once: he looks for new ways and will not find them at the first go. And the one-time university lecturer would be the first to deny all his products the same top mark.

No, a differentiating assessment is truer to Bonhoeffer: recognizing his less brilliant products serves his whole purpose better. Here a minimum of dialectics is more helpful than all general agreement conceded in advance. The reader who does not much like 'Heritage and Decay' may then much more freely and genuinely revel in 'The Ultimate and the Penultimate.'

For this given and rather thankless topic, a differentiation is much easier because it is a predominantly historical topic and not a truly theological one; it is therefore an *opus alienum* which can make the *opus proprium* shine so much the brighter!

B. *The Discrepancy Between Experience and Theory*

This conclusion is not drawn everywhere; a certain degree of dispute may very well continue to exist. Here, however, the thesis is maintained that up till the first years of the war there is an incongruity between Bonhoeffer's personal practice and his writings on *Ethics,* between a highly exposed way of living and his inherited manner of seeing things. Decision and tradition do not walk at the same pace. The gain achieved by risky commitments is first expressed in letters and other statements of the time but not in all essays and professional writings: they, in part, suffer from lagging behind.

If a person did not know Dietrich Bonhoeffer from somewhere else, he or she could never arrive at a correct picture of the man from this *Ethics* — and much less would he suspect the author of the things he was doing and planning just while he was writing those passages.

In this respect his letters and papers from prison provide better and more appropriate information. In the end, the hiatus is close and Bonhoeffer's style agrees with the substance in a way dreamed of by the great poets and creators. The *Letters and Papers from Prison* make up for, catch up with and even surpass his passages in his *Ethics*

139

where henceforth many things must be seen as relativized, even outdated.

The theme of the French Revolution is never taken up again as such, nor is it expressly revised again. But the horizon of thinking has changed, the present and the future dominate the scene — and the Tegel cell. Their impact is so strong that they do not leave any more room for restorative ideas like, say, the reestablishment of a prerevolutionary Europe. Things that in 1940 still sought their expression in traditional categories and views were put in more appropriate words in 1943/44. This development of a few decisive years, discernible in the terminological and the political, in the affective and the intellectual, is something deserving our careful attention.

Bonhoeffer's *Ethics* then may or even should be seen in the light of the *Letters and Papers from Prison* — without smoothing out anything and without levelling anything in it. Let us suppose a real development took place in Bonhoeffer, and a decisive one at that. This would then also mean that there is no way back from the highest discovered, newly climbed summits. Many things will just have to be left behind, some things will have to wither. The way irreversibly leads in one direction only. Not everything can be salvaged. Long live the ambiguous and typically German term *Aufhebung*: in the name of the new, some of the old — also from the texts in the *Ethics* can hitherto serve only one purpose: disappear!

C. *The Shadow of a Suspicion*

Anyone who finds Bonhoeffer's treatment of the French Revolution a problem will soon be faced with other questions. Once the suspicion has arisen, and be it only for such an insignificant and minute reason, it threatens to spread to all kinds of other areas. Be it somewhat justified in the first instance, it would be a pity if it, not being justified at all, should spread its shadow to other material.

We have come to the conclusion that Bonhoeffer's paragraphs on revolution in his *Ethics* are not very successful. The obvious temptation is to not fully accept his judgement on modern times or the Christian occident or his own German times. And yet, his verdict on secularization and the world come of age is important: Should we also disassociate ourselves from him in this field?

No matter what everyone's response may be, one thing is always necessary: *a personal examination*. More strongly perhaps than at times of a preestablished consensus, a critical appropriation is the call of the day — something that will honor best both master and disciples.

This methodological demand is especially valid for Bonhoeffer's *Ethics*. The book will continue to have its own history, if not even make history, by way of and thanks to an attentive 're-reading' in different cultural spheres. If this is done, it will remain a promising treasure chest and an active partner in timely discussion. And on such premises, 'Bonhoeffer and Europe' will have a lasting significance as an open, exciting and promising relationship.

One last thing will have to be said, something that must be spelled out at least by way of intimation and should be taken more seriously by the churches and theologies than is often the case.

140

D. *The Problem of the Turning Point*

Time and again, the question arises about a possible turning point, or possible turning points, in Bonhoeffer's life and thinking: the question may and even must continue to be asked. Beside it, another one arises. It concerns *the time that separates us from him.* History has advanced since 1945; old things continue, many new things have appeared — in all fields. How to measure the new and what to do with it? How to assess the turn that has occurred? And how to bring figures and thoughts of yesterday, of times past, back to new life? The greater the temporal, political and intellectual distance, the less one can avoid such quiet — or unquiet — questioning. This, for instance, is true for ... a revolution. Or for Christ. Or for Bonhoeffer himself.

The time will come to think seriously about the conditions of his continual updating. The example for accepting responsibility he gave us then will not reduce ours today, but will stimulate and nourish it.

To Summarize

Have all these broad and general deliberations now led us as far away from Bonhoeffer's treatment of a historical event as it may seem at first glance? If we try to judge his judgement we will be led automatically to levels that we should one day set out to formulate and to question.

In the letter that invited us to this conference, Bonhoeffer's *Ethics* was paraphrased as 'an ideology of resistance.' This definition should set us thinking. It was certainly not intended to merely emphasize one aspect of the book — resistance, for instance, to the French Revolution and to a modern Europe symbolized and even partly generated by it. Such a side does exist and exists in Bonhoeffer's evolution of thinking — but, let us mark this well, during a special phase of transition and as an undertone, not as a cantus firmus. This evolution, however, led him into a totally different, total life-and-death resistance against National-Socialist totalitarianism.

The ethico-theological thinking that made Bonhoeffer take these steps pushes several people even today to decidedly and firmly resist all dissatisfying and unacceptable circumstances in the world — and, if necessary, in the church. But it also opens up other ways. It contributes to experience of the ultimate in the penultimate and to see highly Christological aspects in the non-theological. It gives us insights and impulses to conduct our business with God in the flesh of the common human and historical reality.

Bonhoeffer's Ecumenical Ethics
in View of Restorative and Revolutionary Tendencies

A CONTRIBUTION TO THE DISCUSSION FROM A CATHOLIC PERSPECTIVE

Ernst Feil

The topic assigned to me was, 'How does a Catholic interpret Bonhoeffer's ethics?' However, the topic seems problematic: What value does a Catholic's interpretation of Bonhoeffer's ethics have? A single individual can hardly represent Catholic ethics, especially since there has been nothing like a closed system of ethics in Catholicism since the end of neo-scholastic theology. Furthermore, there are today in Catholicism special problems and ongoing discussions with respect to ethics as can be seen from official Roman documents. Part of the conflicts are actually in essence related to the foundation of ethics — whether this should be an ethic of faith or an ethic of reason, an ethic of obligation (deontological) or responsibility (teleological), and whether it should, on the basis of its immutable principles, be a constant or a historical, and therefore variable, ethic. Still lying before us seem to be discussions on the question held to be very fundamental, whether there are acts which are wrong in and of themselves *(actio in se ac intrinsece mala)*. Apart from these basic questions there arise other no less weighty differences, especially regarding sexuality and individual ethics, and the concept of society in light of social ethics (cf. the statements accusing the theology of liberation of Marxism).

These comments show how complicated the current situation is. There is, at the moment, no such thing as a unanimously accepted Catholic point of view from which to seek a dialogue with Bonhoeffer's ethics. Nevertheless, there is a point of view basically shared by a great majority of (Catholic) theologians, which could be characterized as an ethic of responsibility, in the sense of an ethic which is to be developed historically. In any case, no one would hold that everything defended by Christians could now be accepted as ethical. Agreement seems to exist on the point that there are behavioral instructions for a Christian life in this world which derive from the moral message of the New Testament and that, accordingly, any separation of faith and world is illegitimate. It should be kept in mind that I comment as but one theologian among many.

I do this by way of taking my topic out of the abstract and applying it to what appears to me to be a pressing question which arose from the following: How and to what extent can Bonhoeffer's ethical reflections help us as the foundation of an ecumenical ethic in our present polarization?

Preliminary Remarks on Bonhoeffer's Ethics

Bonhoeffer did not want to write an 'Ethics' in the sense of a textbook or manual. When in letters from November 18 and December 15, 1943, he reproached himself for not yet having finished the 'Ethik,' and when, thinking he might have his life more or less behind him, he expressed the hope still to complete his 'Ethik'[1], he mentioned an area of study, but no title and no topic. He had been describing the faith of Christians in *Nachfolge*. Later he wanted to write a book on living and acting in the world, under the title, 'Grundlagen und Aufbau der mit Gott versöhnten Welt' (Principles and Structure of a World Reconciled with God), or 'einer künftigen Welt' (of a Future World), or 'eines geeinten Abendlandes' (of a United Occident), with the subtitle, 'Versuch einer christlichen Ethik' (An Experiment in Christian Ethics).[2] While he was writing, the title 'Wegbereitung und Einzug' (Preparing the Way and Entering in) occurred to his mind, in accordance with the division into 'penultimate' and 'ultimate things'.[3]

In the short period between 1940 and 1943, Bonhoeffer concentrated on ethical problems and questions. Before that time — as late as 1939 — he had interpreted Psalm 119 and authored and published *Das Gebetbuch der Bibel*,[4] and for the Croall Lectures in Edinburgh he had considered the topic 'Tod' (Death)[5], a sign that he was not yet dealing with ethics. After this period of consideration of ethical themes — 1944 — he began a new work, 'Bestandsaufnahme des Christentums — Was ist eigentlich christlicher Glaube? — Folgerungen' (Taking Stock of Christianity — What is Christian Faith Anyway? — Conclusions).[6] In between these two periods there is Bonhoeffers's intensive engagement in the resistance and all the work that went along with it, which now concerns us.

1. Bonhoeffer had compiled extensive reading material for his ethical reflections — such as the evangelical ethicists Richard Rothe (1799-1867), Adolf von Harleß (1806-1879), Alexander von Oettingen (1827-1906), and Otto Piper (1891-1982), to whom he added the books of such philosophers as Max Scheler (1874-1928), and Nikolai Hartmann (1882-1950),[7] but finally also the works of Catholic moral theologians such as Otto Schilling (1874-1956).

What especially interests us is Schilling's work, *Lehrbuch der Moraltheologie (Textbook of Moral Theology)*, the second volume of which (Munich, 1928) contains the inscription 'Bonhoeffer 1940.' Various passages in this book have been remarkably well studied, as indicated by the markings, which seem to go back to Bonhoeffer and which are especially heavy in the sections on property (pp. 57-73), *caritas* (pp. 128-141), love of neighbour (pp. 266-270), and righteousness (pp. 274ff., 284f.), as well as truthfulness (pp. 322ff.), and faithfulness and freedom (pp. 331-346). Yet Bonhoeffer makes reference to this book only once in his ethical fragments[8], and there takes a critical stance over against Aristotelian-Thomistic natural theology. Bonhoeffer himself could profit little from such moral theologians who, along with a basic concept developed from Thomas Aquinas, contained a wealth of casuistic instructions (such as whether someone who listens to Sunday mass half asleep must hear a second mass or not).[9] At the same time, Bonhoeffer spoke in a rather friendly way about Catholic handbooks of ethics which, 'in many ways are instructive and more practical than our own,' for which reason they were 'always regarded as casuistic,' while today one is 'thankful for much of what they contain[10].

Bonhoeffer had no basic objections to Thomas Aquinas, whom he came to know primarily through the interpretation of Josef Pieper. Pieper's works *Die Wirklichkeit und das Gute (Reality and the Good)* (1935), *Über die Hoffnung (Concepts of Hope)* (2 1938), *Zucht und Maß (Discipline and Mate)* (1939, with the entry 'Bonhoeffer 1940') and *Thomas von Aquin (Thomas Aquinas)* (1940) are present among the remaining volumes of Bonhoeffer's library. Most of them contain markings from his hand, a sure sign that they were carefully worked through. The recurring theme of 'selfless self-love,'[11] or as in the *Ethik* 'selfless self-assertion' and a legitimate 'Christian egoism,'[12] as well as the *'suum cuique'*,[13] can be found in Pieper.[14]

Another such anthor who gained special significance was Jacques Maritain, to whom Bonhoeffer's thought on the healing of guilt is probably to be traced.[15]

No less important for Bonhoeffer than all these scientific analyses or essays was his consideration of Catholic writers. This is true above all for Reinhold Schneider.[16] It remains to be examined whether Bonhoeffer's statements on the 'impossibility of innocence in history'[17] derive from him.[18] Moreover, Bonhoeffer studied John Henry Newman[19] and Romano Guardini.[20] The sustained influence of Ernest Hello also remains to be further investigated.

Furthermore, Bonhoeffer gained extensive contact with Catholic thought and life during his stay in Ettal,[21] where he not only diligently studied in the monastery library[22] but also obtained, through personal conversation, information on Catholic morality, which he considered problematic, especially with regard to contraception.[23]

It would be an overstatement to say that Bonhoeffer had to change, reconstruct, or revise his own conception after his consideration of Catholic ethics. From early on, Bonhoeffer had developed his conception in such a way that he could without difficulty assimilate the constructive insights from the Catholic tradition. He had gained, of course, at the beginning of his theological development a fundamental impression through his experience with the Catholic church, which he formulated ecclesiologically already in his *Sanctorum Communio*.

'Christus, die Wirklichkeit und das Gute' (Christ, Reality and Good) must be considered the first section of Bonhoeffer's *Ethik* to have been written.[24] The title seems to have been inspired by Josef Pieper's *Die Wirklichkeit und das Gute*. In his own reflections Bonhoeffer takes up the essential and characteristic themes of his theology, namely 'reality,' which is 'the reality of God and the world,' the reality of God only revealing itself when one 'completely immerses oneself in reality,' and the reality of the world, on the other hand, is to be found as 'already borne, adopted, and reconciled in the reality of God.'[25] The way does not lead from 'possibility' to reality, but rather reality is that prius from which all thought, knowledge, and action can and must proceed. And this reality is, contrary to all appearances, ultimately one, so that there are not 'two realms, but only *the one realm of the Christ-reality,* in which the God- and world-reality are united.'[26]

Bonhoeffer does not seek on the basis of this concept to develop a specifically Christian ethic in the sense of one which is limited to Christians, but to make clear to Christians that they must be concerned with the 'poorest of our brothers' beyond their own sphere, because humanity has been taken up into Christ, so that we see in him 'God in the form of the poorest of our brothers.'[27] Although it cannot be conclusively demonstrated, it can at least be accepted on good grounds that Bonhoeffer had in mind here in this passage the Jews who were being persecuted by the National Socialist regime.[28] Precisely by including the persecuted Jews, Bonhoeffer expanded the framework of his ethic to the point where a place was given to those who were otherwise excluded. In this sense the term 'ecumenical ethic' obtains the concreteness it ought to have, embracing those who had been officially consigned to liquidation.

2. In his critique, Bonhoeffer turns primarily against his own typical cultural-Protestant tradition of a variously misunderstood Two Kingdoms doctrine. He protests against any assumption of two 'realms' on the basis of which God and the world are separated from each other.[29] Such a division was never a particular Catholic danger, rather its opposite, a false mixing of both kingdoms, which according to the Lutheran tradition is ultimately responsible for the fact that sin is not taken seriously enough by Catholics, and is not seen as actually affecting 'nature' in a fundamental way.

One positive result which can be confirmed is that Bonhoeffer's ethical starting point in the concretization of incarnation and his plea for the realization of the reality of God in this world as ethical task does not signify confessional disagreement, but, on the contrary, proposes an excellent foundation for a common Christian ethic. This holds even and especially at those times when Catholic moral theology traditionally sought its point of departure too often and too quickly in ethical principles, from which it believed it could deduce a special ethic appropriate to concretization.

With respect to concepts currently under discussion, Bonhoeffer's concept has, of course, the advantage that, in proceeding from 'reality' he immediately conceives of God's incarnation in this world, instead of viewing reality as a reality of the world, as it can be seen in the philosophy and theology of Thomas Aquinas. It is noteworthy that the important study of Alfons Auer, *Autonome Moral und christlicher Glaube (Autonomous Morality and Christian Faith)*[30] likewise begins with the 'Ja zur Wirklichkeit' ('Yes to reality') and refers in this to Josef Pieper's *Die Wirklichkeit und das Gute*.[31] But Auer in no way distinguishes the incarnation clearly enough and from the very beginning as that central point on which reality can and must be constituted and therefore also that in which reality can and must be recognized. Yet there is here no confessional difference, but rather a general Christian corrective to the concepts which are legitimate within Christianity, but which are no longer sufficient for the present stage of our reflection.

3. Bonhoeffer could hardly have written an 'ethics' which, on the basis of certain principles, could have deduced rules and then, in accordance with those rules, could have qualified human behaviour as good or bad. Neither 'system,' 'abstraction,' nor 'idea,' and neither 'principles,' in the sense of 'universal principles,' nor 'norms,' in the sense of 'eternal norms,' could have been the point of departure for Bonhoeffer, since reality could never have been reached by them and the behaviour appropriate to reality could never have been described by them.

In a later section of his *Ethik*, 'Die Geschichte und das Gute' (History and the Good),[32] Bonhoeffer takes up these conceptions when he states that, 'the human being [can] no longer be thought of and recognized other than in Jesus Christ,'[33] and God not apart from the human gestalt of Jesus Christ, and if we make any abstractions from Jesus Christ, whether about the human being or God, they are nothing more than

145

'worthless abstractions,' so that life as 'response to the life of Jesus Christ' is emphatically described by Bonhoeffer as *'responsibility.'*[34] This life is more than we can define,[35] just as we also cannot define 'world' or 'love.'[36]

Bonhoeffer consistently rejects any 'casuistry,' since it attempts to judge concrete 'instances' on the basis of universally valid principles.[37] Rather, as in 1932 with regard to the concrete commandment, so also now it is Bonhoeffer's concern to give an answer to the question 'how Christ takes form among us here and now.'[38]

4. It is surprising how openly today a revival of culture-Protestantism can be called for.[39] Such calls do not take into consideration that at that time, in spite of the separation of the two kingdoms it claimed culture-Protestantism actually realized a high degree of identity with the political system. Such a state-supporting identity is today vigorously promoted under the slogan 'civil religion,' ever since Robert Bellah published his related contribution in 1967.[40] In our country, Hermann Lübbe acts as the most prominent spokesman for this civil religion. There can be no objections if Christians clearly commit fewer instances of insurance fraud than others when adjusting auto damage claims.[41] That the Christian faith requires a corresponding ethos is not only not wrong, but a constituent necessity. For without such a realization in life, faith deprives itself of its own basis, as expressed in the motto 'whatever you did for one of the least of these, you did for me,' and the much less frequently treated counterpart, 'whatever you did not do for one of the least of these, you did not do for me' (Matt. 25:40, 45). The negative version is especially revealing, because it condemns as wrong not only as evil deeds, but also deeds left undone. Therefore it can be no mistake that deeds result from Christian faith which correspond with that faith.

Yet reducing faith to a means for maintaining the political and social order is the death of faith. It contravenes the central proclamation, 'Seek first the kingdom of God...' (Matt. 6:33; par. Luke 12:31). It is precisely here that the error of civil religion is to be seen, namely that it does not primarily serve the acknowledgement and worship of God, but the foundation of the state. To what degree this civil religion proceeds from the presuppositions of culture-Protestantism is conspicuous when Hermann Lübbe, as a result of his defense of civil religion, makes the accusation that Barth could better have 'gone easy on culture-Protestantism in the Troeltschean mould, indeed, even favoured it, instead of having called it an especially prominent sign of that time which could be nothing but a between-time.'[42] In so doing, as Lübbe emphasizes, dialectical theology actually contributed through some of its effects to the downfall of the Weimar era, and helped to turn it into just that 'between-time' that it intended it to be (a play on the title of the journal *Zwischen den Zeiten*). The shaky ground on which Lübbe's conception stands is made manifest in an incidental remark he makes about the Christian 'religion,' which is to be distinguished or separated from civil religion: It might be the case 'that without such ecclesiastically bound religion, culture-religion could not remain tenable.'[43] It is but little comfort when Niklas Luhmann warns against the reduction of religion to civil religion, and discerns that 'it is only in the reflection expressed in credal statements, marks of proper belief, and religious communication (that is, church), that what might be taken as civil religion manifests and specifies itself as religion.'[44]

An opposing concept has also been developed which uses Christian faith for a revolutionary restructuring, if necessary, and it creates for that purpose a corresponding image of God. One who could be considered among the avant garde of this movement is Richard Shaull, who in 1966 said with respect to this subject:

> The God who tears down old structures in order to create the conditions for a more human existence is himself in the midst of the struggle. His presence in the world and is pressure on structures which stand in his way from the foundation of the dynamic of this process... [Only in the center of the revolution] can we observe what God is doing.[45]

One should not say that this was just a wrong turn at the beginning as though, by now, there were no more theology of revolution, but only the theology of liberation as authoritatively developed by Gustavo Gutierrez.[46] And, of course, no one could possibly be against this theology of liberation; it ought rather to be supported, since 'freedom' is clearly a central biblical concept, and especially a New Testament term — which is absolutely correct. People become unsettled, however, when this position is criticized — there are after all very different currents within this liberation theology.[47] Does such repudiation of differentiation, however, not indicate a Volksfront mentality in which it seems necessary, in face of the admittedly violent opponents, to muster all strength and to declare critical reflection as a weakening of fighting strength? If that is so, it would be no credit to liberation theology; liberation theology would then be intolerant of the very thing which is indispensable to theology, namely, critical questioning.

It is evident in an author like Leonardo Boff, who can justly be considered a moderate, that liberation theology also formulates statements corresponding to those of Shaull, though admittedly less pointed. In his work on the doctrine of the Trinity, *Der dreieinige Gott (The Triune God)*, Boff writes that the struggles of the oppressed are 'also the struggles of the Father, Son, and Holy Spirit,' and that, as a result, there arises even 'greater motive for struggle and resistance.'[48] He also writes that 'especially the struggle of the oppressed for their liberation reveals a unique Trinitarian fulness,'[49] and that 'the Spirit is working and fomenting within our conflict-ridden history.'[50] In this last passage, Boff chooses to sketch a hymnic and, to be sure, dramatic panorama of the historical processes in which the poor

> ...join forces,... break down the taboos which keep them under the yoke, ... prophetically condemn the smiths of their chains,... stand up to the violence of the oppressors and tear from them their privileges and unjust positions,... permit themselves their creative fantasies and design the Utopia of a reconciled world, in which all can eat and enjoy life's favour.

It is precisely these processes that Boff characterizes as 'pregnant with the Spirit.'

Completely apart from the question of whether or not a revolution is unavoidable, a theological identification of historical processes on the one hand, and reality and works of God on the other, is carried out here in a dynamic variant which does not retain the otherness of God, especially in the historical acts of God.

As distinct from both versions — civil religion as well as this type of liberation

147

theology — Bonhoeffer decidedly emphasizes 'participation in the powerlessness of God in the world.'[51] He avoids any approval of a *'Deus ex machina'* image of God, who intervenes in our activities as the victorious resolver of conflicts. In his *Ethik,* this aspect is particularly present under the theme *'Gleichgestaltung'* (conformation) to the incarnate, the crucified and the resurrected one. Yet no inner-worldly nor even post-revolutionary triumphalism can be founded on those themes. Bonhoeffer says, moreover, that the person who is conformed to the resurrected one is the 'new person', but 'new in the old. His secret remains hidden to the world.' And a little later he says, 'Although transfigured into the image of the resurrected one, he bears here only the signs of the cross and judgment.'[52]

In the last section worked on by Bonhoeffer before his arrest, he formulates more comprehensively Jesus Christ as the eternal Son with the Father, as crucified reconciler and as resurrected and exalted Lord.[53] Precisely here Jesus is characterized as the Christ who 'was there completely for the world and not for himself.'[54] This is done in such a way, however, that the reality of the cross is not thereby subdued. Therefore Bonhoeffer says:

> A life in genuine worldliness is possible only through the proclamation of Christ crucified; true worldly living is not possible or real in contradiction to the proclamation or side by side with it, that is to say, in any kind of autonomy of the secular sphere; it is possible and real only 'in, with and under' the proclamation of Christ.[55]

Earlier in the same text Bonhoeffer characterized the human person as one who should 'already actually be on the way (not still standing at the crossroads),' and 'already actually have the decision behind him (not constantly still before him),' who should, quite free from inner conflict, 'do the one thing and (though theoretically-ethically perhaps of equal urgency) leave the other.'[56] The Christian is therefore exactly not the one, for Bonhoeffer, who is subject to the 'anguish of the ethical conflict and the decision,' but is a person freed to live, 'freed for unreflected action.'[57] The distinction between *'actus directus* and *'actus reflexus'* which is present throughout Bonhoeffer's work, but was new and more painfully experienced in the decision in the U.S.A. in 1939, had a bearing on this statement; for, according to this distinction, a decision can no longer be ultimately grounded in reflection, but must be risked into the darkness of the future. Therefore, according to Bonhoeffer, decision is not the correct application of ethical principles but, in the end, it remains a risk. 'A historical decision cannot be reduced to ethical concepts. There will always be more : the risk of action.'[58]

Such a decision,[59] which does not always leave the human being torn asunder, is not, however, automatically followed by the salvaging of one's own acts, that is, by self-justification. Bonhoeffer, as no one else, has emphasized the uncertainties of historical action. With all his engagement, which we consider so correct, he asks himself in the important text, 'Nach zehn Jahren' (After Ten Years) 'Are we still useful?'

5. In the *Ethik,* Bonhoeffer decisively carries on the theme of 'Stellvertretung' (deputyship). This is no longer only defined as the deputyship of Christ,[60] nor of the church in imitation of him,[61] nor as the acceptance of guilt by the 'sinless-guilty Jesus

Christ,' through whom 'everyone acting responsibly becomes guilty'[62]; it is much more a question of accepting one's own becoming guilty:

> There is no glory in standing amid the ruins of one's native town in the consciousness that at least one has not oneself incurred any guilt...[63]
>
> Whether an action arises from responsibility or from cynicism is shown only by whether or not the objective guilt of the violation of the law is recognized and acknowledged, and by whether or not, precisely in this violation, the law is hallowed. It is in this way that the will of God is hallowed in the deed which arises from freedom. But since this is a deed which arises from freedom, man is not torn asunder in deadly conflict, but in certainty and in unity with himself he can dare to hallow the law truly even by breaking it.[64]

Such a deed can, however, according to Bonhoeffer, no longer be justified by conscience, according to Bonhoeffer.[65] Bonhoeffer acknowledges that the 'man of conscience' will, in the end, have to content himself, 'instead of a good conscience, to have a salved one.'[66] It is in this sense that he says 'time of inwardness and of conscience, and that means the time of religion as such' is over.[67] What remains is acting without being justified by principle, but surrendering oneself:

> All ideological action carries its own justification within itself from the outset in its guiding principle, but responsible action does not lay claim to knowledge of its own ultimate righteousness. When the deed is performed with a responsible weighing up of all the personal and objective circumstances and in the awareness that God has become *human* and that it is *God* who has become human, then this deed is delivered up solely to God at the moment of its performance. Ultimate ignorance of one's own good and evil, and with it a complete reliance upon grace, is an essential property of responsible historical action.[68]

For us it follows from this statement of Bonhoeffer that we cannot legitimate our actions with reference to his; for then we would be turning his arguments into a principle. It furthermore follows that we cannot spare ourselves the decision. On the contrary, it finally follows that we must accept not only ambiguous acts, but possibly acts of dubious value as well. Of interest here is the *'ultima ratio,'* the extreme borderline case. Catholic moral theology, as it was available to Bonhoeffer, like that of Otto Schilling, developed a 'just war' doctrine that is for us today not only too innocuous, but also flippant, as when Schilling said, quoting Augustine, '... just wars are... such that avenge injustice.'[69] He then goes on to define more fully the grounds for such a 'just war:'

> ... grievous injury to a nation's honour, grievous injury to its property and other important, lawfully established interests, furthermore, assistance in the protection of a people whose rights have been grievously damaged or threatened, the request of neighbouring countries to help them against revolution or tyranny..., the suppression of the Christian religion. ...[and also] if it should be necessary to restrain a hostile tribe which practices severe injustice through pillaging or human sacrifice, or which hinders through violence the peaceful efforts of missions.[70]

On the basis of all these grounds, Schilling can well imagine 'just wars', and under certain circumstances, as *ultima ratio*, even 'offensive wars.'[71] In spite of important restrictions, for instance, the prohibition against taking part in a war which is known to be unjust,[72] the just war doctrine appears so flippant because it excuses serious harm done to innocent people.

It remains to be seen whether, and possibly to what extent, one may follow Bonhoeffer in his statements that the killing of the enemy in war is not arbitrary killing.[73] One will, however, agree with him on the statement that there does exist an extraordinary situation of ultimate necessity (necessitá, according to Machiavelli),[74] which cannot be decided by any law, that there is an *'ultima ratio,'* which Bonhoeffer sees given in the case of war. Yet the *ultima ratio* is 'beyond the boundary of the *ratio*. It is irrational action' and should not be made 'into a rational law' again. The borderline case must not be made the norm. In his evaluation of human action in this borderline case, however, Bonhoeffer remains unambiguous: 'The ultimate question remains open and must be kept open, for in either case man becomes guilty and in either case he can live only by the grace of God and by forgiveness.'[75]

While it is precisely this extreme situation which cannot be excluded today, it also cannot be casuistically determined. Recognition of its existence also rests, after careful analysis of the situation, on a decision, a conclusion, and one, to be sure, which for the sake of right at the same time serves right and injures right. And it can no longer simply be exculpated, simply be qualified as good. There is no more possibility of self-justification. We must risk this action in the given situation, in which there is no more justification of precarious or even evil means for a good end. Yet even at those moments when we are dealing with an action with a double effect — for example, when in war one fends off the enemy but affects civilians in the process — we can no longer simply justify this deed, it is not the permissible action with a double effect, in which the two effects are not of the same level, but an action with a, provisionally stated, double value whose simple justification is no longer possible. We should therefore come to terms with the fact that we are no longer dealing only with an *actio cum duplici effectu* but, once more provisionally stated, an *actio cum duplici moralitate,* with an *actio* with double value, in which good and evil are inseparably contained. To restate it using the quote of Bonhoeffer just mentioned: 'Ultimate ignorance of one's own good and evil, and with it a complete reliance upon grace, is an essential property of responsible historical action.'[76] This appears to me to be a significant contribution of Bonhoeffer to a post-confessional, and perhaps even post-Christian, common human ethic for the extreme situation which, for its part, provides important information on ethics in general.

NOTES

1. *Widerstand und Ergebung,* new edition, pp. 147, 182.
2. E. Bethge, *Vorwort,* in: D. Bonhoeffer, *Ethik,* Munich, 1947.
3. Letter of November 27, 1940, in *Gesammelte Schriften* VI, p. 492.
4. *Gesammelte Schriften* IV, pp. 505-543, or 544-569 = *Dietrich Bonhoeffer Werke. Kritische Gesamtausgabe. Band 5: Gemeinsames Leben; Gebetbuch der Bibel, ed. by* Gerhard L. Müller & Albrecht Schönherr, Munich, 1986 (= DBW 5), pp. 103-132.
5. E. Bethge *Dietrich Bonhoeffer, Theologe-Christ-Zeitgenosse,* Munich, 1967, p. 743, (= DB).
6. July 1944, *Widerstand und Ergebung,* new edition, pp. 413ff.
7. *DB,* p. 803.

8. *Ethik,* p. 355 = Schilling, vol, II, p. 609.
9. Schilling, ibid., p. 250.
10. Letter to E. Bethge, January 20, 1941, *Gesammelte Schriften* II, p. 394.
11. Letter of October 9, 1940, *Gesammelte Schriften* VI, p. 484; and of May 6, 1944, *Widerstand und Ergebung,* new edition, p. 314.
12. *Ethik, p.* 235, *Zettel Nr. (= Z)* p. 18, cf., 19, 25, 28; cf. also, *Ethik,* pp. 240, 168; for 'self-preservation' see Z, 28.
13. *Ethik,* p. 161, Z, 50, 52, 55.
14. The first time in *Zucht und Maß,* pp. 16ff., also under the same title in *Das Viergespann* , Munich, 1964, pp. 208ff.; the last time in *'Gerechtigkeit,'* in *Das Viergespann,* pp. 68ff.
15. *Ethik,* pp. 124f.; Z, pp. 40, 60; contra *DB,* p. 803, where this theme was traced back to Reinhold Schneider; Tödt discovered the underlining of Maritain in the rest of Bonhoeffer's library.
16. Cf. Bonhoeffer's letters of January 19, 1941, *Gesammelte Schriften* VI, p. 510; January 31, 1941, *Gesammelte Schriften* II, p. 396; February 8, 1941, *Gesammelte Schriften* VI, p. 516.
17. Z, 40.
18. Namely from his *Macht und Gnade,* cf. also *Rheinischer Merkur,* May 13, 1988.
19. Mentioned by name, Z, 60.
20. Implied, Z, 61.
21. *DB,* p. 788.
22. Thus his letter to H.-W. Jensen, December 26, 1940, *Gesammelte Schriften,* II, p. 588.
23. Thus his letter to E. Bethge, February 10, 1941, *Gesammelte Schriften* VI, p. 518.
24. *Ethik,* pp. 200-226.
25. Ibid., p. 208.
26. Ibid., p. 210.
27. Ibid., p. 235.
28. Cf. E. Bethge, 'Dietrich Bonhoeffer und die Juden,' in *Konsequenzen* (=IBF 3), Munich, 1980, pp. 172-214, here with reference to the confession of guilt (*Ethik,* pp. 121f.), according to which the church has become guilty 'of the life of the weakest and most helpless brother, Jesus Christ'; cf. also E. Bethge, 'Nichts scheint mehr in Ordnung,' in *Ethik im Ernstfall* [=IBF 4], Munich, 1982, pp. 30-40.
29. Cf. esp., *Ethik,* p. 212, also pp. 101f.
30. Düsseldorf, 1971.
31. A. Auer, *Autonome Moral und christlicher Glaube,* p. 16.
32. *Ethik,* pp. 227-278.
33. Ibid., p. 235.
34. Ibid., p. 236.
35. Cf. ibid., p. 231.
36. Regarding 'love' see ibid., p. 53.
37. Cf., ibid., p. 91; see also Z, 10, 41.
38. *Ethik,* p. 91.
39. Friedrich Wilhelm Graf, in *Lutherische Monatshefte* 25 (1986): 309-312.
40. Robert N. Bellah, 'Civil Religion in America', *Daedalus* vol. 69, no. 1 (Winter 1967), cited in Heinz Kleger and Alois Müller, eds., *Religion des Bürgers: Zivilreligion in Amerika und Europa,* Munich, 1986, pp. 19-41; more precisely, Robert N. Bellah, *Die Religion und die Legitimation der amerikanischen Republik,* (1978), in: ibid. 42-63.
41. Cf., his *Religion nach der Aufklärung,* Graz, 1987, p. 213.
42. Lübbe, p. 285.
43. Ibid., p. 289.
44. Niklas Luhmann, 'Grundwerte als Zivilreligion,' in *Religion des Bürgers,* pp. 175-194, esp. p. 190.
45. Richard Shaull, 'Revolution in theologischer Perspective,' in Trutz Rendtorff and Heinz Eduard Tödt, eds. *Theologie der Revolution: Analysen und Materialen (= es 258),* Frankfurt, 1968, p. 128.
46. 1972, *German edition,* Munich, 1973.
47. Thus Hans Jürgen Prien, ed., *'Puebla,'* in *Lateinamerika: Gesellschaft - Kirche - Theologie,* vol. II, Göttingen, 1981, p. 199.
48. Leonardo Boff, *Der dreieinige Gott,* Düsseldorf, 1987, p. 183.

49. Ibid., p. 255.
50. Ibid., p. 238.
51. July 18, 1944, *Widerstand und Ergebung,* new edition, p. 396.
52. *Ethik,* p. 87.
53. Ibid., pp. 313ff.
54. Ibid., p. 318.
55. Ibid., p. 314.
56. Ibid., p. 301.
57. Cf., ibid., p. 296.
58. Ibid., p. 265.
59. Cf. the references of E. Feil in *Glaube als Widerstandskraft,* Gotthard Fuchs, ed. Frankfurt, 1986, pp. 230-241.
60. *Ethik,* p. 240.
61. Ibid., p. 318.
62. Ibid., p. 256, cf., 259.
63. Ibid., p. 361.
64. Ibid., p. 278.
65. Cf., the few references in E. Feil, 'Gewissen und Entscheidung,' in *Glaube als Widerstandskraft,* pp. 223-228.
66. *Ethik,* p. 70; *Widerstand und Ergebung,* p. 13.
67. April 30, 1944, *Widerstand und Ergebung,* p. 305.
68. *Ethik,* pp. 248f.
69. Schilling, op.cit., vol. II, p. 658.
70. Ibid.
71. Ibid., p. 659.
72. Ibid., p. 663.
73. *Ethik,* p. 169f.
74. Cf., ibid., p. 253.
75. Ibid., pp. 254f., last quote p. 255.
76. Ibid., pp. 248f.

PART III

ETHICS AND NEW FRONTIERS

The Freedom of the Church

BONHOEFFER AND THE FREE CHURCH TRADITION

Keith W. Clements

What significance does the thought of Dietrich Bonhoeffer have for the Free Church tradition, and vice versa? In this paper and that by John de Gruchy on 'The Freedom of the Church and the Liberation of Society' an English Baptist and a South African Congregationalist, respectively, seek to expose their inheritance to the challenge of Bonhoeffer's ecclesiology. Both writers feel deeply rooted in their Free Church traditions, yet are aware that in their respective contexts searching questions are being asked concerning the nature of Christian witness in the social and political sphere. Their enquiry can be summed up in the question: What does it mean for the church to be 'free'?

For many of us from the English-speaking world, the fact that we are meeting here in Amsterdam is of the highest historical significance. For it was this city which, in the late sixteenth and early seventeenth centuries, provided refuge to many of England's Protestants who fled from religious persecution under Elizabeth I and James I. The Elizabethan church settlement was in many ways a masterpiece in its comprehension of both the Catholic tradition of episcopacy and the Reformed doctrine of the Word of God, but it did not satisfy those on the Puritan wing who, having glimpsed at Geneva and Zürich what a true and godly church might really be like, now sought a church order rigorously based on what they saw as the New Testament pattern. Concomitant with their insistence on Scripture was a rejection of ties with the state, epitomized for them in the episcopate of the Church of England and the sovereignty of the English throne over the English Church. A number of leaders of these 'Separatist' groups were imprisoned and executed during Elizabeth's reign, and for some years the Reformed City of Amsterdam provided the nearest haven for the movement until conditions in England ameliorated — somewhat — in the second decade of the seventeenth century.

It was out of English 'Separatism' that Independency (later known as Congregationalism) was born. Here the church exists in two modes: the universal church of all Christ's people, and the local congregation, or *gathered church,* comprising only the committed believers who have 'as the Lord's free people joined themselves, by a covenant of the Lord, into a Church Estate of the Gospel to walk in all his ways made known, or to be made known, according to their best endeavours whatsoever it would cost them.'[1] Moreover, it is in one of the English Separatist groups in Amsterdam, the congregation from Gainsborough led by John Smythe, that a further step along the Independent road was taken which was to be of immense significance: the rejection of infant baptism — frequently identified as the *sine qua non* of a state church — in favour of 'believers' baptism.' The extent to which Smythe and his congregation were influenced by the already-existing Mennonite communities in Holland, the direct legatees of the Anabaptist wing of the radical Reformation, is not clear but in effect in

1609 they constituted the first English Baptist congregation. Under the leadership of Thomas Helwys a number from this community returned to England in 1612 to form in London the first Baptist congregation on English soil.

The Congregational and Baptist churches, emphasizing as they do the primacy of Scripture, the gathered church principle, the requirement of personal faith in Christ for church membership, the right to freedom of conscience in religion and the complete independence of church from state, were to be of immense significance not only in the development of Protestantism but of Western democracy, first in England and then in North America, whither many of the early adherents sailed to seek their freedom. In Anglo-Saxon circles, by 'Free Church' is generally meant this gathered church, state-free tradition (joined, significantly, by Methodism after the Evangelical Revival later in the eighteenth century). It was a tradition which became a crucial bearer of the Reformed faith beyond the European continent, providing a means whereby the social potentialities of Calvinism were released in the creation of an open, activist and libertarian society: 'A Free Church in a free society.'

What does it mean for a church to be 'free'? Further, what is the relation between a church which claims to be 'free', and the liberation of people at large? Can the church which is 'gathered' from society, and independent of the state, really have any ethical contribution to make to the public issues affecting the society from which it distinguishes itself so clearly? Once Dietrich Bonhoeffer is brought into the discussion a whole host of further questions jump up like iron filings onto a magnet. How far did this German Lutheran, reared in the *Volkskirche* of the Reformation, really appreciate the Free Church possibility? How does the 'Confessing Church' which Bonhoeffer sought so ardently relate to the gathered 'Free Church'? In his last prison writings, especially in the 'Outline for a Book', in those concrete proposals for a new form for the church,[2] was he not coming close to the Free Church pattern? Or, when weighed in Bonhoeffer's balance is the Free Church tradition, no less than other patterns, found wanting? What significance, for example, should be attached to his critique of American Protestantism and its emphasis upon 'freedom'?

1

Sanctorum Communio: National Church, Gathered Church, Confessing Church

Any encounter with Bonhoeffer's ecclesiology must of course begin with *Sanctorum Communio,* his doctoral thesis of 1927. What experience or comprehension would the young Berlin theologian have had of the 'Free Church'? In terms of our Anglo-Saxon understanding, on the face of it, very little. He might well have thought of the radical Reformation groups still anathematized in Lutheran catechetics as 'Anabaptists', though represented in modern Germany by the Mennonites, or of the Moravians, offshoots of Lutheran pietism in the eighteenth century. Equally, however, he might have had in mind the Protestant churches which had ceded from the historic *Volkskirche* over doctrinal issues and thus separated from the 'establishment', such as the

Old Reformed Churches (c.1700), the Old Lutherans (1830), or the Evangelical Lutheran Free Church of Saxony (1860). By the same token, of course, the Old Catholic Church which was formed through rejection of the decrees of the Vatican Council of 1870 was a 'free' church.

The 'Free Churches' of an Anglo-Saxon type, however, had not made their appearance in Germany until relatively modern times, in the first half of the nineteenth century. The Baptist movement, for example, began in Hamburg in 1834. Significantly this and other Free Church developments in Germany owed much to British and — especially — American support. For two decades or more, the Free Church movements met with considerable opposition from both church and state authorities in Germany (a factor not without significance in influencing the stance of those Free Churches in the Nazi period — see below). For a time the Baptist movement in Hamburg was dubbed 'the English faith', and *Methodismus* became a synonym for that Lutheran term of abuse, 'Enthusiasm.' As relative latecomers to the German scene, they bore no comparison with the way in which English 'nonconformity' had been a powerful force, socio-political as well as religious, in British history, and they were always to remain a minority on continental soil. But with their strong emphasis on evangelism they were able to implant in German Protestantism the gathered church principle and to make the plea for the independence of religion from state control or patronage. In Wilhelmine Germany of course that was a vain dream. Ostensibly the Weimar Republic offered more hope for that principle, but the Free Churches found that in practice the great *Volkskirche* still behaved as in the old establishment days[3] (a situation not unlike that found in British overseas colonies where the Anglican Church often assumed rights and privilieges which it had at home as the 'Church of England').

When the young Dietrich Bonhoeffer thought of 'Free Churches' therefore, he probably also had in mind these small, rather pietistic groups claiming to be the real inheritors of the Reformation doctrines of justification by faith and *sola scriptura* and claiming to be really putting these into effect, unlike the Evangelical *Volkskirche* which was trapped in rationalism and liberalism. Indeed, the Free Churches often made the claim that had the German Evangelical Church really retained its missionary zeal to its own people, their own formation would not have been necessary. Seen from the outside, there was more than a suggestion of spiritual elitism and exclusivism about the Free Churches, which in turn only led to 'official' church leaders and theologians being still more dismissive of them.

There was, however, at least one notable exception. Ernst Troeltsch in his massive *Die Soziallehren der christlichen Kirchen and Gruppen* (1911)[4] gave a remarkably full place to the radical Reformation groups and the later Free Churches (displaying a notable knowledge of English-speaking church history) in his sociological survey. Troeltsch is now perhaps best known for his distinction between the 'church type' and 'sect type' of Christianity.

> The Church is an institution which has been endowed with grace and salvation as the result of the work of Redemption; it is able to receive the masses, and to adjust itself to the world, because, to a certain extent, it can afford to ignore the need for subjective holiness for the sake of the objective treasure of grace and of redemption.

157

> The sect is a voluntary society, composed of strict and definite Christian believers bound to each other by the fact that all have experienced 'the new birth'. These 'believers' live apart from the world, are limited to small groups, emphasize the law instead of grace, and in varying degrees within their own circle set up the Christian order, based on love; all this is done in preparation for and expectation of the coming Kingdom of God.[5]

There is nothing pejorative in Troeltsch's usage of 'sect.' Indeed, his historical-philosophical judgement was that in balance with the church-type and mystical-type, sect-Christianity was a vital and necessary form of Christian community. Moreover, bearing in mind when he was writing, he offers an intriguing prophecy that Lutheranism is being slowly drawn into the forward march of the Protestant social doctrines, and is being influenced by ascetic Protestantism. This process of development will increase when, as we may expect with certainty, it is no longer supported by the State.'[6]

Troeltsch, however, is primarily of interest to us here in being one of Bonhoeffer's main sources in his attempt to do both theological and sociological justice to the church. As is well known, in *Sanctorum Communio* Bonhoeffer expounds a view of the church wherein revelation is concretized in human community — it is Christ existing as community. That means a heavy theological investment in (very!) human, historical communities which bear the name 'church.' Indeed, as a good Lutheran, Bonhoeffer freely admits that in its visible historical form the church has many more 'nominal members' than 'members of the kingdom':

> It is present, in other words, as a national Church *(Volkskirche)* and not as a 'gathered' church *(Freiwilligkeitskirche)*. How can a church that, as a human community, is by its very nature a community of wills, at the same time be a national church? Such is the sociological formulation of the problem of the empirical church.[7]

Bonhoeffer, however, is not dismissing the principle of the gathered church, but simply defending the existence of a national church. And, as he proceeds to make clear, the justification of the national church lies *precisely in its capacity to enable a gathered church to arise*. The link between the two is the Word, for it is in the preaching of the Word that the church truly gathers:

> The *sanctorum communio,* which by its nature presents itself as a national church, equally demands the gathered church, and continually establishes itself as such; that is, the *sanctorum communio* sustains the others, as it were, in whom the possibility of becoming 'effective' members of the church is dormant, by virtue of the Word which constitutes it and which it preaches.[8]

We are a long way from the 'gathered church' in the Free Church sense of a committed membership, since Bonhoeffer maintains the traditional Lutheran principle that a person can be assumed to be a possible member 'as long as he has made no conscious retraction.' But the dynamics of the relation between national and gathered churches, as introduced by Bonhoeffer, are crucial. The national church *is not justified per se, but only as having the potential to be the visble gathered church under the Word*. It was thus a remarkable and prophetic insight for him now to state, six years before Hitler's accession and seven years before Barmen:

Now for the church there is a point in time when it may not be a national church any longer, and this point is reached when it can no longer see in its national form any way of fighting its way through to becoming a gathered church. But such a step would in the event spring from church politics and not from dogmatics. It does, however, show that the church's essential character is that of a gathered church.[9]

Still Bonhoeffer refuses to disengage from the historical *Volkskirche,* inveighing against the 'many presumptuous attempts at purifying the church from the formation of the perfectionist sects of the early church to those of the Anabaptists and Pietists.'[10] His argument is that it is precisely in this world of sin and death, and hence of historical ambiguity, that God is at work in his hidden way. 'The church is meant to let the tares grow in its garden, for where else can it find the criterion of knowing and judging which of its members are tares?'[11] It is an attitude found again about fifteen years later in *Ethics,* in the passage dealing with judgment (The Pharisee), and still more clearly in the criticism of 'stupidly importunate reformers' and ideologues with their 'idealizing failure, which substitute an abstract notion of good for the unity of creaturely life before the Creator.'[12]

In *Sanctorum Communio,* however, the cruciality of the Word for the identity of the Christian community has injected a kind of restlessness into Bonhoeffer's Lutheranism (and here an interesting comparison could be made with Schleiermacher). It results in his rejection of Troeltsch's church/sect distinction on theological grounds. The Christian sect, too, has the Word (and so has the Roman Catholic community), whatever important sociological differences in structure there may be between these communities. Moreover, the necessary tension between the national and the gathered church returns as an insistent refrain. So on the one hand Bonhoeffer repeats his defense of the historic *Volkskirche* despite — indeed because of — its innate conservatism: 'as an organically developed historical power it possesses greater firmness and lasting power than the voluntary association: historically sterile periods can be withstood by the national church, whereas the gathered church is ruined by such a time.'[13] On the other hand comes the ominous and prophetic warning:

... we can now affirm that the national church and the gathered church belong together, and that it is all too obvious to-day that a national church, which is not continually pressing forward to be a confessing church, is in the greatest inner peril. There is a moment when the church dare not continue to be a national church, and this moment has come when the national church can no longer see how it can win through to being a gathered church ... but on the contrary is moving into complete petrifaction and emptiness in the use of its forms, with evil effects on the living members as well. We have today reached the point where such questions must be decided. We are more than ever grateful for the grace of the national church, but we are also more than ever keeping our eyes open for the danger of its complete degeneration.[14]

'Gathered church', 'confessing church', are here being drawn close together if not identified. The author was clearly being theologically prepared for the coming Church Struggle. He was also being equipped for a critical yet open and creative encounter with the ecumenical community, and not least with the Free Church life he was to meet in the United States and in Britain. This engagement is dealt with fully by John de

Gruchy in 'The Freedom of the Church and the Liberation of Society', together with Bonhoeffer's treatment of the 'exclusive' and 'inclusive' claims of Christ, and their bearing on the church in the *Ethics,* and with Bonhoeffer's vision of the 'church for others' in his prison writings . We therefore do not need to cover the same ground here. There is, however, another important theme in the *Ethics* which has a vital bearing on how we are to understand both the distinction of the church from the world and the relation of the church to the world, which takes cognizance of the 'gathered' nature of the church yet implies that any notion of 'gathering' is by itself inadequate apart from a Christological base.

2

Gathering for Others: the Church as Deputy

Throughout Bonhoeffer's *Ethics* there is an attempt to overcome 'thinking in two spheres.' In Christ, on the Pauline model, God has reconciled the world to himself, and whatever else might need to be said about the world in its sinfulness and godlessness, it is the world which God loves and has somehow 'made one' with himself in the incarnation, death and resurrection of Jesus Christ. Because of the reconciling, mediatorial work of Christ, one cannot have God without the world, nor the world without God, whose rightful rule over the world is manifest in Jesus Christ. It is important to recognize that already in *Ethics*, Bonhoeffer is seeking to explicate what he calls a 'genuine worldliness' on this Christocentric basis.[15] What then, on this unitive view, happens to the church as a distinct entity vis-à-vis the world? And especially, what happens to any notion of a 'gathered church' which, in the Free Church tradition, has been powerfully motivated by a desire to distinguish the people of God from citizenship in general, and from an office of the state in particular?

Bonhoeffer makes several assaults on this problems in *Ethics*. In addition to discussing the exclusive and inclusive aspects of Christ's call, he includes the church as one of the divine 'mandates' in which God-given human responsibility is to be exercised, along with marriage, labour and government.[16] He discusses the respective roles of government and church (note, *government,* not 'state'!). He asks in what sense the church is entitled and obliged to deliver a word to the 'world.' In no case does he rush to disavow his traditional Lutheran insistence on the distinctness of the 'spheres', but seeks to uncover the positive relation between them in the light of the ultimate unity established between all things in Christ. There is one section especially, however, where Bonhoeffer achieves a notable integration between the church as 'gathered' and a total view of humanity as under the lordship of the reconciling Christ. In 'The Commandment of God in the Church,'[17] Bonhoeffer insists that it is the *one* Christ who is Lord and Saviour of the *world* that the church always proclaims. There is not one word for the church, and another for the world. Christ is Lord and Saviour of his people *and* of the whole world, and the church proclaims his commandment 'by summoning all men to fellowship with him.' In Jesus Christ God took upon himself bodily all human being. Henceforth divine being cannot be found otherwise than in human form, and humanity is free to be human before God. 'The ''Christian'' element is not now something which lies beyond the human element; it requires to be in the midst of the human element.' And in view of the incarnation, 'to live as human before God can mean only to exist not for oneself but for God and for others.' Similarly, the cross of Christ marks both the godlessness of the world and its reconciliation, and apart from the crucified Redeemer the reality of the world is not grasped, no true 'worldliness' is possible. Further, it is under the lordship of the risen and ascended Christ that the liberation of creation takes place, for he is the Lord in whom all created things find their true origin, goal and essence. His law is their own true being, therefore, and in his commandment they are neither subject to an alien law thrust upon them nor are they left to some arbitrary autonomy.

The sum of the matter is that 'Jesus Christ's claim to lordship, which is proclaimed by the Church, means at the same time the emancipation of family, culture and government for the realization of their own essential character which has its foundation in Christ.'[18] Bonhoeffer immediately rejects one possible interpretation of this, namely, its equation with the dominon of the church over society and world. The church does have its own specific mandate: to proclaim the revelation of God in Jesus Christ. But first this proclamation being the proclamation concerning him in whom God took *manhood* upon himself, means a community of response to that word:

> In Jesus Christ is the new humanity, the congregation of God. In Jesus Christ the word of God and the congregation of God are indissolubly linked together. Through Jesus Christ the word of God and the congregation of God are inseparably united. Consequently, wherever Jesus Christ is proclaimed in accordance with the divine mandate, there, too, there is always the congregation. In the first instance this means only that men are there who accept the word concerning Christ, and who believe it and acquiesce in it, unlike others who do not accept it but reject it. It means, then, that men are there who allow that to happen to themselves which properly, as an act of God, should happen to all men; it means that men are there who stand as deputies for the other men, for the whole world.[19]

The church is a particular community, with its particular law or discipline relating to itself. But the law which governs its own life cannot and must not be imposed on the worldly order, for then it would be an alien rule. And conversely, 'the law of a worldly order cannot and must not ever become the law of this community.' The church is a means to an end, which is not to dominate or govern society but to proclaim to society the one true Lord of its life. But in fulfilling this instrumental purpose, paradoxically, the church becomes the goal and centre of all God's dealing with the world:

> The concept of deputyship characterizes this twofold relationship most clearly. The Christian congregation stands at the point at which the whole world ought to be standing; to this extent it serves as deputy for the world and exists for the sake of the world. On the other hand, the world achieves its own fulfillment at the point at which the congregation stands. The earth is the 'new creation', the 'new creature', the goal of the ways of God on earth. The congregation stands in this twofold relation of deputyship entirely in the fellowship and disciplehood of its Lord, who was Christ precisely in this, that he existed not for his own sake but wholly for the sake of the world.[20]

There is, then, a proper life of the community as a 'self-contained' entity (and here

Bonhoeffer has sharp criticisms to make of the pastorally and liturgically sparse nature of much Protestantism as compared with Roman Catholic spirituality and discipline), but only on behalf of the world. In writing of the need to insist on the church being free from the alien law of the world order, Bonhoeffer was of course writing with the Barmen Confession behind him. He was also equally, if not consciously, writing with the Free Church tradition at his elbow. But in drawing his notion of deputyship into his ecclesiology — and in a way which was to be continued in the prison theology — he was transcending that usual notion of the 'free' church. For the Free Church tradition, while it has vigorously (and some of us will think justifiably) asserted the distinction of church from world, has been vulnerable to losing interest in the world as such, so long as that 'independency' is maintained. It has been prone to conceiving of itself pietistically as the mark of salvation, the only interest which the world now holds being that of a 'mission field.' ('We remain missionaries!' was the German Baptists' slogan during the early days of the Third Reich.[21]) Or it is content to acquiesce in any socio-political system which leaves it alone. That it is representative of the world before God, Bonhoeffer has shown, and not just the antithesis to that world, need have no deleterious consequences for its own sense of Identity. Indeed, when deputyship is seen as the expression of the form of Christ himself, that identity comes to fulfillment. Equally, it must be said, this later ecclesiology of Bonhoeffer not only transcends the usual 'Free Church' understanding, but takes us beyond his own earlier understanding of the essentially 'gathered' nature of the church in *Sanctorum Communio*. There Bonhoeffer had seen the [*Volkskirche*] as an expression of the fact that the Word is intended for all people. Now it is much more the content of that Word which is to convey that goal, a content to be embodied within the concrete life of the church as deputy 'for the world.'

3

Bonhoeffer and the Free Church Tradition Today: A British Perspective

A theological understanding of the nature of the church and its relationship to the whole of humanity remains high on the agenda, especially in ecumenical discussions.[22] In Faith and Order enquiry, the debate has been both deepened and enriched over the past thirty years by the full-scale entry of the Eastern Orthodox churches, providing a milieu rather different to that known by Bonhoeffer where the parameters were still largely the Western ones of the Roman and post-Reformation churches. Given the Eastern comprehension of the church as the given, eternal, divine community without essential change or development, it would be interesting to know of an Orthodox response to *Sanctorum Communio*! But the contemporary ecumenical scene is also, of course, increasingly shaped by the experiences of 'Third World' Christianity where the questions revolve around the issue of how far Christianity is implicated in, and how far it can be both free from and liberating others from the structural sins of economic and political oppression, racism and militarism.

The Free Church tradition of the West, if honest, feels as vulnerable as any other Christian tradition when faced with the question, *'Today,* are you free enough to liberate the poor and imprisoned of your own and others' societies?' On the one hand, much history supports the Free Church case in the English-speaking world. The democratization of society, the rights to religious and political liberty, the campaign against slavery and the slave trade, the early trade union movement in Britain, the movement for universal suffrage, education and civil liberties — all these were part of the classic Free Church witness. At its best the Free Church movement has asserted the universal implications for *everyone* in society of the 'crown rights of the Redeemer.' It has declared that Christ being head of the church, no earthly power should be allowed to lay hands on the visible community of his kingdom, or to come between any person and his or her God. Equally, Christ being the true Lord of human society (a belief especially stemming fromt the Calvinist root in its heritage), it has at its best dealt roughly with all claims to absolutist authority in society, and has vigorously asserted that the strongest safeguard against the corrupting concentration of power is that the will of the people as expressed in Parliament should be sovereign.

Moreover, is not the presence of any community which visibly and concretely by its very existence testifies to the *distinctness* of the body of Christ from the state making a much-needed witness? Have not disastrous confusions flowed from the near identification of God and Caesar, of heavenly kindom and earthly despotism, which has characterized so much of post-Constantinian Christian and Western history? Is not a supposed dependence of Christianity upon the support of the state an implied statement of disbelief in the power of the Holy Spirit? Has not the 'establishment' of Christianity weakened its integrity as much as it has promoted its 'influence' in the world? Apologists among our Lutheran friends, at least, will have their answer ready: Luther would have been more than willing, at first, to have entrusted the destiny of the church to the gathered congregations, but events dictated otherwise and the godly prince had to be called in. This is not in dispute. But was the question ever asked in the nineteenth century as to what God was doing and saying to his Church in Germany through the growth of the new Free Churches? The tragically negative stance of those Free Churches in comparison with the Confessing Church (see below) cannot be justified, but it was, in part, a reflection of the arrogant and high-handed manner in which the Evangelical Church, no less than the state, had treated their forefathers a century earlier. During the Church Struggle the Free Church leaders professed an inability to feel much sympathy for those who were now being arrested — in the name of that same Evangelical Church. Then, as always, the perspective of minorities can be highly revelatory of aspects otherwise overlooked in the scene at large, as Bonhoeffer himself realized and related in his 1942-43 saying about 'The view from below.'

On the other hand, we are increasingly aware that not *all* history supports the Free Church case. Yes, Free Churches have at times been strongly in the vanguard against social inequities and abuse, and in the promotion of human rights and dignities. A closer examination of history reveals, however, that most Free Church energies have been expended in these directions *where Free Church people themselves have been the most obvious victims* (as in nineteenth-century England for example). In this respect the 'radical liberalism' of nineteenth-century English nonconformity was a powerful movement of *self-liberation* by the rising (but still heavily disadvantaged) artisan and lower middle classes. It was never a proletarian movement. It was no less sincere, worthy or necessary for that. But having gained their civic, religious and cultural rights, British Free Church people largely lost the broader social view, and since the 1914-18 War increasingly espoused a provincial, bourgeois stance, more content to proclaim platitudes about society than engage in any searching critique. Indeed, a case has been strongly argued by one recent church historian that in the 1914-18 War itself, English Free Church 'nonconformity' finally and decisively *opted for conformity to the Establishment* by wholeheartedly supporting the war and abandoning its previous pacifist and internationalist tendencies.[23] The reward was rich: greatly increased public acceptability for the Free Churches who could now be seen to belong in every way to the body politic. The cost appeared to be minimal — after all, the Free Churches were still formally as independent of the state as ever. The price, however, was extracted from the Free Churches' hidden reserves. Less and less could they claim to be offering — as they had early in the nineteenth century — a truly *alternative* kind of society. The most significant social teachers and prophets in English Christianity since 1918 — and indeed the most outspoken 'nonconformists' — have in fact been Anglicans.

Now of course this could just as well be significant of a general historical shift affecting all the British churches, as of any 'decline' in specifically Free Church attitudes. Indeed, concomitant with the growth of ecumenical relationships over the past eighty years has been an increasing awareness among the English churches of a relativization of the distinction between the 'established' and 'non-established' churches. One factor has been the immensely changed position of the Roman Catholic Church, formerly an alien and somewhat recluse minority in England, now to the forefront in every aspect of public Christianity and ecumenical concern, and representing a massive element in non-established Christianity of a kind quite different from that of the Free Churches. Another factor, however, has been the almost tacit acceptance by the Free Churches themselves that for all their formal dissociation from 'establishment', they are nevertheless intimately locked into much of the apparatus of the state, not least in its welfare and educational provision (for instance church youth and community workers are sometimes paid by the local authority, not to mention the fact that ordinands as a matter of course apply for state funding of their theological training). Seen from the margins of British society, and especially, for example, from the experience of some of the back-led churches, *all* the 'mainstream' British churches, Anglican, Roman Catholic and Free Church, must look pretty well 'established' in their social status and command of available facilities.

This is not to imply that important differences do not remain between the Anglican and other churches in England, and particularly in public attitudes and expectations concerning them. But in a society which is increasingly secularized, the Church of England itself, whatever the persistent formal relationships with the Crown and Parliament, has had to come into a somewhat more self-conscious relationship to 'the people' at large, to the state, and to other churches. *Ecclesia Anglicana* is no longer quite such a *Volkskirche*, still less does it now merit the old familiar jibe of it being 'the

Conservative Party at prayer.' Indeed, talk of 'confrontation' between church and state has grown in the United Kingdom in recent years, as significant church leaders, including a number of Anglican bishops, have been increasingly outspoken in their criticism of many of the politicians of the Thatcher Conservative government.

4

Confessing as a Relativizing Act

At this point we find Dietrich Bonhoeffer's questions addressed to the Anglo-Saxon Free Churches as sharp as they were when penned fifty years ago. In one respect it is tempting to say that the Free Churches of his native Germany provide the best verifications of his warnings. 'A state free church is no more protected against secularization than is a state church. The world threatens to break in on the church as much because of freedom as because of association', he wrote reflecting on the churches of the United States in 1939.[24] No churches were more zealous for their independence from the state than the German Free Churches, yet by the time of the First World War, none were more socially, culturally and politically assimilated to German nationalism. 'Die Baptistenkirche ist nicht nur evangelisch, sondern auch gut deutsch', declared a Baptist writer in 1916.[25] Other examples abound — including in 1914 an infamous Baptist exposition of Ephesians 4:4-6 — one Lord, one faith, one baptism — applied to the unity of the *German people*! When the crisis of 1933 arrived, the German Free Churches as a whole adopted the quietist 'middle way' not generally supporting the *Deutsche Christen* but on the other hand enthusiastic in their welcome of Hitler, the saviour from godless Bolshevism and the total abstainer from alcohol. As far as 'freedom' was concerned, the German Free Churches in the Third Reich had few complaints. Indeed the Methodist Bishop Melle and the Baptist leader Paul Schmidt expressed thanks at the Oxford 1937 Conference on Church and State for the 'un-limited freedom' to pursue their evangelistic and pastoral ministries. There is every reason to believe that the authorities were content to allow a continued proclamation which centred on 'Jesus ist *mein* Herr' rather than 'Jesus ist *der* Herr.' Bonhoeffer's dictum that 'where thanks for institutional freedom must be rendered by the sacrifice of the freedom of preaching, the church is in chains if it believes itself to be free,'[26] needed no clearer exemplification.

Bonhoeffer exposes the vulnerability of a 'Free Church' to manipulation by ex-traneous and sometimes sinister forces at precisely the point where it feels itself to be free from the godless world; just as the national church can complacently assume that by its very existence it is upholding the divine order in the world. In both cases the question of the capacity to confess the only one true Lord is at issue. The covenant of the gathered people, with the Lord and with one another, can become the choice to be a church on one's own terms, in order consciously or otherwise to serve one's particular social, political — and religious — interests. It can too readily be an accommodation to the society as it is, rather than providing a critique of it. We have already seen how this

165

has become a temptation to the British Free Churches in their 'suburban captivity.' In terms of freedom they have been left with relatively little to say to a government which has cleverly based much of its appeal on the sanctity of 'personal freedom' interpreted as 'individual choice', yet which is growing steadily more centralized, more authoritarian and more secretive, and which presents an undefined 'national security' as overriding all other considerations. As the churches mark time in face of this advance of state power, their own 'freedom' at a certain level is assured if they stick to their spiritual tasks and do not meddle in politics. Mrs. Thatcher, the candle-lighter of freedom in Moscow, will see to that!

In South Africa the political struggle as presented by the government is frequently seen as one for 'religious freedom' in the face of 'communism', and once more the churches, and especially those of the Free Church tradition, are susceptible. Again, none are more zealous for 'independence' from the state than the Baptists. But tragically no denomination has been more illustrative of *apartheid* in its very structure than that denomination for which 'proclaiming the gospel' has been claimed to be of supreme importance. At least now a point of honesty has been reached whereby the black Baptist Convention has disaffiliated itself from the dominant white-led Baptist Union. In fact all the church traditions of Southern Africa have had to examine to what extent they are primarily locked into the interests of the particular social communities, whether those with power or the powerless. But in particular, claimants to 'Free Churchmanship' are being brought to the bar for examination as to whether they themselves truly are free, let alone liberating. Is a 'Free Church' in such a conflict-ridden situation one which is free to be itself, or one which, in costly discipleship, manifests freedom in moving out beyond itself to identify with the oppressed and powerless outside its own circle?

Bonhoeffer questions our Free Churches as to the theological reality of their 'freedom.' Is it truly the freedom which comes *by* preaching the lordship of Christ, the liberating Lord, however costly and unpalatable a word that might be? Or is it only the freedom *to* preach permitted by the world? That freedom is deeply important. But it is not the final or ultimate freedom, and it can obscure the devastatingly simple question: What, or whom, are we preaching? Bonhoeffer faces the Free Church with the question: Are you a Confessing Church? That question in fact was crucial to him as an aspect of the encounter between the German Confessing Church and the Ecumenical Movement.[27] The question might be expanded thus: Are you concerned not simply to be gathered negatively in distinction from the world, but positively under the Word of the Lord of the world? Have you a Word from the Lord which is significant not only from your own security and sanctity, but for the true welfare of the world of which you are part?

On Bonhoeffer's understanding it is the confessing church which is most truly free, that is, the church which answers the claim of its Lord by putting all rival claims, pressures and possible dangers aside and uttering not only for itself but also its neighbours, on whose behalf it is set in a particular part of the world, the promise and the command for that particular hour. In this perspective, the established State Church, the Free Church, and the Roman Catholic Church, could equally become confessing churches — and could equally be inhibited from becoming so by blindness, fear or inertia. No single structure can guarantee the confessing word and deed, or absolutely prevent it. This is not to make our varied ecclesiological differences irrelevant, but it is to set them in a more significant frame of reference. It certainly means that as history moves on some of us in the Free Churches today are by no means as impatient for the disestablishment of the Church of England as were our parents and grandparents. There simply is little evidence that such a move would by itself 'liberate the Church' to 'speak a word to society' or to 'confront the government.' Put bluntly, the Church of England, no less than the Free Churches, is as 'free' as it wishes to be to say and even to do what it considers to be in the cause of justice, truth and peace. Paradoxically, the most strident calls for the disestablishment of the Church of England these days come from within its own ranks, by those who chafe at the state's role in the appointment of bishops, and at the remaining legal controls on liturgical matters. This desire by some Anglicans for greater 'freedom' in the management of 'the Church's own life' would be unexceptionable, were it not also, in some cases, accompanied by an implicit wish to abandon the public roles with which the Church of England has been endowed — whether one likes it or not — by history. However odd it may seem, this Free Church writer feels uneasy at the tone of some of his Anglican friends' yearning for 'freedom', seemingly motivated by an escapist hankering after freedom from responsibilities. Bonhoeffer's word is apposite: 'The ultimate question for a responsible man to ask is not how he is to extricate himself heroically from the affair, but how the coming generation is to live.'[28]

Churches in the United Kingdom are increasingly speaking and acting together on public issues, and, as not infrequently happens in ecumenical history, it is the historic occasion, the *kairos,* rather than the prepared programme which creates the deepest ecumenical conciousness. In retrospect it is clear that in this regard one of the most significant occasions in the life of modern Britain and the British churches occurred in the summer of 1982 following the successful recapture of the Falkland/Malvinas Islands after the Argentinian occupation. The outcome was marked by a public state service of thanksgiving in St. Paul's Cathedral, conducted by leaders of the Anglican, Free and Roman Catholic churches. Much controversy was aroused at the tone of the service, especially the Archbishop of Canterbury's sermon and the prayers which laid heavy emphasis on the need for repentance and reconciliation, and intercessions for Argentinian as well as British casualties. The government and its supporters in the press expressed patriotic anger at this evident betrayal of the Land of Hope and Glory. Vitriol was especially directed at the Church of England leadership, and it is a widely held view that the Prime Minister's continuing unease with the English bishops — whether over their views on inner cities, or unemployment, or race, or nuclear weapons — owes more to this single unforgivable act than to any other event. It was in a true sense, however mild and symbolic, an occasion of confessing the kingdom of God in face of the rampant claims of the kingdoms of this world. And the lesson is not, hopefully, being forgotten in Britain that it was confession because it was ecumenical and it was truly ecumenical because it was confession. It is unfortunate, I feel, that the Archbishop of York, Dr. John Habgood, should commit himself to the view that

Only the Church of England could have insisted on counter-balancing the nationalistic thrust of the Falklands celebration, precisely because of its relationship to the nation. And the fact that it did so was a direct consequence of its developing relationship with the Anglican communion and other world Christian bodies.[29]

This is to ignore completely both the logic of the various churches' stances and the actual course of events surrounding the episode. That the Church of England played a crucial public role in countering the uncritically nationalistic mood is not in dispute. That it *would or could* have done so without the other churches which were at least as concerned at the chauvinistic attitude, is highly unlikely. The stand taken at the St. Paul's service required the independent-mindedness of the Free Churches which once again were warning that Christianity was not a state monopoly. And no international influence was more crucial at this point than that of the Roman Catholic Church — the 'enemy' in this case was, after all, a predominantly Roman Catholic country!

5

Confessing Free Churches

At this point we contemporary Free Church representatives may well feel that Bonhoeffer is not so much critical of the Free Church traditions as such, but rather is encouraging us to recover those vital elements in our legacy which have tended in recent generations to be lost in the efforts to ensure Free Church survival and growth as ends in themselves. At its most creative points in Western society, the Free Church tradition has been able *both* to assert the distinctness of the gathered, believing community (the 'fellowship of believers') *and* to proclaim the rightful claim of the lordship of Christ over the whole of secular society. The so-called 'nonconformist conscience' of nineteenth-century Britain, summed up in the slogan 'What is morally wrong can never be politically right,' may have been simplistic and open to the charge of being hypocritically selective in its priorities, but it did at least witness to the universalistic concern of the local, covenanted *sanctorum communio*. At the turn of this century, for example, it was John Clifford, minister of Westbourne Park Chapel, London, the 'uncrowned king of militant nonconformity', who was both leading the fight against what were felt to be continuing and unjust Anglican intrusion into religious instruction in schools, and at the same time campaigning against sweated labour and against Britain's last great imperialistic adventure in the South African Boer War (several times his chapel was beset by chauvinistic mobs). The Free Churches can indeed point to cherished occasions in their story where they have not merely claimed freedom to exist, but have exhibited freedom in confession.

Bonhoeffer's challenge to the Free Church tradition has another aspect, however. We note his offhand reference to a 'semi-Pelagian Free Church theology.' Certainly the 'voluntarist' principle can appear to express more self-assertiveness ('Lord, I will follow you wherever you go') than obedience to a given call. Bonhoeffer was justified,

168

in his analysis of the encounter between his Confessing Church and the ecumenical movement, in asking other churches about *their* confessions:

> There can only be a church as a Confessing Church, i.e. as a church which confesses itself to be for its Lord and against his enemies. A church without a confession or free from one is not a church, but a sect, and makes itself master of the Bible and the Word of God. A confession is the church's formulated answer to the Word of God in Holy Scripture, expressed in its own words.[30]

Certainly Free Churches have at times, especially under the influence of late-nineteenth century subjectivity and liberalism, fought shy of any 'credal' emphasis either in their liturgies or their constitutions. But that has not been without reason, for on occasion they have had bitter experience of the use of creeds by religious and secular authorities in attempting to coerce conformity, both spiritual and political. However, Bonhoeffer is not concerned primarily about whether churches have confession in written, credal form (and note again the reservations in his prison letters about how in the Confessing Church itself, actual personal faith in Jesus Christ had been evaded under cover of the abstract 'faith of the Church'[31] — a criticism which finds more than an echo in much Free Church sentiment). He is more concerned about confessing rather than confession, the obedient act rather than a static piece of theology. He criticizes the attitude which 'knows nothing of the significance of the living confession, but regards the confession as a dead system which is from time to time applied schematically as a standard against other churches.'[32] The first item in confession is a confession of sin, and the first confession is the deed. And the nature of confession is not self-proclamation, but response to the given Word of God as it is heard by the church in that particular historical situation.

In this dynamic understanding of confessing as the responsible, obedient answer of the believing community to the claim of the Lord of the church in the particular historical situation (or *kairos),* as revealed in Scripture and enabled by prayer in the Holy Spirit, we are in fact exceedingly close to what at least some of us wil recognise as authentic Free Church theology. A classic exponent was the Scottish Congregationalist, P.T. Forsyth (1848-1921), often described in Britain as a Barthian before Barth thanks to his reaction against liberalism even prior to 1900. In certain respects, however, he also predates Bonhoeffer's 'dynamic confessionalism' in his repeated insistence that the freedom of the church is a *'founded* freedom', and one, moreover, with implications for the whole body politic in society. Thus:

> From first to last... Independency has pursued not a dogma but a polity based on a gospel. Its interest has not been pure doctrine through a church so much as a true church through a gospel, *a true church in a true state*[33] (emphasis mine).

Forsyth was acutely aware of the need for a firm anchorage of the Free Church in that which makes it free — the Gospel (for which read Bonhoeffer's 'Word'). Thereby he was also more aware than most of his Free Church contemporaries of the ambiguous possibilities of a universalistic worldly concern. The Independent (that is, including the Baptist) tradition 'has always had that sense of the real world which was so pre-eminent in Cromwell, and it has had the consequent temptation, when its dogmatic base was shaken or dissolved, of becoming the victim of that world.'[34] Not that he was in the least advocating a non-social, apolitical attitude. Forsyth was second to none in his social and political concern, and in fact was an exceedingly acute analyst of the shifting dynamics and polarities on the Edwardian scene in Britain. But he did recognize the problem of how the church as a gathered community can formulate prescriptions to the extent of a political ethic for the whole of society. Thereby he anticipates to an intriguing degree a number of the queries raised by Bonhoeffer in the later chapters of his *Ethics* where, we have seen, Bonhoeffer raises the question as to how the Confessing Church community can offer a word to the state, or 'solutions' to all the 'problem' areas of life. Forsyth regarded as simplistic the notion that Christianity 'has a direct political ethic,' suggesting instead that 'its direct action is to create a moral soul, and thus a social or national ethos, which then creates the public ethic.'[35] That is in fact what had happened in the contribution of Independency to the creation of Western democracy. Whereas Bonhoeffer saw the justification of the national church as lying in its ability to *become* a gathered or confessing church, Forsyth, by a nice converse, saw the justification of congregationalism consisting in the ability of the church as *free* to do what the church as established has failed to do: to relate Christianity to the whole realm of society and politics — an idea which he recognizes as the authentic 'genius' of the *idea* of establishment. Forsyth's writing, long neglected, can still be highly productive and there are many other parallels with both Barth and Bonhoeffer which cannot be explored here.

Dietrich Bonhoeffer, then, with his presentation of the ethically conscious Confessing Church encourages us, if we are also prepared to face his sharp challenges, to retrace and recover much that is most vital in the Free Church tradition. In the final analysis we have to admit there is a sense in which we feel compelled to concede to Bonhoeffer the last word even over one such as P.T. Forsyth. Historically, as confirmed by our experience both in Britain and South Africa (not to mention Germany), it has proved exceedingly difficult in the twentieth century for the Free Churches to maintain both their distinctness and their universal social commitment. Forsyth's warning has again been confirmed, that the Free Churches can so easily become the victims of the world they recognize (and even evangelize!). Having proclaimed freedom, they too easily allow the world to give them the freedom to occupy an assigned place which presently becomes a ghetto. But Forsyth's suggestion that the task of the church is to create some kind of moral soul in the body politic, has proved equally problematic. Something stiffer has to be built into our understanding of the church as the gathered community to define not only its 'task' but its actual status in relation to the world before God.

As we have seen, in the *Ethics* Bonhoeffer writes of the distinctness of the gathered congregation under the word of God as clearly as any Free Church theologian could. But no less emphatically does he recognize the *deputyship* of the church in relation to the world under God. Such a notion counteracts that perennial tendency of the Free Church to conceive of itself as gathered apart from the world and thereby privileged in its access to God over against the world; or, equally, that tendency to moral superiority which tends to conceive of 'witness' in terms of the self-advertisement of virtue; or just as pertinent, the assumption that the church already knows what is best for the world. The greater freedom which the Free Churches must rediscover is the freedom to stand with the suffering and needs of others. And thanks in no small measure to Bonhoeffer and the Confessing Church, it is being rediscovered. Nowhere is this more evident than in the recent (1977) confession produced jointly by the German-speaking Baptists of the Federal Republic, the Democratic Republic, Austria and Switzerland. The contrast with their earlier pietistic confession of the nineteenth century and from the Nazi period[36] could not be greater. On the church it states:

> The church of Jesus Christ responds to God's reconciling act in praise and worship. Bowing before God *she confesses her guilt* and receives from him forgiveness and the authority for her mission. In evangelization and service the Christian community bears witness to God's salvation *for all men*. She *intercedes* in prayer and in supplication *for all men and nations*[37] (emphases mine, as below).

Certain paragraphs from Section II, 'Christians in the World,' merit quoting in full:

> It is the will of God for the Christian church to be the salt of the earth and the light of the world. The church seeks no dominion in society or over society but is called and empowered for worship of God in the everyday life of this world and thus for the development of shared human life by the power of the Holy Spirit. The church as a whole and each of its members are ready for the responsibility of faith. They speak for God and his righteousness, and in their life as brothers and sisters God's gracious rule can be discerned.

> ... Because Christians rejoice in being accepted by God and called to be his co-workers, they live their faith in bearing witness to Christ personally, in *demonstrating their solidarity with people who are suffering,* in acts of personal assistance, and thus in obedience to the command that we love our neighbours. To take our stand for the truth of Jesus Christ also includes our readiness to accept disadvantage and even persecution.

> Because we have our origin in reconciliation with God, we are called also to serve the cause of reconciliation among men...
> [Christians] strive to eliminate any and all discrimination by person against person and work for peace in the world. The Christians' calling is to be validated precisely when in substantive issues *they must speak a resounding 'No'*. The readiness for reconciliation works for agreement, but it does not mean capitulation in the face of conflict or the suppression of real problems.

> Because we have our origin in God's justification of the ungodly, we are called *to serve the cause of justice among men*. Since Christians live in the liberty for which Christ has set them free, they *oppose every form of dependence that injures human dignity*. In the spirit of Jesus they support corresponding efforts *to liberate men from economic, social and racial oppression*. Accordingly, they contend for the basic freedoms of man, especially for freedom of belief and conscience.

A *rediscovery indeed of that 'founded freedom' which manifests itself in liberating others*. This is still very much a Free Church confession. Dietrich Bonhoeffer would not have written it as it stands. But it could hardly have been written without him and the confessing community he served. Creative figures do not necessarily turn us wholly into their disciples. They also make us reassess and value afresh what is ours already, but perhaps forgotten or as yet unrecognized. That is what Dietrich Bonhoeffer can do for our Free Church tradition.

NOTES

1. Cited in E. A. Payne, *The Free Church Tradition in the Life of England* (SCM Press, 1944), p. 34.
2. D. Bonhoeffer, *Letters and Papers from Prison* (SCM Press, 1971), p. 382ff.
3. See G. Balders, *Ein Herr, ein Glaube, eine Taufe. 150 Jahre Baptististengemeinde in Deutschland 1834-1984* (Oncken Verlag, 1985).
4. English edition, *The Social Teaching of the Christian Churches* (Allen and Unwin, 1931).
5. Ibid., p. 993.
6. Ibid., p. 819.
7. Bonhoeffer, *Sanctorum Communio* (Collins, 1963), p. 151.
8. Ibid., p. 152.
9. Ibid.
10. Ibid.
11. Ibid., p. 153.
12. Bonhoeffer, *Ethics* (SCM Press, 1955), p. 187.
13. *Sanctorum Communio,* p. 187ff.
14. Ibid., p. 190.
15. *Ethics,* p. 263.
16. Ibid., pp. 252-267.
17. Ibid., pp. 258-267.
18. Ibid., p. 264.
19. Ibid., p. 265.
20. Ibid., p. 266.
21. Balders, op. cit., pp. 95-97.
22. See e.g. G. Limouris (ed.), *Church, Kingdom, World. The Church as Mystery and Prophetic Sign,* Faith and Order Paper No. 130 (WCC: Geneva, 1986).
23. A. Wilkinson, *Dissent or Conform? War, Peace and the English Churches 1900-1945* (SCM Press, 1986).
24. 'Protestantism without Reformation,' in *No Rusty Swords,* ed. E. Robertson (Collins, 1965), p. 103.
25. Balders, *op. cit.,* p. 73.
26. *No Rusty Swords,* p. 105.
27. See Bonhoeffer, 'The Confessing Church and the Ecumenical Movement,' in *No Rusty Swords,* pp. 326-344. See also K. W. Clements, 'Bonhoeffer, Barmen and Anglo-Saxon Individualism,' *Journal of Theology for Southern Africa* (paper given at International Bonhoeffer Conference, Hirschluch, DDR, 1984).
28. 'After Ten Years,' *Letters and Papers,* p. 7.
29. J. Habgood, *Church and Nation in a Secular Age* (Darton, Longman and Todd, 1983), p. 10. For some British reflections on the Falklands episode and related issues of national loyalty, see K. W. Clements, *A Patriotism for Today. Love of country in dialogue with the witness of Dietrich Bonhoeffer* (Collins, 1986).
30. Ibid., p. 335.
31. E.g., *Letters and Papers,* p. 381.
32. *No Rusty Swords,* p. 337.
33. P.T. Forsyth, *Faith, Freedom and the Future* (Independent Press, edition 1955), p. 112.
34. Ibid.
35. Ibid., p. 126.
36. See, e.g., W.L. Lumpkin, *Baptist Confessions of Faith* (Valley Forge, 1969).
37. English version in G.K. Parker, *Baptist in Europe. History and Confession of Faith* (Broadman Press, 1982). Note the reference to the confession by the church of its own guilt. In 1984, at the European Baptist Congress in Hamburg, the Baptist Unions of both the German Federal Republic and the German Democratic Republic made public act of confession and repentance for the failure of their churches to speak and act against the iniquities of the Third Reich. This occasion was the fiftieth anniversary of the Congress of the Baptist World Alliance meeting in Berlin in 1934, at which event the German Baptists had made clear their welcome given to Hitler's accession. See K. W. Clements, 'A Question of Freedom? British Baptists and the German Church Struggle,' in *Baptists in the Twentieth Century,* ed. Clements (Baptist Historical Society, 1983), and also Clements op. cit., note 27 above.

The Freedom of the Church and

the Liberation of Society

BONHOEFFER ON THE FREE CHURCH, AND THE 'CONFESSING CHURCH' IN SOUTH AFRICA[1]

John W. de Gruchy

The year 1988 marks the tercentenary of the arrival of the French Huguenots in what is now South Africa. President P.W. Botha's major address at the celebration of this event stressed the fact that the Huguenots came to the Cape in search of religious freedom. This, he maintained, was their most important legacy. What was not mentioned was the fact that the Huguenots, in their struggle for religious freedom, also found it necessary to develop a theology of resistance to an unjust state. Religious freedom was inseparable from political struggle and social liberation.

What constitutes the freedom of the church? Is it to be confined to the freedom of worship or does it, as *The Kairos Document* insists, also include the freedom to engage prophetically in the struggle for justice and liberation in society and, if need be, to resist unjust laws?[2] What is the relationship between the freedom of the church and the struggle for a genuinely democratic society? In the South African context, we may ask more specifically about the relationship between the freedom of the church and the freedoms which are articulated in the *Freedom Charter*, to which many involved in the struggle for a democratic South Africa are committed.[3]

Alongside these fundamental questions is a further query of particular interest to those who regard the Free Church tradition as their heritage, namely, do the churches which claim to be rooted in this tradition really represent its ethos in our present historical context? And if not, what is there in that tradition which needs to be retrieved, restated, and lived out once again in our historical context?

Such questions are fundamental to the struggle of the church in South Africa today, as they are in many other contemporary situations of injustice and oppression. Moreover, as Dietrich Bonhoeffer perceived increasingly clearly, they were fundamental to the struggle of the church in Germany during the Third Reich. So we engage in dialogue with Bonhoeffer in the conviction that his insights can clarify and deepen our understanding of what it means and what it does not mean for the church to be free, and how this relates to the struggle for political liberation.

In anticipation of what is to come, we may state at the outset that the freedom of the church has to do with its freedom to confess Christ prophetically, and therefore to do so contextually and concretely. As in previous attempts to engage in dialogue with Bonhoeffer's theology in relation to the South African context,[4] we begin with a South African case study which illustrates the problem to be considered.

1

State versus 'Confessing Church' in South Africa:
A Case Study

Following the government's clampdown on seventeen extra-parliamentary opposition political organizations and the banning of eighteen community leaders on February 24, 1988, several church leaders, including Archbishop Desmond Tutu, Dr. Allan Boesak, Catholic Archbishop Stephen Naidoo, and the Reverend Frank Chikane, general-secretary of the SACC, issued a strong statement in which they committed themselves to exploring every possible avenue for continuing *'to carry on the activities which have been banned in so far as we believe they are mandated by the gospel.'*[5]

An emergency meeting of leaders belonging to the member churches of the SACC was convened in Johannesburg on Monday, February 29. The meeting prepared a petition to be personally delivered by them to the State President the following day in Cape Town. After a service of worship in St. George's Cathedral on Tuesday, March 1, twenty-five denominational leaders processed to the Houses of Parliament nearby. The procession was halted by the police at the outer precincts of Parliament and the leaders were all arrested, though released shortly thereafter.

In their two-page petition to President Botha and members of Parliament, the church leaders expressed their strongest exception to recent state action: 'We believe,' they stated, 'that the Government, in its actions over recent years, but especially by last week's action, has chosen a path for the future which will lead to violence, bloodshed and instability.' Referring to the church, they reiterated what had previously been said:

> The activities which have been prohibited *are central to the proclamation of the gospel* in our country and we must make it clear that, no matter what the consequences, we will explore every possible avenue for continuing the activities which you have prohibited other bodies from undertaking.

They then listed these activities:

> We will not be stopped from campaigning for the release of prisoners, from calling for clemency for those under sentence of death, from calling for the unbanning of political organizations, from calling for the release of political leaders to negotiate the transfer of power to all the people of our country, from commemorating significant events in the life of our nation, from commemorating those who have died in what you call 'riots', or from calling on the international community to apply pressure to force you to the negotiating table.

Those familiar with the better moments in the history of the Free Church tradition will readily detect in such an utterance a powerful affirmation of that tradition's attempt to defend human rights and liberties as an integral part of the mission of the Christian church.

In a political address shortly after the church leaders' protest march, the State President roundly condemned the march as an act of civil disobedience.[6] The same theme was echoed on South African television, in the government-oriented press, and in statements issued by the leadership of the Dutch Reformed Church. Severe personal attacks were made on Archbishop Tutu and Dr. Boesak.

The next moment occurred in the growing conflict related to the impending execution on March 19 of the 'Sharpeville Six.' These six blacks had been condemned to death for their alleged part in the murder of a black town councillor in Sharpeville in 1984. For many within the black townships, town councillors are a symbol of the government's policy and are regarded as sellouts and traitors to the cause of liberation. This does not mean that murder can be condoned, but in this particular instance it was legally debatable whether the accused were in fact guilty. In an attempt to prevent the execution at the last moment, Archbishop Tutu met with President Botha on Wednesday, March 16. The meeting went smoothly while the Archbishop presented the case for a reprieve. But once that had been dealt with the President presented the Archbishop with a letter in response to the church leaders' petition. The President then severely admonished Tutu for his role in the illegal march on Parliament, angrily accusing him of supporting terrorism. 'You owe all Christians an explanation of your exact standpoint.' Botha wrote in his letter:

> for we are all adults, and the time for bluffing and games is long past. The question must be posed whether you are acting on behalf of the kingdom of God, or the kingdom promised by the ANC (i.e. the African National Congress) and the SACP (i.e. South African Communist Party)? If it is the latter, say so, but do not then hide behind the structures and the cloth of the Christian church, because Christianity and Marxism are irreconcilable opposites.

The letter concluded with the President questioning the right of the church to become involved in 'secular power-play.' After a heated exchange of words, Tutu left, and the attacks on him and other church leaders were continued on television and in the government-oriented press. The leaders of the Dutch Reformed Church also issued a statement condemning the actions of Archbishop Tutu and Dr. Boesak.

The following day a gathering of Anglican bishops, assembled in Pretoria for a long planned meeting with leaders of the Dutch Reformed Church, issued a statement in which they indicated that they had cancelled the talks in view of the attacks made upon the Archbishop. They went on to make it clear that such action would not split the leadership of the Anglican church. Moreover, they insisted that Tutu's actions were in accord with Anglican church policy and not dictated by the ANC or SACP. On the contrary, they argued, the totalitarian and dictatorial actions of the State in banning political organizations promoted 'Marxism and revolution.' Taking the strongest exception to 'Mr. Botha's abuse of the Archbishop at their meeting,' the bishops stated that if the authorities took 'action against Desmond Tutu and Allan Boesak for their witness to the gospel, it will be an attack on the Church of Christ and it will precipitate a major State-Church confrontation.'

A subsequent meeting on March 22 of all the Anglican bishops came out with a clear statement of support for their Archbishop and the other church leaders. The bishops questioned

> the right of the State President to arrogate to himself, as we believe he has done, the right to define what

is spiritual or to decide what is valid Christian witness... *The Church has a spiritual responsibility not only to individual Christians but to the lives of nations and we shall endeavour to meet that responsibility.*

Affirming their commitment to oppose apartheid, they rejected the alternatives which the State President had put to Tutu:

> The State President would have it that South Africans must choose between the Government's programme and atheistic Marxism. We reject this definition of the choice and reaffirm our commitment to a just, democratic and sharing society reflecting the values of the Kingdom of God.

For several years now (the beginnings may be traced back to the launching of the Programme to Combat Racism in the early 1970s) the South African government has sought to divide those churches critical of apartheid, and, in a variety of indirect ways, to woo their more conservative and moderate members, both black and white, into new ecclesiastical organizations. More recently the state has attempted to undermine the authority of the church leaders, thus weakening their base and support. With its control of television, the state has been able to attack them with impunity, and there has been little opportunity for reply or for the challenging of misinformation and distortion. In this the state has been ably assisted by right-wing American fundamentalists, and by a coterie of right-wing Christian groups and organizations in South Africa.[7]

The government clearly wants to convey to the world that its reformist policies are Christian and moral, that it does have the support of most of the people, black and white, except radicals (both right-wing and left-wing), Communists and terrorists, and that it is determined not to surrender power to those who would destroy 'Christian civilization.' The actions of the church leaders are therefore depicted and rejected as part of the 'total onslaught' against South Africa by the Communist world and therefore destructive of the freedom of religion and the church. As President Botha said in his letter to Archbishop Tutu: 'You are no doubt aware that the expressed intention of the planned revolution by the ANC/SACP alliance is to ultimately transform South Africa into an atheistic Marxist state, where freedom of faith and worship will surely be among the first casualties.' Likewise, in a letter to the Reverend Frank Chikane, President Botha wrote: 'I request you urgently not to abuse the freedom of religion and worship, and the goodwill of the people and the Government of South Africa for the pursuance of secular and revolutionary objectives.'

Nothing could pose the problem of the freedom of the church more sharply. President Botha's challenge reflects one very dominant position within Christian tradition, namely, that the freedom of the church has to do with the space it is given by the state in which to function. His challenge also reflects the rhetoric of the religious right in many Western countries, not least the United States, for whom any kind of socialist state, whether democratic or not, means the death of religious freedom and the end of the freedom of the church. Moreover, the simplistic identification of all effective protest as Communist inspired, or as leading inevitably to a Communist state, is not only a propaganda ploy, but it also reveals a perception of social reality and of the meaning of Christian faith and witness which is totally at variance with that of the church leaders and many other Christians and churches in South Africa and throughout the world.

If, however, we cast our minds back to the Weimar Republic, and therefore to the historical context within which Dietrich Bonhoeffer began to develop his theology, we are reminded that the position articulated by President Botha (or his theological advisors) is not very different from that adopted by both the Vatican and evangelical church leaders at that time.[8] Indeed, the fear of Bolshevism and the consequences which its expansion would have for the church united the majority of Christians in Germany and made them open to National Socialism. We turn, then, to reflect on the way in which Bonhoeffer responded to this challenge and more specifically to the question of the freedom of the church in order to clarify the issues involved and to provide us with a way of relating to them in confessing Jesus Christ

2

The Freedom of the Church for Christ and Humanity:
exploring a Dialectic in Bonhoeffer's Ecclesiology

In what follows, we shall trace a trajectory on the Free Church and the freedom of the church in Bonhoeffer's theology from *Sanctorum Communio* to his prison reflections, giving special attention to some of the key insights found in his *Ethics*. We will assume that the development of Bonhoeffer's ecclesiology is determined by the development of his Christology, and therefore that his understanding of the freedom of the church is shaped by his understanding of the freedom of God in Christ. We will also take for granted that Bonhoeffer's ecclesiology was affected by the changing circumstances of his historical context and the various ways in which theology developed.

James Woelfel has rightly spoken of the 'dialectic reality' of Bonhoeffer's ecclesiology.[9] This dialectic is grounded in the way in which Bonhoeffer relates the divine and human natures of the church,[10] and finds expression in a variety of ways in his ecclesiology. The trajectory we shall trace on the Free Church and freedom of the church clearly shows one dimension of this dialectic, that between the church as a public institution with a national responsibility, and the church as a gathered, confessing community. Both elements are held together in tension, albeit in different ways, from *Sanctorum Communio* to the prison letters.

2.1. *Sanctorum Communio as Volkskirche and Free Church*
In his discussion in *Sanctorum Communio* of the relation between the empirical and the essential church, Bonhoeffer insists that the 'kingdom of Christ or the church' is 'present to us in concrete historical form' as a national church (*Volkskirche*) and not as a 'gathered' church (*Freiwilligkeitskirche*). The major reason he gives for this derives from the nature of the proclaimed 'Word':

> The sanctorum communio, with the preaching of the Word which it bears and by which it is borne, extends beyond itself and addresses all those who might belong to it, this is part of its nature.[11]

177

Bonhoeffer is here affirming the responsibility which the church has for the nation in which it is set as a whole. In doing so he insists that this is not only because we have no right to separate the 'wheat' from the 'tares,' but because it is of the essence of the church and the nature of the proclaimed 'Word' which brings it into being and sustains it.

Nevertheless, Bonhoeffer is aware that the idea of the 'gathered' church, which is central to the free Church tradition,[12] is also of the essence of the church. By 'gathered' church is meant a church comprised of committed rather than nominal members, the latter being the real danger within a national church. In fact, as early as 1924, when as a student he had visited Rome, Bonhoeffer seriously questioned whether the Protestant church should ever have allowed itself to become a state church, and whether in doing so it did not betray its Reformation heritage.[13] So it is not surprising that Bonhoeffer wrote in his dissertation:

> The *sanctorum communio,* which by its very nature presents itself as a national church, equally demands the gathered church, and continually establishes itself as such: that is, the *sanctorum communio* sustains the other, as it were, in whom the possibility of becoming 'effective' members of the church is dormant, by virtue of the Word which constitutes it and which it preaches.[14]

Thus, alongside his stressing the national character of the church as part of its *essence,*[15] Bonhoeffer also states that 'the church's essential character is that of a gathered church.'[16] Indeed, in his critical discussion in *Sanctorum Communio* of Weber and Troeltsch's 'church and sect' typology, Bonhoeffer later insists that the church 'is only a church insofar as it comes to be effectively willed by persons, i.e., as a gathered church.'[17] That is as strong an affirmation of Free Church ecclesiology as possible, emphasizing in particular the voluntary character of the church. But, for Bonhoeffer, it did not mean as a consequence a rejection of the church as *Volkskirche.*

Bonhoeffer regarded this dialectical relationship between *Volkskirche* and 'gathered' church as 'genuinely Lutheran.' It was not understood, as in the early Barth, as a dialectic between institution and event, or in Augustinian terms, as a division between the 'visible' and 'invisible' church. On the contrary, such false dichotomies were always rejected by Bonhoeffer as can be seen in his paper 'What is the Church?', where he insists that the two natures of the church, the human and the divine, coexist as one concrete reality in the world. This, too, is typical of genuinely Free Church ecclesiology. But unlike the Free Church tradition, in *Sanctorum Communio* Bonhoeffer insists that the *sanctorum communio* relates to the world, or is structured in the world, in a dialectical way both as *Volkskirche* and 'gathered' church.

The dialectic of *Volkskirche* and *Freiwilligkeitskirche,* or national and 'gathered' church, is one which derives from the nature of the proclaimed Word. The priority of the Word demands structures which enable the church to exercise its responsibility for the life of the nation as a whole (*Volkskirche*), and this in turn requires that the church be a confessing community of faithful people under the Word ('gathered' church). Both are visible and public, both are of the essence of the church as a divine-human reality called into being by the nature of the proclaimed Word. But they are distinct and complementary.

In one of the sections of *Sanctorum Communio* which was deleted from the published edition of 1930 (though included in the English translation as part of the text and now published in the notes of the new critical edition), Bonhoeffer included in his discussion on 'church and sect' the affirmation that 'the national church and the gathered church belong together', but with this critical qualification:

> it is all too obvious today that a national church, which is not continually pressing forward to be a confessing church, is in the greatest inner peril. There is a moment when the church dare not continue to be a national church, and this moment has come when the national church can no longer see how it can win through to being a gathered church.[18]

Such a moment occurred with the advent of the *status confessionis* in Nazi Germany. But this did not mean, as Bonhoeffer suggests in this statement, that he turned away from affirming the *sanctorum communio* as *Volkskirche* in favour of the establishing of a confessing Free Church. On the contrary, he decisively rejected this option. The question is why he did so.

2.2. *The Confessing Church as Reichskirche Not Free Church*
During the initial days of the *Kirchenkampf*, especially after the infamous Brown Synod in September 1933, the leaders of the emergent Confessing Church seriously considered establishing a Free Church. The idea of a Free Church was certainly very attractive for Bonhoeffer himself (had he not already embraced one element within the tradition by becoming a pacifist?) and he explored the possibilities for its establishment. Karl Barth was also strongly committed to the idea.[19] But after the Barmen and Dahlem synods and the launching of the 'Confessing Church'[20] there was a decisive turn away from any proposal for constituting the Confessing Church as a Free Church. On the contrary, Bonhoeffer assertively claimed that the Confessing Church was not a movement or a voluntary association alongside of the true national church, or an alternative church, but *the* Evangelical Church in Germany.[21] Writing from London on July 12, 1934, to Henriod of the World Alliance in Geneva, Bonhoeffer objects to the notion expressed by Henriod that the Barmen Synod has resulted in the constitution of a church which is distinct from that of the official German church.

> I think you are misrepresenting the legal construction of the Confessional Church in this point. There is not the claim or even the wish to be a Free Church besides the *Reichskirche,* but there is the claim to be the only theologically and legally legitimate Evangelical Church in Germany...[22]

The irony of this development becomes obvious when we recognize the extent to which the ecclesiology expressed in *The Cost of Discipleship* is, in many respects, that of the 'gathered' church and even a voluntary association. But for Bonhoeffer, the very idea of the church as a divine reality, political-ecclesial considerations aside, ruled out any notion of a voluntary association, even though it always included what was essential to the 'gathered' church. The 'gathered' church is not only of the essence of what Bonhoeffer captured in his distinction between 'cheap and costly grace', but also in his insistence on the boundaries of the church, its separation from the world, and the

179

visibility of the Christian community in the life of the world. It was not for nothing that Bonhoeffer had to defend himself against the charge of having become an Anabaptist!

The question must therefore be asked: why did Bonhoeffer so categorically reject the idea of the Free Church to which he was previously attracted and which, in important respects, is implicit in the ecclesiology of *Nachfolge*? First of all it must be stated that Bonhoeffer, in insisting on the Confessing Church as the true *Reichskirche*, was certainly not supporting the idea of a *Volkskirche* as understood by the *Deutsche Christen*.[23] In fact he no longer appears to use this word in any positive sense. For the *Deutsche Christen* a *Volkskirche* was a nationalist, *völkisch,* and therefore culturally and racially determined church that served the self-interests of the *Volk*. Bonhoeffer categorically rejected any such ecclesiology.

Secondly, Bonhoeffer wanted to insist, for theologically grounded political reasons, that the Confessing Church was not a sect or hole-in-the-corner affair, but *the* true Evangelical Church of the German people in continuity with the church of the Reformation. It was *this* church which had the real interests of the nation at heart, not the false 'official' church that had sold out to National Socialism. The true church of Jesus Christ had a responsibility to the German nation as a whole. It was not a Free Church, especially if by that was meant a voluntary association of people who had no responsibility for the welfare of the nation.

Thirdly, and this is the theological nub of the matter, the Confessing Church did not have to be a Free Church in order to exercise its freedom. Indeed, to become a Free Church under the circumstances would have meant that it would not have had the space or freedom in which to fulfill its prophetic task. Its freedom to do this derived from its faithful confession of Christ to the nation, not from any attempt to be constituted as a Free Church. Nevertheless, to be *the* Evangelical Church in Germany at this point in history, in order to be *for* the nation, it had to confess Christ *against* the nation and thus emphasize in its life the essence of the church as a 'gathered' church. In this way the dialectic between *Volkskirche* and *Freiwilligkeitskirche,* and therefore the essence of the church as both national and 'gathered', was maintained. The proclamation of the Word made this a necessity.

What this all meant was never more clearly spelled out by Bonhoeffer than in his remarkable essay on 'The Church and the Jewish Question' in 1933. For it is there that he speaks of the church's responsibility to act on behalf of the victims of society both for their sakes and, not least, for the nation and the state itself.[24] Indeed, we are here reminded most strikingly of the insistence of the South African church leaders that the church had the responsibility to do those humanitarian tasks which government action now prevents other organizations from doing. Bonhoeffer makes it abundantly clear that the freedom of the church is contingent upon such prophetic witness and action. Indeed, in this remarkable essay he anticipates what he would later refer to as the 'act of free responsibility' on behalf of the oppressed.

2.3. *The Freedom of the Church as Necessity not Possibility*
Bonhoeffer's knowledge of the Free Churches in Germany naturally determined the way in which he discussed the idea of a *Freiwilligkeitskirche* in *Sanctorum Communio*.

Later, as a student at Union Seminary and as a pastor in London, he encountered the tradition more directly and fully in its North American and British setting. There it had developed differently and played a much more significant ecclesiastical and public role for historical and cultural reasons. Bonhoeffer's essay on 'Protestantism without Reformation', written in August 1939, and therefore at the end of his participation in the *Kirchenkampf*, demonstrates his developed understanding and grasp of the strengths and weaknesses of this tradition, but also of its contextual character. Moreover, Bonhoeffer has by now clearly shifted away from relating the freedom of the church to a particular form of church structure. This comes out clearly in his comparison of Protestantism with and Protestantism without Reformation.

Bonhoeffer appropriately sets his comparison in the context of a discussion on 'Freedom':

> America calls herself the land of the free. Under this term today she understands the right of the individual to independent thought, speech and action. In this context, religious freedom is, for the American, an obvious possession. Church preaching and organization, the life of the communities can develop independently, without being molested. Praise of this freedom may be heard from pulpits everywhere, coupled with the sharpest condemnation of any limitation of such freedom which has taken place anywhere. Thus freedom here means possibility, the possibility of unhindered activity given by the world to the church.[25]

How different this was from the German cultural ethos and the historical agenda of the evangelical church, especially within the Third Reich. The difference was rooted, of course, in the distinct ways in which Europe and the United States had historically developed, and which led to very different ways of resolving the problem of relating church and state.

In the land of the Reformation the doctrine of the two kingdoms was operative in such a way that the church was prevented from exercising any politically critical or prophetic function. There the church might well have entered the political arena as the established *Volkskirche* which, by definition, had a national responsibility. But its very relationship to the state hamstrung its prophetic role. In the New World, on the other hand, the separation of church and state should have led even more decisively to the withdrawal of the church from the political arena. But, as Bonhoeffer discerned, it actually meant 'the victory of the church over any unbounded claim by the state.'[26] Indeed, in the United States 'the *church* claims for itself the right to speak and act in all matters of public life, for only so can the kingdom of God be built.'[27]

The question Bonhoeffer raises so sharply in this essay is, therefore, whether the cultural and political ethos of a nation, or the formal relationship between church and state, is really determinative for a proper understanding of the freedom of the church. Is the freedom of the church really contingent on being an established church or a free church? For Bonhoeffer this is clearly not the case. With emphasis he writes:

> *The freedom of the church is not where it has possibilities, but only where the Gospel really and in its own power makes room for itself on earth, even and precisely when no such possibilities are offered to it.* The essential freedom of the church is not a gift of the world to the church, but the freedom of the Word of God itself to gain a hearing.[28]

Bonhoeffer sees some real dangers for the church when it understands its freedom as a gift of the state, that is, as a result of some agreement with the world whereby the church becomes either established or technically free, or indeed, as Bonhoeffer detected in the United States, when it attempts to build the kingdom of God on earth.[29] Either way, this speeds up the process of secularization whereby the church in fact becomes captive to the world and surrenders its freedom under the Word of God. Thus, Bonhoeffer insists,

> Freedom as an institutional possession is not an essential mark of the church. It can be a gracious gift given to the church by the providence of God; but it can also be the great temptation to which the church succumbs in sacrificing its essential freedom to institutional freedom.[30]

Without recognizing the fact, the church is then in chains even though it regards itself as free. This has, indeed, been a trap into which many within the Free Church tradition have fallen, not least within South Africa. The freedom of the church is not a possibility derived from the state, but a necessity derived from the Word of God. The proclamation of the Word creates the freedom and space which the church needs to fulfill its task in its historical context. Hence,

> Only where this word can be preached concretely in the midst of historical reality, in judgment, command, forgiveness of sinners and liberation from all human institutions is there freedom of the church.[31]

Thus the freedom of the church is no longer contingent upon its formal relation to the state, but upon its concrete witness to the Gospel and therefore to genuinely human liberation.

2.4. *The Exclusive and Inclusive Claims of Christ*

Our discussion thus brings us to the important chapter in Bonhoeffer's *Ethics* on the 'Church and the World' where this relationship between the freedom of the church and human liberation is brought to a head. The dialectic which in *Sanctorum Communio* found expression in the relationship between *Volkskirche* and 'gathered' church is no longer focussed on the structure of the church but on its ability to respond to the inclusive and exclusive claims of Christ over the whole of social reality.

   In the opening section, Bonhoeffer refers to one of the 'most astonishing experiences during the years when everything Christian was sorely oppressed,' namely, the fact that the defenders of the endangered values of truth, justice and freedom found common cause with those Christians who remained faithful to the gospel.[32] In an Anglo-Saxon context, such as North America, this would not have been a cause for astonishment, quite the contrary. But in Germany, where there had been an historical estrangement of the values of the Enlightenment from the Christian church, an alienation exacerbated by developments within the Weimar Republic, it was an astonishing fact.[33] When all other opposition to injustice and oppression was being systematically denied by the state, the church was being forced to become the protector of the values of truth, justice and human freedom *in pursuing its mandate of proclaiming the claims of Christ*. For the origin of these values, Bonhoeffer asserts, is none other than Jesus Christ.[34]

This leads Bonhoeffer to his perceptive discussion on the claims of Christ which are at the same time inclusive of all who struggle for truly human values ('He that is not against us is for us,' Mark 9:40), and exclusive of all who deny Christ in denying such values ('He that is not with me is against me,' Matthew 12:30). This, as Bonhoeffer argues, is not simply a theoretical position, but one which has in fact taken place quite concretely in the confessing church.

> The exclusive demand for a clear profession of allegiance to Christ caused the band of confessing Christians to become ever smaller... then, precisely through this concentration on the essential the Church acquired an inward freedom and breadth which preserved her against any timid impulse to draw narrow limits, and there gathered around her men who came from very far away, and men to whom she could not refuse her fellowship and her protection; injured justice, oppressed truth, vilified humanity and violated freedom all sought for her, or rather for her Master, Jesus Christ.[35]

The freedom of the church is thus dependent upon her faithfulness in confessing Christ, irrespective of what this means in terms of the size of her space in the world. 'The greater the exclusiveness, the greater the freedom.' The true freedom of the church is an inward freedom derived from 'its concentration on the essential.'

Yet this exclusiveness must not be allowed to degenerate into fanaticism, any more than the church's openness must lead to the secularization or self-abandonment of the church. Geffrey Kelly rightly states that 'Bonhoeffer intuited a dynamic unity between church and world in which the secular and the Christian prevent each other from assuming any static independence apart from their mutual relationship in Christ.'[36] The clue lies in the genuine confessing of Christ over the whole of reality. 'The more exclusively we acknowledge and confess Christ as Lord, the more fully the wide range of his dominion will be disclosed to us.'[37]

Bonhoeffer thus ends his discussion by denying that this espousal by the church of humanizing values should be understood as an apologetic ploy designed to further its triumphal expansion in the world. On the contrary, in faithfully confessing Christ before the world it becomes ever more clear how much these values have their origin in Christ, and therefore confessing him as Lord includes their affirmation in word and deed.

It follows, then, that the church does not have to justify its commitment to the struggle for truth, justice and freedom; on the contrary, these values have to be understood and therefore justified in terms of their origin in Christ. At the profoundest level their true meaning can only be discerned in Christ.

> It is not Christ who must justify himself before the world by the acknowledgement of the values of justice, truth and freedom, but it is these values which have come to need justification, and their justification can only be Jesus Christ. It is not that a Christian culture must make the name of Jesus Christ acceptable to the world; but the crucified Christ has become the refuge and the justification, the protection and the claim for the higher values and their defenders that have fallen victim to suffering.[38]

Thus the discovery of the freedom of the church in the process of affirming those values which liberate from oppression, rather than dehumanize, is Christologically grounded, indeed, grounded in a theology of the cross. For 'it is with the Christ who is persecuted and who suffers in his church that justice, truth, humanity and freedom now seek refuge...'[39] In this way, then, the church exercises her public, national task, for it protects these values without which a nation cannot live in justice and peace, and it sides with those who are committed to the struggle for the liberation of the nation from oppression. Yet, in doing so, it does not forsake its identity as church, as the community of gathered disciples. In Christ it discovers that its identity as a confessing community and its relevance as a public institution are inseparably bound together in the service of truth, justice and freedom.

2.5. *Deputyship and the 'Act of Free Responsibility'*
Bonhoeffer's discussion in the *Ethics* of 'The Structure of the Responsible Life', where he deals with Deputyship and Freedom, is not primarily about the church but about the individual Christian in his or her life before God and neighbour.[40] Indeed, we now find ourselves at the heart of Bonhoeffer's own moral struggle, as well as that of the conspirators, that small band of men who were, in their own way, not against but for Christ. Now we are face to face not with the freedom of the Church but our personal freedom, for at that moment in the historical saga the church had squandered and lost its freedom. All depended upon free men and women who knew their responsibility and who were prepared to act on behalf of others, even if it meant sacrificing their own liberty or even moral righteousness in order to do so. Now it is 'the free venture' which 'knows itself as the divine necessity.'[41] So the dialectic between responsibility for the nation (*Volkskirche*) and the need for personal commitment ('gathered church') is now personalized.

The act of deputyship on behalf of the nation and its victims was also an act of deputyship on behalf of a church that had failed to exercise its freedom. This failure paradoxically began, as Bonhoeffer perceived, when its main consideration became its own freedom in relation to the state. It stood up for its own cause rather than the needs of the world.[42] From the beginning, the *Kirchenkampf* was about the freedom of the church to be the church, not about the freedom of the church to speak and act on behalf of the Jews and other victims of Nazi terror. The issues debated at Barmen and Dahlem were vital, but the issue not debated was even more vital. In hindsight, the Confessing Church missed the real point of the confession it was making because it failed to discern the connection between prophetic witness on behalf of human rights and freedoms and the freedom of the Gospel and the church. Likewise, by focusing on church-state relations and not the rights and liberties of Nazi-victims, the Vatican concordat prevented the Catholic church from exercising its prophetic freedom.

Thus it was that Bonhoeffer turned away from the Confessing Church to engage with others who were committed to human rights, truth, justice and freedom and, in the 'act of free responsibility' on behalf of the victims, surrendered his life.

2.6. *The Church for Others as the Truly Free Church*
Our tracing of the 'freedom of the church' trajectory in Bonhoeffer's ecclesiology must

end by referring briefly to the way in which it is expressed in his prison theology. There we discern the same dialectic of which we have been speaking, though it is couched in radically new language and concepts. The ecclesiology of *Letters and Papers from Prison* is an ecclesiology which is open to the world, a church which is obedient to 'Jesus, the man for others.' In this way it fulfills the intention of the national church as a church for all people, a church concerned about the nation and issues of social justice and righteousness. It is a public church at the centre of the city rather than a privatized church gathered on the periphery, as many modern day so-called 'Free' churches have become.

Yet, at the same time, it is a church which has given up on all the privileges of the traditional church, with its clergy depending entirely on the freewill offerings of its members.[43] This means, in effect, that the 'gathered' church has become a voluntary association and that Bonhoeffer's ecclesiology is now, in the best sense, Free Church, though different from what the Free Church denominations have become in either the new or old worlds.

Moreover, the church without privileges, while open to the world and existing for others, nevertheless practices the *Arkandisziplin*, a life of worship and prayer that characterizes the community of committed disciples of a truly 'gathered church.' The church is the community of those who are both 'called forth' from the world, and yet who belong 'wholly to the world.'[44] That is how the dialectic of the national or public, yet free and 'gathered' church works itself out in Bonhoeffer's final theological thoughts.[45] And it is in this way that it truly confesses Christ. In fact, Bonhoeffer's vision of the church in prison is indicative of what the Confessing Church might have been if it had listened to the counsel of Karl Barth and decided to relinquish any claim to being the *Reichskirche* in 1934. But whether that would then have been right and appropriate is now impossible to say unless, that is, in doing so, the Confessing Church had become free to speak and act prophetically for the victims of terror.

3

The Confessing and Prophetic Church as the truly Free Church: The Freedom of the Church in South Africa

The problem of defining what constitutes a Free Church is widely recognized. Indeed, it has been suggested that the confusion is so great that the concept 'in its traditional sense is no longer useful.'[46] Nevertheless, there is good historical reason to confine its use to those 'gathered' churches which refuse any state establishment and are therefore comprised of members who freely commit themselves to Christ and the community of faith. This tradition has been embodied historically in the Baptist and Congregational churches in South Africa.

The problem is, however, that this understanding of the church has become increasingly universal. In fact, since 1875 when the 'Voluntary Principle' Bill was adopted by the Cape Parliament, and later by the Constitution of the Union of South Africa in

1910, there has been no state church in South Africa; though because the Dutch Reformed Church has functioned as the *Volkskerk* of the Afrikaner, it has, in many ways, been a 'state' church.[47]

In situations like South Africa it might well be argued, then, that the Anglican Church, despite its Erastian heritage, is now a Free Church. Indeed, this is particularly pertinent precisely because of its strong opposition to the state and its apartheid policies. The same could be said of other churches which are not Free Church by tradition, such as the Roman Catholic Church. In fact, the 'levelling' of all churches to the formal status of 'free church' opens up ecumenical possibilities otherwise very difficult, especially in enabling the churches to become confessing communities.

In other contexts the same would apply. Certainly the Catholic 'base communities' in Latin America embody something of the essence of the Free Church tradition, and it is not for nothing that Nicholas Lash has suggested 'that none of the changes in Catholic Christianity which have occurred in recent decades are of more far-reaching potental significance than what we might call the recovery of the ''congregationalist'' element in Catholicism.'[48] It might also be argued that many of the African indigenous churches in South Africa embody the key elements of the Free Church tradition as 'gathered' and 'voluntary.'

But just as it may now be true that other church traditions embody crucial elements of the Free Church tradition, by historical circumstance perhaps more than by choice, it may also be asked to what extent the churches of this tradition have lost their vision of what it means for the church to be free today. To what extent is their historical protest and affirmation a thing of the past rather than a contribution of the present? Is it not now urgently necessary for those elements in the tradition which are of vital importance for the witness of the church today to be retrieved? Indeed, it might be asked, is not this process of retrieval in fact not taking place before our eyes as the churches in South Africa struggle to confess their faith in action and so fulfill their responsibility to the nation?

What is of crucial importance in all this is not whether the Free Churches per se continue, but whether the church in every context freely and prophetically confesses its faith in Jesus Christ over the whole of reality. In other words, what is at stake is not a tradition that must be preserved in some formal way, but the freedom of the church in the service of the gospel of the kingdom of God. And this is precisely the essence of a truly 'confessing church', whatever its formal relationship to the nation.

In the same way as the definition of the Free Church has become problematic, so also the traditional ways of relating church and state within a Constantinian framework have also become largely problematic since the Reformation.[49] This is not to suggest that the statutory separation of church and state, or the constitutional defense of religious liberty — formal as they may be in some places, as well as absent or curtailed in others — are no longer important. On the contrary, the safeguarding of a proper formal and legal relationship between church and state and the safeguarding of religious liberty for all faiths are of great importance. This is certainly of fundamental importance for the Free Church tradition. But these formal arrangements do not constitute the freedom of the church to proclaim the gospel in its fulness. As Lukas

Vischer has put it:

> Reflections on the proper relationship between church and state are, therefore, in the last analysis, only of secondary importance. They can help us to describe the ideal conditions for the witness of the church. But the witness itself stems from another source.[50]

In the light of our discussion, we turn again to the case study with which we began. President Botha is articulating a position traditionally held since Constantine and reaffirmed at the time of the Protestant reformation, namely, that the freedom of the church is something which is granted and guaranteed by the state. Although this understanding of ecclesial freedom was challenged by the Radical Reformers and their heirs within the Free Church tradition, it was assumed and accepted by the Magisterial Reformers. President Botha's theological advisers stand in that tradition, the tradition of the Lutheran two kingdoms reinterpreted by neo-Calvinism.

But President Botha's position is also one which was widely held by both the Vatican and the Evangelical Church in Germany during the Weimar Republic, namely, that those Christians who support a liberal or social democratic form of government are aiding a Marxist takeover, and that if a socialist or Marxist state comes into being, it will inevitably mean a denial of the freedom of the church. Therefore, as was argued in Germany and Rome in the 1920s, largely based on the experience of the church in Russia after the revolution, it is better both for the future of the state and the church, and therefore for the preservation of 'Christian civilization', that Christians unite in opposition to the forces of liberalism, socialism, and Marxism, even if this means the denial of some democratic liberties and the acceptance of some form of totalitarian government.[51] The freedom of the church, in this scheme of things, is something to be defended against what others perceive to be the forces of liberation, rather than be an instrument of social freedom and democracy.

As far as the church leaders in South Africa and, more broadly, the 'confessing church', are concerned, the policy and power of the nationalist government must be opposed in obedience to the gospel and in the interests of truth, justice, and freedom, and therefore a peaceful future. These are the policies which are destroying 'Christian civilization', not the other way around. The only way forward is through negotiations in which all people, including political exiles and prisoners, are free to participate as equals, and not on the basis of ethnicity. Such a step alone will prevent the escalation of violent conflict and lay the basis for a united nation as envisaged in *The Freedom Charter*.

This highlights and brings us back to the problem which the churches see in the recent action taken by the government against left-wing socio-political organizations. Such action seriously reduces the possibility of negotiation, and prevents certain necessary and humane social tasks from being undertaken by the churches, which brought them into conflict with the state. The churches see this as part of their responsibility on behalf of both the nation and the victims of apartheid. If they surrender this responsibility, they actually surrender their freedom, even though they may gain space from the state.

187

Thus, on the one hand, the South African authorities insist that there is religious freedom in South Africa, and moreover, that the government and its policies are the sole guarantee of that freedom and the future of Christianity in South Africa. On the other hand, the church leaders understand the freedom of the church not as a possibility given to it by the state but as an evangelical necessity, an integral part of its divine mandate, which includes its calling to participate in the struggle for justice and liberation in society, if need be, in resistance to the state. This, in essence, is what the freedom of the church and therefore a free church is about. And it is this which the 'confessing church' in South Africa is discovering in its attempts to be faithful to the gospel.

NOTES

1. This paper relates to that of Keith Clements' on 'The Freedom of the Church: Bonhoeffer and the Free Church Tradition.' Both of us are rooted in the Free Church tradition (Clements as an English Baptist and myself as a South African Congregationalist), yet we are also concerned about the failure of that tradition to be true to its confessing and prophetic ethos in our respective situations. It is our shared conviction that Bonhoeffer provides critical insights and resources which can help us retrieve those elements within the Free Church tradition that are essential for the church as a whole (and not just the so called 'Free Churches') if it is to be a confessing and prophetic community today. By 'confessing church' in South Africa is meant that coalition of churches and church groups which reject apartheid as a heresy and share in the struggle for a more just, non-racial and democratic South Africa.
2. *The Kairos Document: Challenge to the Church,* Revised Second Edition, Institue for Contextual Theology (Johannesburg, 1986).
3. On the Freedom Charter, see Raymond Suttner and Jeremy Cronin, *30 Years of the Freedom Charter* (Johannesburg: Ravan, 1986).
4. John W. de Gruchy, *Bonhoeffer and South Africa: Theology in Dialogue* (Grand Rapids: Eerdmans, 1986).
5. This and the extracts which follow will be found in full in 'Documentation' in the *Journal of Theology for Southern Africa,* No. 63 (June 1988). The emphasis here and in what follows is intended to highlight crucial elements in developing a theology of a confessing and prophetic, and therefore a free church.
6. South African law not only denies the right of such public protest, but is particularly severe on any such action within the vicinity of Parliament.
7. See Harald Winkler, 'Final Report of Pilot Study on Right Wing Church Groups,' Department of Religious Studies, University of Cape Town, 1988.
8. See Klaus Scholder, *The Churches and the Third Reich,* Volume One, 1918-1934 (London: SCM, 1987), chapters 8-10.
9. James W. Woelfel, *Bonhoeffer's Theology: Classical and Revolutionary* (Nashville: Abingdon, 1970), chapter 7.
10. See his draft paper on 'What is the Church?' (1932) in *No Rusty Swords* (London: Collins, 1970), p.149f.
11. Dietrich Bonhoeffer, *The Communion of Saints* (New York: Harper & Row, 1960), p. 151.
12. See John W. Grant, *Free Churchmanship in England: 1870-1940* (London: Independent Press, n.d.), p. 6ff. On the difficulty of defining what is precisely meant by a 'Free Church' see Donald F. Durnbaugh, *The Believers' Church: the History and Character of Radical Protestantism* (London: Macmillan, 1968), p. 4ff.
13. Eberhard Bethge, *Dietrich Bonhoeffer* (Munich: Chr. Kaiser, 1967), pp. 89-90. See also Durnbaugh, op. cit., p. 185.
14. *The Communion of Saints,* p. 152.
15. Woelfel overstates the case when he says that Bonhoeffer 'never conceives of its essence in institutional

but rather in personalist terms.' Woelfel, op. cit., p. 176. This does not gainsay the fact that the *sanctorum communio* is fundamentally, of course, a 'community of persons.'

16. Ibid.
17. Ibid., p. 186.
18. Ibid., p. 189f. See the new critical edition of *Sanctorum Communio* (DBW 1) edited by Joachim von Soosten (Munich: Chr. Kaiser Verlag, 1986), p. 288, n. 410.
19. See Durnbaugh, op. cit., p. 185.
20. Eberhard Bethge, *Dietrich Bonhoeffer* (London Collins, 1967), p. 250.
21. Ibid., p. 414f.
22. Dietrich Bonhoeffer, *Gesammelte Schriften,* Band 1 (Munich: Chr. Kaiser, 1958), p. 201.
23. On the ambiguous meaning of *Volkskirche* see Scholder, op. cit., p. 209. Similarly, on the significance of the use of the term *Reichskirche* at that time, see ibid., p. 280 and p. 283.
24. Bonhoeffer, *No Rusty Swords,* p. 217f.
25. *No Rusty Swords,* p. 99f.
26. Ibid., p. 104.
27. Ibid.
28. Ibid., p. 100.
29. Dietrich Bonhoeffer, *Ethics* (New York: Macmillan, 1976), p. 104f.
30. *No Rusty Swords*, p. 100.
31. Ibid., p. 101.
32. Dietrich Bonhoeffer, *Ethics* (New York: Macmillan, 1976), p. 55f.
33. Scholder, op. cit., chapter 1.
34. Bonhoeffer, *Ethics,* p. 56.
35. Ibid., p. 58.
36. Geffrey B. Kelly, *Liberating Faith: Bonhoeffer's Message for Today* (Minneapolis: Augsburg, 1984), p. 97.
37. Bonhoeffer, *Ethics,* p. 58.
38. Ibid., p. 59.
39. Ibid.
40. Bonhoeffer, *Ethics,* p. 224ff.
41. Ibid., p. 249.
42. Dietrich Bonhoeffer, *Letters and Papers from Prison* (London: SCM, 1971), p. 381.
43. Ibid., p. 382.
44. Ibid., p. 280f.
45. Ibid., pp. 280, 382f.
46. Peter Meinhold quoted by Durnbaugh, op. cit., p. 8.
47. See John W. de Gruchy, 'Religious Liberty and the Freedom of the Church: Reflections from within the Context of South Africa' in *Faith and Freedom: A Tribute to Franklin Littell,* ed. Richard Lobowitz (New York: Pergamon Press, 1987), p. 129f.; David Bosch, 'The Fragmentation of Afrikanerdom and the Afrikaner Churches' in Charles Villa-Vicencio and John W. de Gruchy (eds.): *Resistance and Hope: South African Essays in Honour of Beyers Naude* (Cape Town: David Philip; Grand Rapids: Eerdmans, 1985), p. 61ff.
48. Nicholas Lash, *Theology on the Way to Emmaus* (London: SCM, 1986), p. 199. See also Leonardo Boff, *Ecclesiogenesis: The Base Communities Reinvent the Church* (New York: Orbis, 1986).
49. See *Church and State: Opening a New Ecumenical Discussion* (Geneva: WCC, 1978), p. 7f.
50. *Church and State,* p. 15.
51. See Klaus Scholder, *The Churches and the Third Reich,* volume one, 1918-1934 (London: SCM, 1987), chapters 8-10, especially p. 224.

Hopeless and Promising Godlessness

Martin Kuske

Theses for the Fifth International Bonhoeffer Society Conference
Amsterdam, June 13-19, 1988

1. In his *Ethik,* Bonhoeffer considers godlessness in Fragment III, 'Ethik als Ge-staltung', pp. 74f., 109f. ('Ethics as Formation') and in Fragment VII, 'Das "Ethi-sche" and das "Christliche" als Thema', pp. 314f. ('The "Ethical" and the "Christian" as a Theme'). He speaks of 'hopeless' and 'promising' godlessness on pages 109 and following.

2. On pages 74 and 314 and following, Bonhoeffer argues more on a theological-principial basis, and on pages 109 and following he argues more on a theological-historical basis.   •

3.1. The love of God, which does not withdraw itself 'from reality into remote noble souls... embraces even the most abysmal godlessness of the world' (p. 75).

3.2. The context here defines godlessness — based on German fascism — as in-humanity in practice.

4.1. This character also brings with it the hopeless godlessness of the West, since it divinizes man, proclaims nihilism, and leads to self-destruction. It is 'religion born of enmity toward God.'

4.2. Bonhoeffer first (p. 109) classifies very different forms of godlessness together under the type 'hopeless godlessness', and then focuses on that godlessness which masquerades as religious and Christian when in fact it is pious and hopeless and has corrupted the churches. Is Bonhoeffer dealing primarily here with the support which the majority of evangelical Christians in Germany gave to fascism?

4.3. Whatever the case, promising godlessness, with its anti-religious and anti-church expressions, is 'the protest against pious godlessness.' Moreover, it preserves 'the heritage of a true faith in God, and a true church.' Are the 'good' of chapter II, who resist fascism, representatives of such a promising godlessness?

5. The unusual thing about the statements on the godless world in Fragment VII is that Bonhoeffer here connects godlessness with the cross of Jesus Christ. Through the cross, the whole world became godless, and the cross of reconciliation is liberation to live in the midst of the God-less world. This life — as promising godlessness — is a renunciation of a divinization of the world.

6.1. With his remarks on godlessness in *Ethik* Bonhoeffer fulfills the task he described in the foreword to *Nachfolge,* that what matters for those who 'take' the narrow way of churchly decision, 'is that they at the same time "remain with the weak and the godless in the fullness of God's 'philanthropy' (Titus 3:4)"' (*Nachfolge,* p. 11).

6.2. With those remarks Bonhoeffer also prepares for what he would write on July 7, 1944, about suffering with people and the 'suffering of God for the godless world' and also about how 'The mature world is godless, and perhaps precisely on that account closer to God than the immature world.'

7. Bonhoeffer's statements on godlessness, which have won a definite place in history, oblige Christians and churches to measure their own godlessness and that of others against the event of God's love become flesh, crucified, and raised, in order in this way to be liberated for life with others, for being-for others, which is the real task of life (*Fragmente aus Tegel,* 1978, pp. 151f.).

Hopeless and Promising Godlessness:
Elaboration of the Seven Theses

1. To begin, I would like to express in a somewhat more personal manner what I have stated in principle and in general in the seventh thesis. For me, as an evangelical pastor in the G.D.R., the concept of 'promising godlessness' is inviting and attractive. It opens a door, and surprising developments manifest themselves. Jesus' parable of The Prodigal Son (Luke 15) is changed: the son who leaves his father's house, proves himself, masters life, fails here and there, but also is successful. He does not lead a life that ends up in a pigsty, but puts to use his gifts and abilities in order to live with others and for others. His father hears about it and is proud that his son has proved himself among foreigners, that his upbringing has borne fruit. He visits his son and is pleased with him. His son is capable. He had made him capable of fulfilling the task of living-together-with-others. The father writes his older son a letter in which he bids him to also join his younger brother. The older son comes and lives and works together with his brother. And the joy of the father became yet greater. That is what I associate with the concept of 'promising godlessness.'

2. And what do I associate with the other concept of Bonhoeffer, with 'hopeless godlessness'? — the words of the Church Council of the German Evangelical Churches in 1939 and 1941.

In the pulpit proclamation on the occasion of the harvest celebration of 1939 it says:

> The God who guides the destiny of the nations has blessed our German nation with yet another equally abundant harvest again this year. As the dispatches can confirm in these days with pride, the struggle on the Polish battlefields is coming to an end... How can we thank our God enough! We thank Him that He has given our weapons an early victory... We praise You above, O Guide of battles, and beseech you that you might continue to stand by us.[1]

On June 30, 1941, eight days after the attack of Hitler's Germany in the Soviet Union, the Church Council sent Hitler the following telegram:

> You have driven the Bolshevist threat from our own land, my Führer, and are now calling our nation and the nations of Europe to the decisive conflict against the mortal enemy of all order and all Western Christian culture. The German Evangelical Church is with you in all our prayers, as are our incomparable soldiers who now with such powerful blows advance to destroy this pestilent hoard so that in all Europe, under your leadership, a new order might arise and all subversion, pollution of the Most Holy, and violation of the freedom of conscience might be put to an end.[2]

3. My thoughts, prompted by these two concepts, are one thing, but Bonhoeffer's statements on godlessness in his *Ethik* are somewhat different. Theses one through five are an attempt to summarize them. I would now like to add a few questions to those posed in theses 4,2 and 4,3.

The *first* arises from theses 3.1, 4.1, and 4.2: Can there really be a hopeless godlessness when God's love also embraces the world's most abysmal godlessness? Compare *Ethik* V:

> There is no piece of the world, no matter how lost, no matter how godless, that was not accepted by God, reconciled to God, in Jesus Christ. Whoever looks on the body of Jesus Christ in faith can no longer speak of the world as if it were lost, as if it were separated from Christ, can no longer separate himself from the world in clerical arrogance. (p. 218)

The *second* question arises from thesis five: the *whole* world has become godless through its rejection of Jesus Christ. What does the *whole* world mean? It is a general, universally valid statement, made by Bonhoeffer in the context in which he inquires about the proclamation of the command of God by the church. 'God's command cannot be found and known in detachment from time and place' (*Ethik*, p. 294). But is not the *whole* world a timeless and spaceless concept?

Behind these two questions stands a *third*: How are theological-principial and theological-historical arguments related to each other? I myself have difficulties with theological-principial, theological-general, theological-universally valid arguments.
4. But also with respect to Bonhoeffer's concrete statements that are not timeless and spaceless, but are bound to space and time, what does Bonhoeffer mean by the 'religion of Bolshevism' (*Ethik*, p. 109)? The Bolshevists were, after all, convinced atheists, Lenin tolerated no form of searching for God in the ranks of the party!

Bonhoeffer's statement stands, in my opinion, in tension with a passage in a sermon he preached in 1932, and with his answer to a question posed by Visser 't Hooft of September 1941.

On June 19, 1932, Bonhoeffer preached on Colossians 3:1-4 and stated:

> For we *are* chained to this earth. It *is* the place where we stand and fall. An account is taken of what happens on this *earth*. And woe to us Christians if we are brought to shame when it is said to the godless at the end: Well done, good and faithful servant. You have been faithful with a few things; I will put you in charge of many things. Come and share your master's happiness — for *he* was faithful on this earth to the earthly task that had been given to him, for *he* had made the most of the talents which had been entrusted to him. While it must be said of us Christians: and throw the worthless servant outside, into the darkness — for we had hidden our talents in the earth, in order to strive for what was above. The Russian film 'Der Weg ins Leben' has left an unsettling inpression on many people. We saw how unkempt, criminal youths were brought together by a superior leader and were changed from vagabonds to men through volunteer and structured labour. The unsettling part of it was that the building where this labour commune was set up was a monastery church. The spiritual had been driven out, worship and prayer had ceased, but now a new time and a great earthly purpose streamed through its halls — to lead people out of the earthly night to the earthly light. Strive for that which is on *earth* (*Gesammelte Schriften* IV, p. 70).

In September 1941 Visser 't Hooft asked Bonhoeffer what he actually was praying for under the current circumstances — the German army was making unbelievable advances into Russia. Bonhoeffer replied, 'If you want to know, I pray for the defeat of my country, for I believe that it is the only way to pay for all the suffering that my country has caused in the world.'[3] The question remains. What did Bonhoeffer mean by the 'Bolshevist religion'?

I think it is advisable, especially in light of the 'New Thought' of M. Gorbachev, to handle that expression of Bonhoeffer's very carefully. In his book *Umgestaltung und neues Denken für unser Land und für die ganze Welt (Perestroika and the New Thought for Our Nation and the Whole World)* the Marxist atheist Gorbachev recounts the following story:

> I do not believe I will betray any great secret if I repeat an episode which I heard from Amintore Fanfani. He told of one of his conversations with the world-famous film director Eduardo de Felippo. They were speaking about the complicated international situation, and De Felippo asked, 'What remains for us to do?' Fanfani answered him: 'To trust in God.' De Felippo replied: 'Then we humans should act in such a way that we lay no obstacles in God's way.'

Gorbachev follows this with 'This insight, that we are all responsible for the destiny of the world, is therefore today especially profitable and worthwhile.'[4]

5. In spite of this open question, thesis 6 maintains its validity. Bonhoeffer's comments on godlessness in his *Ethik* are a step along the path of reflection on the phenomenon of godlessness, not in terms of principle and universal validity, but historically, concretely, and discriminatingly, on the basis of its intervention on behalf of the weak, poor, abused, homeless, and hungry (second verse of the poem 'Christen und Heiden' ['Christians and Heathens'] who, together with the 'good' of Fragment II of the *Ethik*, struggle against fascism. In *Widerstand und Ergebung*, Bonhoeffer goes a step beyond the *Ethik* in that he binds the phenomenon described in Fragment II, in which the defenders of reason, education, humanity, tolerance, autonomy, are children of the church who have grown independent and run away (*Ethik*, p. 60), to the cross of Jesus Christ, and in so doing, so to speak, regards those runaway children as those who have been abandoned by God in order that they might be able to become independent and mature. Godlessness is thus not only, and not in the first place, an act of man, but an act of God.

NOTES

1. Karl Herbert, *Der Kirchenkampf*, Frankfurt 1985, pp. 226f.
2. As cited by Werner Krusche in 'Schuld und Vergebung; der Grund christlichen Friedenshandelns,' *Zeichen der Zeit* 38 (1984), p. 301f.
3. As cited in Bethge, *Dietrich Bonhoeffer*, p. 834 cf. also p. 824; cf. also, however, the section 'The Russian Problem' in the discussion of William Paton's book, *The Church and the New Order*, in *Gesammelte Schriften* I, pp. 370ff., in which Bonhoeffer warns against taking too lightly the danger which 'Russia, in our judgment, continually poses for all.'
4. Op. cit., Berlin, 1987, p. 265.

Bonhoeffer's Picture of Women

Renate Bethge

This certainly is no comprehensive study. René van Eyden has done the necessary research. So I will just touch on some of my experiences in the Bonhoeffer family and compare them with figures in Bonhoeffer's *Fiction from Prison* and also with his views on women in the sermon for my wedding.

1

The Place of Father and Mother

Bonhoeffer grew up in a setting where men and women had their special and distinctively different places. But also between the men and between the women there were big differences. The mother had a very different place from the kitchen maid, the father a different one from the gardener or the carpenter. Yet all were respected adults. Children were not supposed to give impudent answers to any of them.

It is difficult to say whether father or mother had a more prominent place in the family. The father was a very respected personality in his work, that is, in the University, with his assistants and patients, and somehow this transmitted itself to the family as well. The father was seen much less by the children than the mother, so his worth may have grown by rarity. And the mother herself cared that the picture of the father appeared spotless and that things went the way he liked it, that he had peace and quiet for his work. He really was an impressive person — but that is a different point. That the father was very fond of the mother and chivalrous toward her and also cared that the others behaved in the same way, was obvious.

Some people of the generation of my mother and Dietrich, who had been in the Bonhoeffer home in earlier times, thought that the mother was the dominating figure in the family. She had quite a staff (at times seven persons) to help her organize and do the work in the big household with the eight children and many guests. About the way she educated her children, I have talked and written before — also in Eberhard's Bonhoeffer biographies. Her children and grandchildren and their education was most important to her. She was always ready to put everything at stake for it. So, when her son Klaus passed his fifteen minutes swimming test and did not dare to jump into the water, which also belongs to the test, she jumped into the deep water, fully dressed without being able to swim, as she had once heard that one would come up by oneself. Luckily the swimming instructor was there to pull her out. How much this encounter strengthened the courage of Klaus I do not know.

The mother was strict. But she had the most wonderful imaginative thoughts for games and feasts, gifts and food for children, also for puppet shows to play and for books to read to them.

She liked to give big parties not only for children, but also for the adults. These

194

parties were famous because she always had some original ideas for them: special games or dances, little funny skits and the like. I have met people much later who still remarked with excitement about these parties.

The mother was the soul and the spirit of the house. I never saw her cooking or sewing, but always in discussions with much planning about family matters and still more often — as it was in the Nazi period — about the political and the church situation. She liked discussions, and it is said that even on walks in the holidays she was so wrapped up in them that she hardly saw the landscape or the mushrooms, which were the interest of her husband. She was consulted by everybody. What she said was listened to and how she planned things was accepted. Also the way to the father had to go via her. My mother reported that when she was already married and had gone directly into her father's room, the mother had asked her why she had done that without first asking her.

The mother had studied to be a teacher 'for higher education for girls.' So she taught all her children during the first school years, each one with a few little friends of his or her age. But — though she had fought to be allowed to study, which was not done by girls in her day — later on it was not really important to her. Apart from this teaching at home she never took it up. Her life was full without it. Also she did not push her daughters to study. None of them completed a professional education, though all of them started one before they married. She saw the main role for women in having a good marriage — and she certainly had a very happy one — to be a good mother and to keep and direct a house. The house was of course not seen as an isolated place, but as a part of a community and a country, which you always had in view and in mind. This role was also seen by the family as very important and not inferior to a man's role. Of course, my grandmother's house, with all that it implied, was a little kingdom — not to compare with the later houses of their daughters, let alone granddaughters.

There was also a remarkable academic woman in the family, a younger cousin of the mother, Charlotte Leubuscher, who had studied economics and taught in Berlin at the Technische Hochschule (or Technical University). So she often visited the Bonhoeffer house. This aunt apparently was not held in highest esteem by the Bonhoeffer children, since, for all her intelligence, she was too much of a teacher. The children made fun of her. I saw her in Berlin only, when I was a small child, as she left Germany very soon after the Nazis took power, because of her Jewish father. But I came into closer contact with her when we lived in London and was quite impressed by her unusual and witty personality. Yet I can imagine that children could not see that. It may be also that she had become more open-minded when she grew older. Anyway, this aunt apparently could not serve as an example for the girls, nor did she especially impress the boys.

So the picture of women for Dietrich was dominated by the woman who is at home, looking attentively after those who are under her care: husband, children, servants and the wider family and the many friends. This caring role extended also to people who needed help of any kind; the woman who listens, who gives advice, who radiates a sense of humor, who knows literature, who is quick — sometimes too quick — in her judgement, who is well informed and aware of the problems in the world. These women were especially important in the Nazi period. They discussed problems, gave support and also were able to unobtrusively set up hours of pleasure and relief in their homes for family and friends, even in hard times. So Bonhoeffer wrote from prison: 'Most people have forgotten nowadays what a home can mean, though some of us have come to realize it as never before. It is a kingdom of its own in the midst of the world, a stronghold amid life's storms and stresses, a refuge, even a sanctuary.'[1] Bonhoeffer could not have praised the result of the women's activity more.

2

The Women in Bonhoeffer's Fiction from Prison

This kind of woman with whom Bonhoeffer had lived from the beginning and which he similarly had found in the family of his fiancée, he describes — though in a strongly onesided way — in his *Fiction from Prison*. The cold and malicious atmosphere in prison made them appear to him in an idealized way. His women in that book, as women in his time were expected to do, find fulfillment in their 'female role' and see it as God-given and natural. So, for instance, young Klara answers the question, whether she wants to become a pianist: 'No, I never thought of that. Also, I don't have enough of what it takes, and I don't want to do something halfway. I'll stay at home and some day I'd like to get married and have a family.' And Bonhoeffer goes on: 'The simplicity and warmth with which Klara said this made it clear that she wasn't speaking of her personal happiness but of her vocation.' And then: 'She wasn't one of the daughters of our time... who wasted their days with cocktail parties, tea dances and adulation of film stars. She also was not one of those emancipated half-men. But she also was no future old maid who, with her virtue and excellence, would walk through the world a living reproach to all others. She was a born mother who had experienced the joy of a good family life from childhood and now carried it within her as a possession she could never lose.'[2]

This Klara has quite a likeness to my mother, Dietrich's sister Ursula, three and one-half years older than he. But in comparison to Ursula, Klara's 'female qualities' are even enhanced. Yet there is a certain self-critical soberness which is to be found in the beginning of Klara's answer here, and the certainty about the meaning of her role as a woman is the same with Klara and Ursula.

3

Where Are the Other Women?

Though I recognize rather familiar women in Bonhoeffer's fiction, I am astonished that he did not also describe a different type of woman which he also could find in his family, of course in his grandmother, but also in his generation, even among his sisters. These were women who were not altogether content only with their female role, though they mainly kept to it, who spoke more aggressively, who focused their activities more strongly on things which were not directly connected with house and family. I wonder why there is only the one sister, Klara, who is mainly his older sister, Ursula (in parts also his twin sister Sabine). It seems that he was especially fond of Ursula, that he felt secure in her own security. Ursula was the one who was always approachable, living next door to the parents, and the one to whom Dietrich went when he had — rightly — to reckon with his imprisonment during the next hours. She then gave him strength of body – feeding him with good things before he was taken away — and of mind — with her sympathetic, self-controlled and courageous way.

But probably this was not all. He may have seen in Ursula and in her stability, more than in anybody else, the continuation of the tradition in which he had grown up, which, under the Nazis and especially now in prison where everything that was of value to him seemed to vanish, was more important to him than ever before. About the value of this tradition he writes in different places during his prison period, for instance: 'The consciousness of being borne up by a spiritual tradition that goes back for centuries gives one a feeling of confidence and security in the face of all passing strains and stresses.'[3] The bearers of this tradition were mainly the women, and especially women as he describes them in this drama and novel. Of course there the older women, especially the grandmother, are described as much more original and lively than Klara or Renate, the young girl of the other family, supposedly the later bride of the main character Christoph. Why Bonhoeffer in this fiction did not concede more originality to the women of his own generation — he being, to a large extent, Christoph — is difficult to understand. It may be that he felt threatened or just disturbed by the more demanding way of such women. But it is most likely that the troubled atmosphere in prison made him wish strongly to think only of understanding, friendly women who kept to their path. I cannot imagine that he would have written like this under normal conditions.

In one of the letters, when he heard from his fiancée that she likes books which he is not so fond of, Bonhoeffer writes to Eberhard how strongly he hopes for an agreeing wife: 'I would very much like my wife to be as much of the same mind as possible in such questions. But I think it's only a matter of time. I don't like it when husband and wife have different opinions. They must stand together like an impregnable bulwark. Don't you think so? — Or is it another aspect of my "tyrannical" nature?' he at least adds, somewhat sceptically. I think it is also very important that the Klara-type was for him in accordance with Christian teaching.

4

The Christian Wife

This Christian teaching about women, as Bonhoeffer sees it, taken in a rather doctrinaire way, is one of the few things which sometimes really surprises me in the *Ethics*, *Creation and Fall* and other places, and also especially in the sermon for my wedding (in *Letters and Papers from Prison*).

I only speak here about my wedding sermon. Here Bonhoeffer writes all too often about the role of the wife to help and to serve the husband who has all responsibility: 'You, Eberhard, have all the responsibility... and you, Renate, will help your husband and make it easy for him to bear that responsibility, and find your happiness in that.' He would never have said anything of the like directly to me or to any other woman whom I know — but here in the wedding sermon he wrote it. Yet there is no place where Bonhoeffer points to the duty of the wife when he does not also point to the duty of the husband. Also, like a little excuse for the strict statement that 'the wife's honour is to serve the husband, to be a help meet for him', Bonhoeffer adds: 'as the creation story has it (Gen. 2,18).'[4]

Perhaps he himself is not quite happy with this requirement of the Bible — at least thinking of me — but he feels that it should be especially after what he had taught about wedding sermons — as we have heard from René van Eyden — now marrying his friend, one of his former pupils. Wondering about this sermon, I sometimes also thought that the reason why Bonhoeffer brought out so strongly the serving role of the woman and the responsibility-role of the man was to help Eberhard to make his voice also heard in the big Bonhoeffer family, because he knew how strong his family was, being used to plan and decide everything (and this of course mainly on the part of the women).

5

The Strength of the Weak

In daily life, Dietrich never had or gave the feeling to a woman that he, as a man, was superior to her. None of the men in the family did that, nor did the women feel this way. So I get angry when I read dialogues in the many fiction and film manuscripts about Dietrich Bonhoeffer and his family where the men — of course mainly Dietrich, but also the others — talk down to the women in a teaching manner and when the women are described as simple and frightened. As a matter of fact, the women were cunning and strong, never showing fear towards the Nazis, hardly even to each other, in order to keep up the spirit. They, as women were, even more outspoken and straightforward to the Nazis than the men. They had no jobs to lose and as women enjoyed a certain fool's license which they all used, especially effectively Dietrich's sister Christine von Dohnanyi, when she was taken prisoner on the same day as Dietrich and her husband. She was very well informed about the resistance, having also helped with inconspicuously passing on important news to other conspirators, but now played so well the uninformed and naïve housewife, giving keenly wrong answers and asking stupid questions, so that she was released.

The women fought up to the end for their men, even after death sentences (for my father and Klaus Bonhoeffer). The men in prison felt upheld by the women. But I think Dietrich is also right with his two-sided view — though I never liked this passage — when he points to the 'free, composed confident walk' of these 'women who — like their mothers before them — have always known themselves safe under the protection of their fathers, husbands or brothers and safe within the realm of their families. But these women will also walk like that when disaster strikes and forces them to stand alone; that protection under which they once lived surrounds them at every step, even in the hour of greatest desolation, like an invisible power that no one dares to touch.'[5]

NOTES

1. Dietrich Bonhoeffer, *Letters and Papers from Prison* (London: SCM, 1971), p. 44.
2. Dietrich Bonhoeffer, *Fiction from Prison*, pp. 97, 98.
3. Bonhoeffer, *Letters and Papers*, p. 165.
4. Ibid., p. 44.
5. Bonhoeffer, *Fiction*, p. 95.

Dietrich Bonhoeffer's Understanding of Male and Female

René van Eyden

Dealing with the subject of male and female in Bonhoeffer's works, I personally experience something like a conflict of loyalty in my commitment both to Bonhoeffer studies and to critical reflections from the viewpoint of theological women's studies. I have taught for twelve years in this field at the Catholic Theological University in Utrecht. We have discovered that these two streams of liberating theology are not easy to conciliate. However, Bonhoeffer's reflections, in particular those from the last period of his life, open visions and perspectives which, in my opinion, are relevant also for theological women's studies.

1.

Bonhoeffer's Theology on Woman's Place

At several occasions Renate Bethge has explained how strongly Bonhoeffer's theological thought is based on the facts of his family background.[1] I will not dwell on these and other biographical data and will restrict myself to some relevant passages in his writings.

A. *Texts on Man and Woman*
When we read Bonhoeffer's writings about the relation between man and woman, there are very few relevant passages.
— In a course on spiritual care, which he gave on many occasions between 1935-39, he taught the students what should be included in a wedding sermon. 'Under the Lordship of God, marriage also should have its order that the man in the marriage is lord while loving his wife and the wife is subservient to her man while likewise loving her husband' (*GS* V 413). Marriage is God's order. The man as lord has God as Lord above himself, whilst the woman is subservient to both.
— In an interpretation of 1 Timothy (dating from 1938) for students in the seminary of Finkenwalde, Chapter 2:8-15: 'The husband is the head of the woman and the family. He is the priest. He intercedes with God for his household.' Then he points to the danger of disorder in the relation of husband and wife. 'Enthusiastic teachings will always strive to convince women by holding out a prospect of special rights for them. For Paul the order is clear: women share fully in salvation and in the truth. But they have another calling than the man. The glory of women is not to be sought in the public sphere, rather in modesty and in propriety, i.e. clothed in the secret mantle of unostentationsness. So has God given to woman her vocation in her subordination under her husband' (*GS* IV, 367f.).

In these texts Bonhoeffer did not present an anthropological doctrine of man and woman, but rather theological insights into the position of man and woman based upon a theological understanding of the Bible and a Scriptural ethic. His pronouncements about man and woman are only intended as the clearest possible interpretation of the Bible. A correct proclamation avoids an application to one's own situation. In the canonical form of the Bible it is God himself who speaks to us his word in the words of men. 'It is one and the same God who speaks in each word of the Bible' (Finkenwalder Homelitik. *GS* IV, 253). 'The only method of presentation is the direct exposition of the matter of the text as the witness to Christ' (Vergegenwärtigung neutestamentlicher Texte. Vortrag in 1935. *GS* III, 303f.).

Bonhoeffer is well aware that this interpretation contradicted contemporary tendencies. What is asserted in the exposition of the subject of man and woman (see 1 Tim. 2:8-15; Col. 3:18-19; Eph. 5:22-23) 'is not simple conservatism, but rather a biblical order' (*GS* IV, 369). That this 'biblical order' is incongruent with the stance which Jesus adopted towards women and his intention with respect to the community of his disciples was for the church in Bonhoeffer's time still inconceivable. Theologians such as Elisabeth Schüssler Fiorenza, among others, have shown that 'Jesus radically questioned social and religious hierarchical and patriarchal relationships. The fatherhood of God radically prohibits any ecclesial patriarchal self-understanding. The Lordship of Christ categorically rules out any relationship of dominance within the Christian community (Matt. 23 : 7-12). According to the Gospel tradition, Jesus radically rejected all relationships of dependence and domination.' She describes the gradual patriarchalization of the early christian movement. 'This process... climaxed in the identification of women's leadership with heresy... was also operative in the selections and formulation of the canonical New Testament which in turn serve to reinforce and to legitimize the patriarchalizing tendencies in the patristic Church'.[2]

Even in Bonhoeffer's time there were a few women who attacked the biblical basis of male domination. The letters which Henriette Visser 't Hooft wrote to Karl Barth in 1934 are impressive examples of this. She asked Barth if he could justify 'The man is the head of the woman', in I Corinthians 11:3 and Ephesians 5:23, and went on to criticize sharply the traditional interpretation, also Barth's, who rejected the concept of 'mutual interest' of man and woman and continued to maintain the hierarchy of God-Christ-man-woman. Her answer is: 'I believe that there is more than superiority, namely love alone. Love knows neither superiority or inferiority: Christ died on the cross'.[3]

The fundamental question underlying the criticism of Bonhoeffer's views on man and woman is this: Which biblical hermeneutic legitimates it? How does he interpret the relationship between Bible and revelation? And to what extent does he regard himself as bound by Luther's interpretation of the Bible?

Bonhoeffer himself was well aware that there was a great need for responsible hermeneutic and he had also intended to write a book on that subject after *The Cost of Discipleship*. But more important undertakings prevented him from carrying out this plan. While still a student he had already produced an essay (1925) on the relationship between a historical and a pneumatological exegesis in which we see the extent to which he had been influenced by the biblical interpretation of dialectical theology of

Karl Barth and E. Thurneysen, and the hermeneutics of Luther.[4] What he taught later in Finkenwalde on the subject of a correct interpretation of the Bible had already been worked out in this early text.

In *Ethics*, Bonhoeffer's doctrine of the divine mandates is relevant for our subject, namely the divine mandate of marriage.

Lutheran theology talks about 'orders of creation' (*Schöpfungsordnungen*). As early as 1932 Bonhoeffer rejected that notion and coined the phrase *Erhaltungsordnungen*, the 'orders of preservation'. He deals with this extensively in *Schöpfung und Fall*. But he dropped it quickly enough, when W. Künneth and P. Althaus adopted it in order to legitimate their interpretation of the *Zwei-Reiche-Lehre* ('two-kingdoms-doctrine').

In his *Ethics* Bonhoeffer developed the theme of the orders of preservation, but from then on he called them mandates. Four interconnected social structures: work, marriage, state and church have been instituted by God for all humankind as the structural framework for investigating what God wants in the world. These mandates are definite historical forms of the command of God. Characteristic is their setting in a Christological interpretation of the reality of the world: under the dominion of Christ, the world reaches true worldliness which Bonhoeffer calls Christonomy (*E* 316; *Ethics* 299).

Another characteristic of the mandates is the relation of *Oben* and *Unten*, above and below: 'The bearers of the mandate do not receive their commission from below; their task is not to expound and execute desires of the human will, but in a strict and unalterable sense they hold their commission from God, they are deputies and representatives of God... In this way, by virtue of the divine warrant, there is established in the sphere of the Mandates an unalterable relation of superiority and inferiority' (*E* 306; *Ethics* 289) (in the German text: *Oben und Unten*).

The warrant for ethical discourse is imparted to a person on the basis of an objective position in the world. The ethical therefore implies certain definite sociological relations which involve authority. Without this objective subordination of the lower to the higher, and without that courage to accept superiority which modern man has so completely lost, ethical discourse is dissipated in generalities (*E* 288; *Ethics* 272). This is applicable to the mandate of marriage, 'The oldest of all human institutions' (*E* 185; *Ethics* 174).

In the mandate of marriage this 'above and below' is expressed in the relation of the members of the family; in this context Bonhoeffer refers to the subordination of children to their parents. 'The parents are for the child the representatives of God, for they have brought him into the world and are his educators by God's commission' (*E* 223; *Ethics* 210). Here not only the father but also the mother is doubtlessly intended, although his examples only speak about 'father and child,' 'father and son,' 'father of the family' and 'fatherhood.' The warrant or authorization for ethical discourse by the mother is assumed, but is not specifically mentioned anywhere.

The question which now interests us is this: Does the relationship of above and below, superiority and inferiority, also apply to the spouses? Does the mandate of marriage include relationships of dominance determined by God himself between husband and wife? Although Bonhoeffer does not say this explicitly in *Ethics*, it is presupposed when he associates the marriage of man and woman with what is said in

Ephesians 5:31f. about the relationship between Christ and the Church (*E* 223; Ethics 209). Thus he implicitly accepts what Paul himself says in this context: 'Just as the Church is subject to Christ, so must women be to their husbands in everything' (Eph. 5:24).

Although Karl Barth was impressed by Bonhoeffer's understanding of the divine mandates, he posed several critical questions, e.g.: 'Are such oppositions of "above" and "below" always adequate and necessary (Bonhoeffer's theory of the mandates smacks of North-Germanic patriarchalism)?' (KD III 4,22) (1951).

One can say that K. Barth had hardly the right to speak, for in the same volume he treats at some length the teaching of revelation that God ordered a *Vorordnung* of man, and a *Nachordnung* of woman, a 'superordination' of man, and 'subordination' of woman (KD III 4, 187ff.). The Lutheran theologian H. Ringeling has characterised Barth's position as 'pure romanticism, just possibly coloured with a touch of Swiss'.[5]

And yet the question remains: why is there so much emphasis on the relationship of authority between people above and people below? Part of the answer could be, with reference to Tiemo Rainer Peters: Bonhoeffer's doctrine of mandates and his Christonomy were a theological rebuttal of the principles of the Nazi state: *Gleichschaltung*, total control, etc.: 'The emphasis of the eschatological "from above' as opposed to "from below' contains as a rule polemical, political thrust: to demonstrate theologically the relativity and accountability of every mere earthly power from below'.[6]

The second part of the answer is given by Frits de Lange: Bonhoeffer's doctrine of the divine mandates is a 'conservative construction for which bourgeois Germany in the 19th century functioned as a model: a bourgeois pattern of values was retranslated in terms of above and below in the *Ethics*'.[7]

To conclude: the traditional religiously based patriarchal structure of marriage and family was legitimated theologically and ethically in Bonhoeffer's doctrine of the mandates.

The inheritance of a patriarchal culture, in the form of a bourgeois pattern of values, prevented Bonhoeffer from achieving a more critical insight into the specific situation of woman in a man's world and a man's church. This also explains why he was not really concerned about the specific problems which the Nazi ideology and the politics of the 'Third Reich' entailed for women.

The basic elements and convictions of Bonhoeffer's theology are found combined in the 'Wedding Sermon from the Cell of May 1943, a valuable *document humain* for his most intimate friends (WEN 53-59). The things he taught in Finkenwalde about a wedding sermon, and his ideas about the mandate of marriage which he developed in his *Ethics*, are brought together here as characteristic of his thinking before the change in his perspective which took place in April 1944. To quote a few sentences:

— 'Your love belongs to you alone and personally, but marriage is something surpassing the individual, it is a state and an office.' It strikes us that here he does not apply his own term 'mandate,' but applies the terms 'state' (*Stand*) and 'office' (*Amt*) as found in traditional Lutheran doctrine.

God establishes an order which enables you to live together in marriage... In setting up your household you are completely free, but in one thing you are subjected to a law: the wife should be subordinate to her husband, and the husband should love his wife... As the head he is responsible for his wife, for his marriage and for his house. The place where the wife was put by God, is her husband's house...

In connection with this he expresses his conviction:

The beginning of the dissolution and breakdown of all human order is there when the serving role of a wife is seen as subordination... and the exclusive love of a husband for his wife as a weakness.

Quite a different perspective is seen in the baptism letter of May 1944 (WEN 321f.): the awareness of a radically renewed world.

All forms of thinking, talking and organizing in matters of Christian life and work should be born anew. There will be a new language, perhaps completely a-religious, but as liberating and redeeming as Jesus' language, ... the language of a new justice and a new truth.

All the same, Bonhoeffer's comment on the Hernhuter Losungen, written on June 7, 1944 (*GS* IV, 592), reveals a new approach: here he discusses the theme of a husband's and wife's mutual support. Such a mutual support in body, soul and mind is the essence of marriage; and this is something permanent, even when the war situation prohibits their being together. Thus it appears that, because of their mutual support in all aspects of life, Bonhoeffer sees husband and wife as equals. Both in his wedding sermon and in this comment, his starting point is Genesis 2:20: 'a help meet for him' (the equal of man), but the elaboration leads in different directions.

B. *Bonhoeffer's Writings in General*
Bonhoeffer's androcentric approach is shown in various ways:
— In separate identifiable places: for instance, in a sermon for the wedding of a vicar (Albrecht Schönherr and Hilde Enterling: *GS* IV; 460f.) he addresses the couple from a man's perspective: the woman is asked to assist her husband, in such a way that he can carry out his pastoral vocation. Her own development is not mentioned, or rather, it is supposed to consist in serving her husband. In *The Cost of Discipleship*, there is a chapter on adultery and lust. The title which he gives to this chapter is 'Woman.'
— An underlying problem is that the language, the concepts and the elaboration of Bonhoeffer's themes have an androcentric flavour and perspective. Present-day women, when reading his text, notice this. They often feel excluded.

2.

Bonhoeffer's Reception in Women's Studies in Theology

Both Bonhoeffer's personality and theology have deeply influenced various forms of liberation theology. At the Bonhoeffer symposium of 1976 in Geneva, Julio de Santa

Ana read a paper on the influence of Bonhoeffer on liberation theology in Latin America, and John de Gruchy discussed Bonhoeffer as a dialogue partner in theological thinking in South Africa.

At the Third International Bonhoeffer Conference, of 1986, in Oxford, John Godsey discussed 'Bonhoeffer and the Third World: West Africa, Cuba, Korea.'

Oddly enough, Bonhoeffer's theology is not paid much attention to in another form of liberation theology: women's studies in theology.

A. *Ambivalent Reactions*

The words of a female student of theology, taking part in a seminar on Bonhoeffer's *Ethics* at Marburg, are fairly representative of many women who study Bonhoeffer: 'All of us had great expectations as we started studying Bonhoeffer, well aware that he is one of the very few theologians we can link up with.' But she was disappointed, especially as a woman, with Bonhoeffer's outspoken patriarchal view of life, and with the picture of woman that emerges in *Letters and Papers from Prison*, and especially in the wedding sermon.[8]

A group of women who held a Bonhoeffer week in Berlin in April 1986 had a similar experience. Two women who had known Bonhoeffer personally spoke with appreciation of what he meant to them. And together they read 'Thy Kingdom come' (*GS* III 270-285). But this is how the report of this meeting ends:

> It is impossible just to adopt or apply theological *topoi* from Bonhoeffer's very masculine theology to women. Our feeling of relationship is with the praying and acting Bonhoeffer, rather than with the theologian.[9]

Many women think in this respect the man Bonhoeffer is better than the theologian Bonhoeffer (as F. Littell once said in another context).

B. *In Feminist Theology*

1. In some cases, Bonhoeffer's androcentric pronouncements are flatly rejected. For example, Mary Daly: 'God can be used oppressively against women... in an overt manner, when theologians proclaim women's subordination to be God's will.' And among the authors she mentions are Barth and Bonhoeffer.[10]

Elisabeth Moltmann Wendel:

> How strongly traditional bourgeois ideas were connected with a theology of God-given patterns is shown in a biblical study Bonhoeffer wrote in 1938 [...] 198. But in the end this theological thinking got cracked. The adult Christian, who frees himself from subservience to authorities, was discovered; but the adult woman still remained in obscurity.[11]

Elisabeth Moltmann-Wendel contrasts this 'order of creation' with the 'order of Christ':

> The ancient order of creation entailing women's subordination to man, has been replaced by the order of Christ, which gives them equal status. This already heralds something of the Kingdom of God. For women, this means a new dimension in Christian and social commitment.

The traditional Christian views of marriage, which supposed different roles and functions for man and woman, have been replaced by a view of marriage as a partnership of free equals.[12]

Maria de Groot, a Dutch theologian and poet, expresses her disappointment quite frankly. After rereading *Widerstand und Ergebung* she closed the book sadly: 'Women are absent. It seems to be a Greek book; a men's culture.'[13]

More significant, however, than these incidental criticisms, is the fact that the most important feminist theological authors of recent years do not even mention Bonhoeffer. He is not found for instance in the works of Elisabeth Schüssler Fiorenza and Rosemary Radford Ruether.

2. *Working out the Inspiration*

In his study *Die feministische Eroberung der Theologie,* Uwe Gerber repeatedly points to a relationship between some of Bonhoeffer's theological concepts and certain views in feminist theology, even if Bonhoeffer is not explicitly referred to. To give an example: the feminist concept *Kirche der Schwesterlichkeit* (Church of Sisterhood) reminds one of Bonhoeffer's final ecclesiology: The church only makes sense if it exists for other people, and all functions, ministries and structures should support that task.

Some women theologians have started a dialogue with Bonhoeffer and develop material he offered. Carter Heyward is impressed by the 'logical insights' in *Letters and Papers from Prison*:

> Bonhoeffer's Christology is set here in a vision of 'religionless Christianity', the personal presence of Christ in history as 'the man for others', and the help rendered by a 'powerless and suffering God.'[14]

Dorothee Sölle offers, among other things, a historical evaluation of Bonhoeffer's view on 'deputyship' (Stellvertretung) and the powerlessness of God in his creation. She also wrote a subtle analysis of Bonhoeffer's poem, 'Wer bin ich?' (*Die Hinreise.*)[15]

Conclusion

It would be anachronistic to berate Bonhoeffer's 'male chauvinism' from today's vantage point. However, according to Thomas Day, Bonhoeffer's ethical thought holds a male myopia extreme even in his time. 'Subordinate, but equal is a twist of mind easy for the superior. It made Bonhoeffer's perspective oppressively male'.[16]

Bonhoeffer's life was situated in a historical climate that is different from ours. We cannot merely repeat the theological answers he gave. But what we can analyze is how his ideas as a theologian guided his responsible activity in concrete circumstances, and this may teach us how to do the same now.

Bonhoeffer's texts can be seen 'as threads in a texture which Bonhoeffer also, for some time, helped to complete — threads that are or can be connected, but can also prove to be loose ends and break off'.[17]

It is we who weave on and insert new patterns in the context of a new praxis of partnership and mutuality between women and men. We can reach a new understanding of the witness of the Bible. Created in the image of God and called to be disciples of Jesus, women and men are not bound by hierarchical relationships, but as equals they are responsible for their own development and for their life together. We honour the legacy of Bonhoeffer when we attain 'the language of a new justice and a new truth' (WEN 328), creating an ever new 'polyphony of life' (WEN 331). In this respect his famed paragraph, 'Der Blick von unten' ('We have for once learned to see the great events of world history from below, from the perspective of the outcast,' [GS II, 441]) is challenging us to develop a perception of the specific repression of women in a patriarchal society and culture. Bonhoeffer's central beliefs continue to inspire people involved in struggle for liberation. I am committed to see students of theological women's studies discover the relevance of Bonhoeffer's legacy for their feminist reflections. In a world come of age, we have to build a Christian community of discipleship of equals.

NOTES

1. Renate Bethge, *Bonhoeffers Familie und ihre Bedeutung für seine Theologie*. Berlin 1987 (Gedenk-stätte Deutscher Widerstand).
2. Elisabeth Schüssler Fiorenza, 'You are not to be called Father'. Early Christian History in a Feminist Perspective. In N.K. Gottwald (ed.), *The Bible and Liberation. Political and Social Hermeneutics*. Maryknoll, NY. 1983, 394-417.
3. Henriette Visser 't Hooft, Unausweichliche Fragen (u.a. Briefwechsel mit Karl Barth 1934). In Gudrun Kaper u.a., *Eva wo bist du? Frauen in internationalen Organisationen der Ökumene*. Gelnhausen-Berlin-Stein 1981, 11-36.
4. Dietrich Bonhoeffer, *Referat über historische und pneumatische Schriftauslegung*. In DBW, Band 9 '*Jugend und Studium*', 305-323.
5. H. Ringeling, *Die Frau zwischen gestern und morgen. Der sozial-theologische Aspekt ihrer Gleich-berechtigung*. Hamburg 1962, 25.
6. T.R. Peters, *Die Präsenz des Politischen in der Theologie Dietrich Bonhoeffers*. München-Mainz 1976, 77.
7. F. de Lange, *Grond onder de voeten. Burgerlijkheid bij Dietrich Bonhoeffer*. Kampen 1985, 264 f.
8. E. Bethge, *Bekennen und Widerstehen*. München 1984, 216.
9. Erika Fechner, Dietrich Bonhoeffer – ein feministische Auseinandersetzung. In *Dietrich Bonhoeffer 1986. Texte zum 80. Geburtstag*. Berlin 1986, 109-119 (Evangelisches Bildungswerk Berlin).
10. Mary Daly, *Beyond God the Father*. Boston 1973, 19.
11. Elisabeth Moltmann Wendel (Hg.), *Frauenbefreiung. Biblische und theologische Argumente*. München-Mainz 1978, 65.
12. Quoted by Uwe Gerber, *Die feministische Eroberung der Theologie*. München 1987, 117.
13. Maria de Groot, *De vrouw bij de bron. Fragmenten intuitieve theologie*. Haarlem 1980, 87.
14. Isabel Carter Heyward, *The Redemption of God. A Theology of Mutual Relation*. Washington 1982, 211-212.
15. Dorothee Sölle, *Stellvertretung*. Stuttgart 1965. Dorothee Sölle, *Die Hinreise*, Stuttgart 1975.
16. T.I. Day, *Dietrich Bonhoeffer on Christian Community and Common Sense*. New York-Toronto 1982 (dissertation from Union Theological Seminary), 122.
17. F. de Lange, Wie zijn ziel behouden wil. Dietrich Bonhoeffer als man uit één stuk. In: *Het leven is meer dan ethiek. Studies aangeboden aan prof.dr. G.Th. Rothuizen*. Kampen 1987, 152.

Bonhoeffer and Gandhi: Measure and Movement for a Political Ethic of Resistance

Jurjen Wiersma

To begin with, I would like to make some introductory remarks. Firstly, it is rather complicated to deal with the relationship between Bonhoeffer and Gandhi. For what is at stake here — to put it briefly — is that East is East and West is West. In this respect we are perhaps more alert and conscientizised than our forefathers were fifty years ago. They were fully captives of their Western and Euro-centered biases. In fact, Dietrich Bonhoeffer was no exception. For him Gandhi was a 'heathen Christian,' a qualification which demonstrates that he also approached Gandhi in terms of a Western phraseology. Even Bonhoeffer, who turned out to be such an ecumenical theologian and a liberal commentator, underscores the fact that Indian character and culture often present something which baffles and disturbs Western observers.

Secondly, I would like to quote at some length from *A History of Europe,* the formerly eminent standard work in the field of history by H.A.L. Fisher, who declared in the edition of January 1936:

> Mr. Gandhi has many qualities which, had his lot been cast in a Western land, would have brought him to the front of political life: personal charm, ardent patriotism, brilliant dialectical ability, a keen eye for publicity, sublety in attack and defense, a distinguished command of the English language. Such qualities, pertaining as they do to the Western category of political virtues, are easily appreciated by Englishmen. But this little Hindu lawyer who has given so much trouble to the British *Raj* as organizer of a boycott of British goods and as the leader in a campaign of civil disobedience, presents other aspects which perplex and elude. An indubitable saint yet as a member of the money-lending caste a friend to usury, an ardent patriot yet as a politician the beneficiary of the worst slum properties in India, a declared opponent of Western modernism yet not averse from (sic) availing himself of the convenience of a Ford car, Mr. Gandhi is an epitome of those picturesque and baffling contrasts which offer so remarkable and exciting a challenge to the patience and prudence of the West.

This all sounds rather condescending to people of the last quarter of the twentieth century, at least to us. Now, after being alerted a little and hopefully equipped with a sensible capability to discern between East and West, let us go ahead and turn to the subject matter of this essay, i.e. the connection — and the construction of a connection — between Bonhoeffer and Gandhi.

A Passion

The young German theologian Dietrich Bonhoeffer (1906-1945) clung to his passion for India. There was many a time that he wanted to go there. In particular, he wished to make acquaintance with Mohandas Gandhi, India's prominent political strategist, not with Tagore, an artistic and intellectual aesthete, and not even with Ambedkar, the militant leader of the outcasts. A meeting with Gandhi was what Bonhoeffer passionately strived for. Through the interaction of mutual friends, Gandhi himself invited Bonhoeffer in a letter on 1 November 1934, in which he gave some practical advice as well:

> With reference to your desire to share my daily life, I may say that you will be staying with me if I am out of prison and settled in one place when you come. But otherwise, if I am travelling or if I am in prison, you will have to be satisfied with remaining in or near one of the institutions that are being conducted under my supervision. If you can live on the simple vegetarian food that these institutions can supply you, you will have nothing to pay for boarding and lodging.

The trip, however, did not occur, because Bonhoeffer became the head-tutor of the seminary of the Confessing Church. But it is still challenging to do research into this Indian option. Who actually was this Bonhoeffer around 1935? As far as his upbringing and education are concerned, he had become a complete person; he had found his identity and felt himself a theologian of character.

He himself wrote about this newly found identity from London on 14 January 1935:

> I believe that I have eventually landed on the right track. It often makes me feel very happy. But yet I am still afraid that I conform to the opinions of other people and will not go far enough but will stagnate. In fact, if I were earnest about the Sermon on the Mount, then I should become inwardly perfect and thoroughly sincere. Its text is a unique source of inspiration, which stimulates a person to spend his life in the imitation of Christ. It is now time for the people to stand together for this life, for there are things which deserve unremitting zeal. I believe that peace and justice are such things, for this is what the imitation of Christ is about.

However, Bonhoeffer felt he could not cope with the situation, which became more and more dominated by Hitler and his applauding hordes. Therefore, he wanted to be trained by Gandhi in India in order to confront and to be more prepared in Germany for this approaching danger. The 'India-fragment' is a fairly small part of Bonhoeffer's legacy, but if we take it seriously, its implication is major and radical.

Latent Alternative Potentiality

On the one hand, I am tracing the cultural background of these two men back to its latent potentiality. Gandhi, in particular, activated the negation of violence which had become anchored in his society, although through the centuries the Indian society was not altogether exempt from violence and atrocities.

Through his contributions of *Satyagraha* (the love of truth) and *Ahimsa* (nonviolence), Gandhi undeniably enhanced this latent non-violent tendency in India. Moreover, he stressed that on every page of the *Bhagavad Gita*, one of the holy scriptures of Hinduism, there was only love.

For example: If Arjuna had to fight, then Gandhi saw this as a witness to love and non-violence, for Arjuna had to act without any maliciousness and to fight the two largest enemies, i.e. eagerness and anger. Also, Arjuna must not discriminate between friend and foe and he must confront temptation in order to be free from pain and delectation.

Only an Ardjuna, who personifies the essence of this alternative potentiality and who destroys the devil within himself, can live a life that is compatible with renunciation. This is one of the fundamentals of Hindu philosophy. One must first become less human to then become more human.

Bonhoeffer, in turn, revealed himself as 'a citizen at his best.' Not only did he use the finest qualities of his cultural environment, but he also delved into the sealed treasures of his alternative potentiality for the world, which had been severely damaged by Nazism. Bonhoeffer sought a contrast world. But still he was powerless; his inability to act tipped the balance. Therefore, Bonhoeffer wanted to meet Gandhi. This hiatus had to be overcome in India.

The journey did not occur. In consequence, Bonhoeffer's political service to the resistance against the Führer unfortunately did not get further than the drawing board. But it is my intention to take it further, for in this sense we must learn to become his heirs too.

United Europe?

On the other hand, I am making an attempt to do research into the Bonhoeffer-Gandhi relationship, with the intention of following the tracks they left behind. The first was in defense against the distress into which the Nazis were about to plunge the world, the second in defense against British colonialism. If we actualize their specific involvement, by implication we have to oppose the current modes and methods of both militarization and colonialization, which in one way or another oppress the contemporary world, 'the free Western world' as well.

Here lies the original and actual significance of Bonhoeffer's passion to go to India, which ought not to be seen as an effort to escape from a sinking ship; on the contrary, he was battling to save it. Therefore, along with Gandhi, the politically and socially conscious German theologian sought a contrapoint for his terror-ridden world.

In this context, contrapoint must be understood in sociological terms. It then means a blazing furnace of resistance against the dominant value system. My hypothesis is, that we are adequately working in the spirit of Bonhoeffer and Gandhi if we engage ourselves in the praxis of civil defense and, at the same time, abandon military defense and neo-colonial policy, as well.

Military defense is becoming less feasible, now that we have a vast and frightening number of nuclear weapons. Consequently civil defense, which I see as the alternative to our military defense, is becoming essential. Whereas the former goes hand in hand with the concept of participatory democracy, the latter is as a rule inextricably connected with the concept of an 'Obrigkeitsstaat.' We badly need the praxis and strategy of civil defense (passive resistance), not so much for the protection of our territory, as for the maintenance of our democracy, our national identity, and our culture. In our time we must be thoroughly trained for this kind of defense: all people, young and old, black and white.

Inclusive Action

Ultimately, the trio Bonhoeffer, Gandhi and civil defense implies a mode of social performance which I call inclusive action. Theologically, this action can be seen as a strategic expression of the notion of reconciliation. Also in this respect, we must faithfully follow the tracks Bonhoeffer and Gandhi left behind. Clearly, they both could not live in the divided and hostile world of their time. They wanted peace, justice, and reconciliation.

In this context we must pose the question, can we really be content with the political development towards a 'United Europe'? Would it not be an exclusive, socio-politico-economical stronghold of self-preservation? Would it not coincide with the military apparatus of NATO and with the economical fortress of the EC? If this is the only way for development towards Bonhoeffer's contrast world, then we must have serious doubts, for it is more a development towards might than right; the powerful seem to have better chances than the weak, and 'being-with-others' seems to score lower than 'being-against-others.'

In my ethical vision, we cannot rely on this process, but we ought to resort to inclusive action. This is, as I see it, the only justifiable praxis and strategy to survive in our times. Theologically, I orient myself toward the encouraging words of Matthew 11:28-30: 'Come to me, all of you who are tired from carrying your heavy loads, and I will give you rest. Take my yoke and put it on you, and learn from me, for I am gentle and humble in spirit; and you will find rest. The yoke I will give you is easy, and the load I will put on you is light.' This is a text on which Bonhoeffer preached on 8 July 1934.

Without doubt, the triptych that I present is exacting but certainly not shattering. It is not without fighting and suffering, 'lutte et contemplation', as the Taizé Brothers would say. Christologically, it is to be interpreted as a light load. This conclusion I have drawn ecclesiologically implies that the Christian congregation lives and acts consciously, always ready to fight and to suffer. With such an attitude the congregation is able to transcend the limits of a *theologia crucis,* and to listen to those admonishing words that Luther once spoke to academic theologians: *crux, crux, et non est crux* (cross, cross and no cross). That means, we can get beyond the tragic stagnation in which both Bonhoeffer and Gandhi sadly broke down. It is true, we can and we must go farther in the tracks they left behind, choosing old Europe as our vantage point.

Books which may be consulted
Bethge, Eberhard. *Dietrich Bonhoeffer — eine Biographie* (Chr. Kaiser, München; 1967).
Bonhoeffer, Dietrich. *Gesammelte Schriften* (Chr. Kaiser, München; 1965 etc.). Vol. II, pp. 120, 182, 185 and 288. Vol. V, p. 526: 'heathen Christian.'
Gandhi, Mahatma. *The collected works* (Navajivan Publishing House, Ahmedabad; 1934). Vol. LIX, p. 273: letter to D. Bonhoeffer.
Gandhi, M.K. *Het verhaal van mijn experimenten met de waarheid — een autobiografie* (SVAG i.s.m Gandhi Vredescentrum Nederland, Zwolle; 1986)
Rudolph L. I. and S. Hoeber Rudolph. *The modernity of tradition — political development in India* (The University of Chicago Press, Chicago and London; 1967).
Wiersma, Jurjen. *Inclusief handelen — met Bonhoeffer en Gandhi op weg naar sociale verdediging* (Ten Have, Baarn; 1988).

The Understanding of Bonhoeffer in India

Poulose Mar Poulose

The church of India has been called out to proclaim the good news of 'abundant life' to a nation where forces of death are operating. In a society where injustice, oppression, hunger and such forces of death prevail, proclamation of the abundant life requires a radical commitment in the service of justice and the total liberation of humanity in the name of Jesus. It is illegitimate to speak of spiritual emancipation from the bondage of sin without speaking at the same time of material emancipation from the demonic political and economic forces which enslave the oppressed peoples of our country. Keeping the spiritual and the material realities together is what the exodus of Israel from Egypt was about. Therefore, if the church in India is to be honest to its calling, it should risk its money and prestige and all the resources at its command, and move into a biblical ministry of justice and wholeness to the poor and oppressed, that they may have life, and have it abundantly. In this context, to do theology is to seek to discern and articulate those normative patterns of abundant life which both judge the forces of death and unjust institutions of our society, and at the same time point us toward the realization of a new order where justice, peace, and freedom are established.

There is a new awakening among the people of India, and they have begun to struggle for the fulfillment of their hopes and aspirations about the future. Theology is not the main subject of this struggle, but justice is. Theologians are not the avant-garde of the 'new heaven and new earth' that the people visualize. It is the struggle of the people, especially the struggle of the poor, for their life. It is not we who should theologize this struggle. God himself has chosen sides. He has chosen to liberate the poor by delivering them from their misery and marginality, and to liberate the rich by bringing them down from their thrones. We are invited to take the side of the poor, to claim solidarity with them in their struggle. But the attitude of the church is that of the benevolent master rather than that of the suffering servant. This paternalistic attitude tempts the church to make the claim that they have all the answers for the problems of the masses. In the midst of the vexing problems of the suffering people, however, it is not true that only Christianity has the answers. In fact, it was Bonhoeffer's opinion that the Christian answers are no more conclusive or compelling than any of the others (cf. letter of May 29, 1944).

In the following, what I am trying is to set out six criteria for doing theology in the Indian context in view of Bonhoeffer's theology. They are not put forth with any particular kind of logic. As a matter of fact, they are so interrelated that it is not possible to ascribe priority to any one.

1.

Bonhoeffer wanted the faith to be understood as a demand to live radically in the midst of the world. Accordingly, the task of theology is not to build up a metaphysical system, but to consider the traditional testimony to faith as a thing to be answered for in the present. Bonhoeffer said:

> ... it is only by living completely in the world that one learns to have faith. One must completely abandon any attempt to make something of oneself, whether it be a saint, or a converted sinner, or a churchman (a so-called priestly type!), a righteous man or an unrighteous one, a sick man or a healthy one. By this worldliness I mean living unreservedly in life's duties, problems, successes and failures, experiences and perplexities. In so doing we throw ourselves completely into the arms of God, taking seriously, not our own sufferings, but those of God in the world — watching with Christ in Gethsemane. That, I think, is faith; that is *metanoia*; and that is how one becomes a man and a Christian (cf. Jer. 45!). (*Letter of July 21, 1944*)

This is the direction in which he would have the biblical and theological concepts drive. They are to be interpreted in terms of responsible involvement in the world. Metaphysical and individualistic terms cannot perform that function.

Theology is dependent on a text — the gospel, and it is the task of theology to make the word of God relevant to contemporary people. The gospel can be timely only as it assumes new and bold forms in relation to the actual historical situation and the particular needs of the people in their own time. This is not to deny the rich heritage of the sages like Augustine of Hippo and Gregory of Nyssa, neither does it mean that we should write off the wisdom found in the *Summa Theologica* and the *Church Dogmatics*, but it is to emphasize that God's good news comes to a different focus in different times and circumstances, that the Gospel should be retold again and again in new terms appropriate to the ongoing historical experience and cultural activity of the people in their time. Today in India this means that we have to consider seriously the hopes and aspirations of the people and their struggles for the fulfillment of these hopes and aspirations.

2.

It was said that theology is dependent on a text — the Gospel. But we cannot confine the function of theology to the mere ordering of the word of God as it is revealed in the Bible. We must take seriously every text that is relevant to the coming of God's word to the world — not only the texts of the church tradition but also of non-Christian and non-religious traditions, and particularly the texts which voice the world's opposition to God. The theologian has the responsibility of listening to God's word of judgement and grace in such risky writings. Perhaps it may even be said that a new Bible is being written, not with ink and paper, but with the actual struggles of the people, and it can be read only with our participation in that struggle. Of course, there is risk involved in this, but taking risk is also part of the faith. In other words, the subject of inquiry should be both the traditional testimony to faith and the risky involvement in the struggles of the people.

3.

Since modern secular man cannot accept the premise of transcendent reality, today there is an increasing tendency in some theological circles in India to be diffident in engaging in God-talk. This is an incorrect solution to a misidentified problem. Our theology fails, not because it speaks of God, but because the God of whom we speak is unrelated to the world in which men and women live. God is separated from the world. Although we cannot make God speak, we can equip people to hear, and we can do this in such a way that what they hear may also be understandable to them.

Bonhoeffer insisted that the preached word should grow from the knowledge of present circumstances and should be intensely concrete. This anticipated a totally secular language for the fundamental Christian truths. He knew that our theology, and likewise our proclamation, is constantly faced with the problem of translation. He had already expressed this idea earlier in *Ethics*, that in ethics as in dogmatics we cannot just reproduce the terminology of the Bible. The altered problem demands altered terminology. A church in and for the world understands itself only in the language which is the impelling force of the world's present vitality — for example, in the language of science, business, politics, etc. Thus, he firmly believed that the language for the renewed proclamation can be drawn from the secular world. In the 'Thoughts on the Day of the Baptism of Dietrich Wilhelm Rüdiger Bethge,' Bonhoeffer wrote:

> It is not for us to prophesy the day (though the day will come) when men will once more be called so to utter the word of God that the world will be changed and renewed by it. It will be a new language, perhaps quite non-religious, but liberating and redeeming — as was Jesus' language; it will shock people and yet overcome them by its power; it will be the language of a new righteousness and truth, proclaiming God's peace with men and the coming of his kingdom.

One thing is quite clear from what Bonhoeffer says: the criterion for the under-standability of our theological language should not be how well it is understood by the believer, but by the non-believer. Today, I am afraid, we have made the faith of the believer as a requirement for his/her understanding of our theology. 'Believe what we tell you,' the theologian seems to say, 'have faith, and you will understand,' failing to recognize that if his theology is not understandable it can hardly elicit faith. This reversal of criteria of understandability results not only in making theology into a foreign language to the non-believer, but also in stifling the faith of the believer.

4.

The church must work out its theology in the context of the new community which is now taking shape. Of course, that community cannot be defined by the existing ecclesiastical institutions. It transcends the boundaries of Christian religion and of religion as a whole. The religious vitalities which we cherish move outside those religious structures. God in Jesus Christ is bringing humanity together in new and different ways. Therefore, theology should not be merely an academic exercise within an esoteric Christian community; it must take into consideration the larger outer world. As Bonhoeffer said:

> The church must come out of its stagnation. We must move out again into the open air of intellectual discussion with the world, and risk saying and doing controversial things, if we are to get down to the serious problems of life. (Letter of August 3, 1944)

Responsible involvement in the world also means active political participation, identifying with the oppressed and exploited, fighting for the cause of civil liberty and human rights and joining those who struggle for their freedom. The theologian should take the risk to lead the church for a collaboration with the spirit of liberation in the secular world today.

5.

It has been said that Bonhoeffer's life was an interpretation of his theology. The climax of that life was in the act of resistance against tyranny and subsequent climbing up on the gallows. It reminds us that a relevant theology in our time proceeds by an act of negation, or protest, or judgement upon the status quo. The prophetic lineage by which we trace our own identities maintains that tearing down must always come before the building up. Crucifixion is the precondition of resurrection. Death of the old is required if there is to be life for the new. To negate the negative is at the same time to affirm the possibility of that new reality which lies beyond us. Negation is not nihilism. Negation of war is the affirmation of peace. Negation of repression is the affirmation of freedom. Not to challenge the forces of death is to condone them. And to condone them is to become a part of the problem.

6.

The relevance of Bonhoeffer in India is to be understood also in the context of religious pluralism. A meeting of religions is a must in India for the promotion of a healthy community. Today men and women of all faiths in India have begun to become aware in a new way of their solidarity in the face of the challenge of common problems and tasks in building a common society on new foundations. People have begun to ask questions about what the significance of the ultimate religious concern is in the common striving for the truly human existence. There is a constant search for the ultimate ground of man's personal being. In these days Christianity is losing its ancient body. It finds it difficult to live in its traditional form.

Bonhoeffer's concept of transcendence gives us some clue to the form of Christianity in the context of religious pluralism. Our relation to the transcendent God is the reconciliation seen in Jesus' freedom to live for others. Our relation to God, whose transcendence is reconciliation seen in Jesus' freedom to live for others, is not a 'religious' relationship to the highest, most powerful, and best being imaginable — that is not authentic transcendence — but our relation to God is a new life in 'existence for others', through participation in the being of Jesus. The transcendental is not infinite and unattainable tasks, but the neighbour who is within reach in any given situation. God in human form — not, as in oriental religions, in animal form, monstrous, chaotic, remote, and terrifying, nor in the conceptual forms of the absolute, metaphysical, infinite, etc., nor yet in the Greek divine-human form of 'man himself', but 'the man for others', and therefore the Crucified, the man who lives out of the transcendent.

('Outline for a Book')

God's transcendence is manifested not in 'religion' but in a new orientation of human being toward life: existing for others after the pattern and in the power of Jesus' utterly selfless life.

Jesus' 'being there for others' means that the transcendent is met in the concern for others as given to us in the life and way of Jesus, and our faith is nothing but 'participation in this being of Jesus.' Transcendence thus refers to the transformation the sovereign and eternal God has effected upon the concrete human situation in terms of reconciliation, redemption, the restoration of health, the healing of social and political divisions, etc., and it is an ongoing process. Accordingly, transcendence must be grasped, not as it has so often been in the past, in spatial terms referring to the God 'up there' beyond the affairs of human life, but specifically in terms of what God has effected historically and is doing now on behalf of man.

Bonhoeffer's concept of transcendence leads us to a renewed understanding of faith which becomes more meaningful when we live in dialogue with non-Christian religions and secular ideologies. Dialogue is a way in which we express our humanity. Those who believe in God who is living and active must hold that his Spirit is present always. They therefore enter into dialogue in expectation and hope, not solely or primarily for the conversion of the other, but for enlightenment and enrichment of themselves as they enter more deeply into the 'unsearchable richness' in Christ. A dialogue of this nature will certainly lead us to the fulfillment of the prophetic words of Schleiermacher: 'New developments of religion, whether under Christianity or alongside of it, must come and that soon.' (*On Religion*, translated by John Oman [New York: Harper & Row, 1958], pp. 252-253.)

What Has the Japanese Church Learned from Dietrich Bonhoeffer?

Hiroshi Murakami

1.

The Japanese Church is guilty. The church did not stand on the gospel of Jesus Christ during World War II and resist our country which was committing sins against the surrounding countries of Asia. Rather the church adapted itself to state policy, thereby supporting that policy. That is to say, the Japanese church fell into the same situation as the German Church. There is, however, a great difference between the two churches. In Germany the 'Confessing Church' was founded and fought against the Nazi regime; furthermore, only a half a year after the end of the war, that church confessed its sin officially (Stuttgart Declaration of Guilt) and made a new start toward the future. In comparison, in Japan there was no resistance by the church and the 'declaration of guilt' (Confession on the Responsibility of the United Church of Christ in Japan During World War II) came about twenty years after the war (1967). We are still asking how this difference came about.

It is not, therefore, only out of intellectual interest that since the end of the war the Japanese Church has been strongly interested in the resistance history of both the German Confessing Church and Dietrich Bonhoeffer. Rather we should say that we 'encountered' them when questioning the theological existence of our church, especially when we concentrated on the problem of our sin.

Already in 1964, the first biography of Bonhoeffer written by a Japanese appeared. Most of his works were rapidly translated into Japanese and now we have a Japanese *Gesammelte Schriften* in nine volumes. In 1978, the Japanese Section of the International Bonhoeffer Society was founded, and in the ten years since we have consistently and productively carried on our studies. All of this indicates how important Bonhoeffer's theology is for our church.

In 1985, based upon our studies up to that time, we confessed the sin of the Japanese Church in the name of our Society. This 'Declaration of Guilt' is, of course, not the official declaration of our church, but is an invitation to discuss this very important issue. It is a discussion which we feel is inevitable in Japan. We can see here an essential development of what we have learned from Bonhoeffer.

2.

The Japanese Church is still young (the first Protestant Church was founded in 1872, in Yokohama) and small (the number of Christians, including Catholics, is only one percent of the whole population), but she recognizes herself as a member of the

217

worldwide body of Christ. This belief is derived originally from the Bible; however, it has been essentially deepened by the theological reforms of the twentieth century. We Japanese Christians owe our deepened understanding especially to two European theologians, Karl Barth and Dietrich Bonhoeffer. They have made it clear to us that the church is the body of Christ, 'the form of the earthly-historical existence of Jesus Christ' (Barth). Bonhoeffer spoke in the same sense of 'Jesus Christ existing as the church.' These men have also made it very clear that this concentration on Christology also has a global range. Christ is the Lord not only of the church, but also of the world. To live as a Christian, therefore, necessarily means to take responsibility for history. When Pastor Suzuki declared, at the time he was elected to be moderator of the United Church of Christ in Japan (Kyodan), that we should stop promoting a parallelism of church and world, he was led by this new theological consciousness.

Furthermore, it became clearer to us that the Lordship of Jesus Christ should not be understood in terms of supremacy, but rather through a dynamic relationship with the 'Kenosis' of the Son of God on the cross. Here Bonhoeffer has helped us very much, because he opened the way to the 'view from below' and thus prepared the soil for new theologies such as 'liberation theology' and 'Minjung Theology.' In this sense, the Japanese Church has learned a lot from Bonhoeffer.

3.

Now we have to look back more concretely at the historical sins of the Japanese Church. The modern history of Japan from the Meiji Restoration up to the defeat of 1945, might be generally characterized as a period in which every effort was made to maintain independence against Western colonialism. To this purpose Japan rapidly modernized all sectors of society. In order to motivate and encourage this social revolution, Japan developed the system of Tenno (Emperor) absolutism, which became the spiritual mainstay of the nation. Furthermore, Japan quickly adopted the Western pattern of colonialism in order to gain economic strength. As Reinhold Niebuhr noted, this is one of the greatest 'ironies' of history. Japan was able to avoid becoming a colony of Western countries, but became itself a colonial power. Japan began to invade neighbouring countries, first taking Taiwan in 1895, Korea in 1910 and then establishing a puppet government in the northeastern part of China (Manchuria) in 1932. It was, so to say, the beginning of the end.

What did the Japanese Church do during those years? On the whole, the church followed the national policy and not God's will. The reason might be that theological consciousness was not deep enough. It might also be that the minority complex of the Christians contributed; however, be that as it may, the church supported the militaristic policy of our government and accepted as a fact the colonial rule of Japan all over Asia. Furthermore, in accordance with a 1941 law aimed at mobilizing all religious bodies, the church began calling itself 'The United Church of Christ in Japan', and did everything that the government required. This 'church', which was analogous to the 'Deutsche Christen', justified the war. Its first president went to the central shrine of

Shintoism at Ise and worshipped, and forced Korean Christians to do the same. Many of them were killed by the police because they would not obey this order. This 'church' proclaimed itself the only true church and thus the leader of Asian Christianity because it had the emperor as God. To be sure, there were those who criticized these developments and there were even martyrs; however, most of these actions were those of individuals and their voice was small. 'The Confessing Church in Japan' did not come into existence.

This is a short sketch of the history of our church. The church is responsible for the unspeakable suffering of so many innocent Asian people. Without awareness of these sins and repentance there could be no new start for the church after the war. On this point Bonhoeffer has helped us to achieve a clear and deep consciousness. An especially important, essential contribution to the Japanese Church is his assertion on the necessity of the church recognizing, confessing, and taking upon itself the sins of the nation (*Ethik*).

4.

We cannot deny that, like all the people, the Japanese Church was also deeply disappointed and exhausted after the war. Be that as it may, our sense of responsibility was very weak. When the government appealed to all Japanese to repent, the Kyodan also published a short statement on the 'tragedy of the war' which, however, was unclear as to where the problem lay. After the war, then, almost all of the church's leaders were able to stay in their leadership positions, claiming that 'the militaristic government was guilty; we are victims.' When the tide turned and we entered the so-called 'Christian boom' era, the church was excited and happy to find a new chance in this development, and the church forgot its responsibility for the past.

To compare the Japanese Church with the German Church again, we might look at the Treysa Conference in August of 1945, the touching speech by M. Niemoeller and the subsequent discussion on the sins of the German Church, the Stuttgart Declaration of Guilt in October of 1945, and subsequent developments. We know of course that there were and still are problems in the German Church as well. Nevertheless, with respect to these grave issues, I note a great difference between the German Church and the Japanese Church.

The Japanese Church, therefore, must confess its sins, not only those committed during the war, but also those committed after the war. In spite of its moments of truth, why did the Kyodan's 'declaration of guilt' have such little impact? The reason may be that, with respect to the problem of the responsibility for sin, the Japanese Church did not reach the same theological depth as Bonhoeffer did in his *Ethik*. In this respect, it is symbolic that in the discussions surrounding the 1967 Declaration of Guilt we did not reflect deeply enough on his *Ethik*, even though it had already been translated into Japanese in 1962.

5.

The Japanese Church has learned much from Bonhoeffer, especially from his profound thought on the sins of the church. As a result, the Japanese Church has had an opportunity both to reflect on what it did in the past and to examine what it is doing in the present situation. However, that is not all. As we move towards the future, Bonhoeffer's theology has a compelling effect upon us. For example, the image of future Christianity which he pursued while in prison, even if fragmentary, gives us courage. Furthermore, his expression of 'the church for others' has a decisive influence on many Christians in Japan today. While considering what and how the church should be, Japanese Christians receive insight from Bonhoeffer. The same can be said for his emphasis on 'prayer and doing justice among people.'

Today the Japanese Church faces several concrete tasks. I would like to describe just two of them.

1.   The Japanese Church should pay more attention to the problem of 'human rights.' Bonhoeffer was one of a small number of people who raised their voices on behalf of the Jews. We who have learned so much from him cannot close our eyes to the issue of 'human rights.' We must see clearly that behind the prosperity which Japan enjoys today there is much discrimination and oppression. The so-called 'Burakumin' [dark-skinned underclass - ed.] and other minority groups are still discriminated against within Japan itself, and neo-colonial structures can be found throughout Asia. Pollution-causing industries move into developing countries and destroy both the social structure and the natural environment. Besides these issues we can identify 'sex-tourism', Asian women working in Japanese 'go-go bars', support of the South African apartheid system through massive foreign trade, and so on, as important human rights issues. We cannot sing Gregorian chants with our eyes closed to these problems.

2.   Above all we must emphasize our responsibility for 'peace.' As a result of its reflection on the tragedy of war, Japan adopted a new constitution in which it was decided 'to renounce war forever.' We believe that this is a correct decision. Furthermore, as the first victim of the atomic bomb, we will not cease to cry out, 'No more Hiroshimas!' Hence the three non-nuclear principles (not to have, not to produce and not to introduce). Here we have a historical task which God has given to Japan.
A categorical imperative in the present world situation is to break the vicious circle of nuclear armament. Japan, located as a chain of islands between East and West, is in an ideal position to contribute to this process. Nevertheless, Japan is already involved in the nuclear strategic system of the United States. The 'teeth' have been taken out of our 'peace constitution.' The three non-nuclear principles exist now in name only. Japan seems to have abandoned its historical responsibility by becoming an 'unsinkable aircraft carrier' of the United States, and by lending a hand in intensifying East-West tensions.

The church has been given the word of God, the gospel of reconciliation, and has to continually proclaim it in this situation. Following the definite example of the Reformed Church of the Netherlands and of the Federal Republic of Germany, the Japanese Church must proclaim clearly and repeatedly that these genocidal weapons are absolutely against the will of God. Here, too, we have to learn from the peace ethics of Dietrich Bonhoeffer. Our aim is neither 'pax Americana' nor 'pax Sovietica', but the peace of Christ, peace in Christ, the peace of righteousness.

The Lord of reconciliation gives us a sure and steady hope that the vicious circle of fear and distrust can surely be broken. This hope comes from the promise of the kingdom of God. Standing upon this hope and following Jesus Christ, let us advance unceasingly on the way of peacemaking. In addition, the Japanese Section of the International Bonhoeffer Society would like to say that the proposal for the 'World Council for Peace' should be welcomed by all Christians on the earth. Towards that purpose, we will do our best.

Documentation:

Confession of Guilt by Today's Japanese Church

Prepared by the Japan Bonhoeffer Society

I

As we stand at the close of the fortieth anniversary of the conclusion of World War II, we reflect deeply on the historical responsibility which has been entrusted to our church as the body of Christ. Above all we are reminded with deep pain of the fact that the Japanese Church, like Peter, denied the Lord during the war. We should not have set out on postwar reconstruction without first acknowledging this sin. But the acknowledgement that is called for now does not consist in accusing those who were in charge at that time. In order for us to engage ourselves responsibly in present and future history, including also the generations born after the war, we must accept the guilt of the past as our own. This we take to be the meaning of the words 'historical responsibility.' It is for us a heavy, yet joyous and creative task. Now that Japan claims to have turned the decisive corner, finally liquidating the postwar politics supposedly imposed upon it, the Japanese Church is once again reminded of the scene in which Peter was asked three times by the risen Lord whom he had thrice denied: 'Do you love me?' In this question we see the Lord's forgiveness of fallible Peter, his inexhaustible love, and his new commission. The confession of sin to follow below is our humble and wholehearted response to this question of the Lord.

1. We believe that the Gospel was brought to our country by God's grace and according to God's unfathomable will, founding the church, the body of Christ. We confess with gratitude that we are accepted as members of the world wide communion of the saints. Based on the testimonies of the Old and New Testaments, we confess that 'Christ is the Lord,' with the saints from generation to generation. Faithful obedience to the One who is vested with 'all authority in heaven and on earth' must be the ultimate goal of our life and prayer.

2. We confess that all churches in the world, despite the tradition of faith and rich gifts for which we are to be thankful, have repeatedly fallen into errors. The two-thousand-year history of the Christian church is not a history of glory. The church often rebelled against the divine commission and sinned against its neighbors with whom it was called to live. History is full of instances in which the church did not believe the sovereignty of Christ, abused it in lending support to oppression and invasion and even justified or condoned massacre and war in the name of the Lord. To deny or conceal this fact is to be unfaithful to the crucified Lord.

3. The Old and New Testaments describe plainly the sin and guilt of the prophets and

apostles. We believe and confess that precisely therein the God who justifies the sinner truly lives. The biblical proclamation received its true power from their sincere confession of sin. So the church must have the freedom boldly to confess its sin. If the church tries to justify itself, to save its reputation, to glorify itself with its own ideas, and to defend that glory, there is no way for it to be justified by God.

4.   We believe and confess that the God of grace leads the church that repents and confesses its sins, not to destruction but to new life. This is the testimony of the Old and New Testaments and the experience of the churches in the world. With the 'Stuttgart Declaration' (1945) and subsequent declarations, the German churches started their steps toward restoration and re-entered the ecumenical fellowship. The 'Confession on the Responsibility of the United Church of Christ in Japan during World War II' (1967) was intended to serve the same purpose. These confessions are not complete of themselves, but require that we make them our own and apply them critically in our present context.

II

1.   In this unredeemed world the state is assigned a certain role by God. But that role should never be absolutized. No power on earth save Christ on the cross is the Lord. With this confession the Japanese Church was given the firmest possible foundation to resist the ideology that makes the emperor into a living god. But we did not do what we should have done on this foundation: Not only did we not resist this deification, we conformed ourselves to it too naively, knowing or not knowing it to be wrong, and we yielded ourselves to the Shinto-shrine worship. We also yielded to the state's policy to unite all Christian powers as the 'United Church of Christ in Japan [Kyodan]' and finally ended up willingly supporting the militaristic policy of the state. We even abandoned the minor denominations that were persecuted because of their faith. Thus with words and deeds the church denied its confession, 'Jesus is the Lord.' We now confess that this weakness is still present in the constitution of our church and we seek the forgiveness and mercy of the Lord.

2.   When our government invaded our neighbor countries and destroyed the lives and dignity of brothers and sisters there, our church sinned with it. We did not rightly realize the sin being committed; we condoned it, supported it, and even acted as the unlawful leader of Asian churches. There were voices in criticism, but they were feeble, and there was almost no action in protest. Our church diverted its attention from the greater social evil in the world and fled into the traditional refuge of individual salvation. Our church shares responsibility for the indescribable affliction of millions of innocent people in Asia. We confess the guilt of war and seek from our heart the forgiveness of our neighbors.

3.   We also confess the sin of our church committed after the war. It was at first totally absorbed in rehabilitating itself from fatigue and breakdown, and did not grapple

sincerely with its own guilt. Then, the past was too easily submerged in the mission of a booming Christianity in the new age. When we compare ourselves with the German church which started discussing its own guilt right after the conclusion of the war, it is obvious that our sense of guilt was very frail. The church was the last to sense the pain of Asian neighbors when Japan was attaining marvelous economic restoration by exploiting the wars in Korea and Vietnam. Instead we availed ourselves of the country's prosperity and devoted ourselves to self-expansion. The Kyodan cut off the churches in Okinawa without pain when the San Francisco Treaty of Peace was concluded between Japan and the United States in 1951. It also lagged conspicuously in its effort to solve the problems of discrimination against the Burakumin (the so-called outcast groups) and in protecting the human rights of Korean residents in Japan. It was only in 1967 that theological awareness of the historical responsibility of the church finally grew enough to produce the so-called 'Confession on the Responsibility of the United Church of Christ in Japan during World War II.' Yet even this confession could not secure the consensus of the whole church. It was often met with slander and neglect, and now is in danger of being forgotten.

4.   We further realize the grave responsibility of the church toward the present and the future. Japan has now grown into one of the world's few economic superpowers, and the people are infatuated with this prosperity, the other side of which is the emergence of serious problems in education, medical and social welfare, and not least in international relations. Especially noticeable is the nation's open attempt to build up its military force, which cannot be done without the *de facto* evisceration of the people's vow of international peace as stipulated in the Constitution. The three non-nuclear principles (that once regulated the flow of nuclear weapons through Japan's territory) are already reduced to mere formalities. Our state is now lending itself to the East-West tension by taking part in the nuclear strategy of the United States. These considerations add gravity to the responsibility for peace with which the church is entrusted in the Gospel of reconciliation. Have we not been given the insight of faith to see that weapons of mass destruction are absolutely irreconcilable with God's will? At the same time are we not granted the confident hope of terminating the vicious circle of hatred and fear? The church can and must create, neither *pax americana* nor *pax sovietica,* but *pax Christi.* What is called for in this connection is, first, to perceive rightly the nature of the alarming events around us and to carry out in practice an effective common resistance. On the fifteenth of this August (WW II Memorial Day), Yasuhiro Nakasone became the first postwar prime minister who dared to pay an official visit to Yasukuni Shrine (where the souls of the soldiers of past wars are revered as quasi-deities). This is not only an unconstitutional act that infringes upon the (people's) freedom of religion, but it is a shameless attempt officially to restore the Yasukuni Shrine to a center of the state-religion that was the spiritual core of Japanese militarism (up until forty years ago). It is an outright defiance of the goodwill of all people in the world who wish peace.

It is hence a time of utmost importance for the future of Japan and of the whole earth.

Our sincere prayer at this moment is to live the life of witness to the Gospel with brothers and sisters in Christ throughout the world, and to take up sincerely the responsibility we have for generations present and yet to come.

Come Creator Spirit!

What Would Bonhoeffer Say Today to Christian Peacemakers?

G. Clarke Chapman

Bonhoeffer applied the term 'pacifist' to himself from 1932 until mid-1939;[1] but can the label be generalized to include the rest of his life? A brisk debate on that issue arose in the 1970s in the English Language Section of the International bonhoeffer Society, beginning with the superb book by Larry Rasmussen[2] and its thesis that 'Bonhoeffer's resistance activity was his Christology enacted with utter seriousness.' He concludes that the later Bonhoeffer defected from his earlier pacifist principles: 'All the twisting possible cannot make the author of *The Cost of Discipleship* a volunteer for assassinating even Adolf Hitler.'[3]

Such a shift, however, seems inconsistent with Bonhoeffer's own words from Tegel: 'I'm firmly convinced — however strange it may seem — that my life has followed a straight and unbroken course, at any rate in its outward conduct.'[4] Eberhard Bethge likewise refutes Rasmussen's view, 'as if Dietrich had moved from a conviction of non-violence to a conviction of using violence.' The violent murderer instead was Hitler, and 'the murderer had to be stopped.'[5] Bethge holds that Bonhoeffer was consistent to the end: 'I think he would have said: Of course I'm still in your terms "pacifist", even in doing this (participating in the conspiracy) and I took... all the consequences...'

Unfortunately there is a price to Bethge's defense: pacifism comes to appear a naive luxury, dependent on secure circumstances and gentlemanly enemies. It concedes that 'realism' requires unscrupulous force to be met by force. But is there some other way to defend Bonhoeffer's 'straight and unbroken course'? Yes, says Dena Davis: less 'twisting' (Rasmussen) is needed, if one takes as central Bonhoeffer's interest in Gandhi.[6] Thereby pacifism becomes more robust und flexible, encompassing the several phases of Bonhoeffer's lifelong 'Christology enacted with utter seriousness.'

Bonhoeffer first wrote of his great interest in Gandhi in 1928. Unfortunately his plans for a study leave in India were disrupted by the crises of 1934. But, says Davis, Bonhoeffer's thought continued to parallel that of Gandhi in three notable ways: 1. Both conceived of non-violent resistance as a positive, holistic force in the active pursuit of justice. Pacifism is not passivity, shunning contamination or compromise. 'To do nothing for fear of doing violence is cowardice, in Gandhi's view, an un-Christian obsession with one's own moral purity, in Bonhoeffer's.'[7] 2. Faith means being there 'for others': Bonhoeffer returned to Germany in 1939, and Gandhi reached out to the untouchables. 3. For both, voluntary suffering and a willing self-sacrifice characterize this existence for others.

Thus Davis dissents from Rasmussen by viewing Bonhoeffer's lifelong concern with peace and justice issues, shown as early as his 1930-31 contacts with black Christians in New York. Indeed, Davis claims, it is *The Cost of Discipleship* period that is the anomaly, a temporary lapse of his social activism occasioned by the narrow concerns of the church struggle. But both before and after that period Bonhoeffer saw non-violence as inseparable from active resistance in the name of justice.

This completes the summary of the U.S. debate on Bonhoeffer's 'pacifism.' I prefer the more activist term 'peacemaker', but certainly both are labels open to many interpretations. More important, as our title suggests, is what peacemakers today may learn from him!

The first step, I suggest, is to ponder anew his vision of Christocentric existence: 'All concepts of reality which do not take account of Him are abstractions...'[8] Secondly, we must study our own concrete situation, the nuclear age. And thirdly, to gain perspective, it is helpful to concentrate on that segment of Bonhoeffer's life which most nearly matches our situation.

But which period of his career to choose? Should we select 'Bonhoeffer the political resister' of the early 1940s? This, however, may support a model of the theologian as reluctant collaborator with violence, all for the sake of a higher good. Granted, for the oppressed of the Third World such a model does have relevance; indeed a number of themes from the later Bonhoeffer have become significant for liberation theology.[9]

But for us today in the industrialized First World, there is a danger in such a focus: it could slip too easily from an image of Bonhoeffer the eventual conspirator to one of Bonhoeffer the reluctant Cold Warrior. His turn to conspiracy in planning *limited* violence, namely tyrannicide inside a police state, could be mistaken for complicity in threatening *limitless* violence, the international balance of nuclear terror. The Cold War, however, is not comparable to the contained ferocity of living within Hitler's Germany. The situation of the early 1940s was not just a potential but an actual holocaust — administered efficiently and under war-time conditions. Today by contrast the evil is much more diffuse — geopolitically, ideologically, and stretching indefinitely into a future of nuclear stalemate. Yet nowadays the Hitler analogy is misused by modern Rambo patriots glamorizing heroic violence. Sadly, such jingoism may appeal to Bonhoeffer's example, even though he himself accepted the conspiracy as only a measured and prayerful response to an exceptional crisis.

So which period of his career ought to be our focus? The answer for us is, I maintain, not Bonhoeffer the political conspirator of the 1940s. Rather it should be Bonhoeffer the peacemaker of the early 1930s.

There are sobering parallels of that earlier decade to our own. In a time of neither war nor peace the clouds were gathering, punctuated by brief incursions and surrogate bloodshed. At home, democracy was undermined by social and economic unrest, racial hatred, and covert uses of power. In short, massive evil was not yet an entrenched reality against which only conspiracy could act. Instead it was an ominous possibility against which society should mobilize.

Therefore let Christian peacemakers today focus on the Bonhoeffer of 1932-34.[10] Peace, he contended, must be the concrete command of the Gospel for this hour. Not that international peace is an end in itself, but it is a means (an 'order of preservation') towards the end, namely justice and an openness to faith in Christ. The very struggle for national security is itself insecurity, mandating endless countermeasures.

There is no way to peace along the way of safety. For peace must be dared... To demand guarantees is to mistrust, and this mistrust in turn brings forth war... The hour is late... We want to give the world... a Christian word. We want to pray that this word may be given us today.[11]

The word needed was a new confessing of faith, at a time of *status confessionis*. Granted, Bonhoeffer's use of this portentous phrase concerned the Aryan clauses,[12] but anti-Semitism was merely a component of a broader alien spirit. That spirit was 'totalism,' an absolutist ideology incompatible with the Lordship of Christ. As defined by psycho-historian Robert Jay Lifton, totalism is misguided response to the decay of traditional symbols that formerly shielded humanity from death anxiety. It manipulates language in the service of genocide. It is a pseudo-scientific attempt to enforce purity from contamination, suppress dissent, and gain absolute control over life.[13] The terror of death is averted through turning it into a worship of death — which in turn is imposed on 'the Enemy.' A prime modern example of totalism, says Lifton, is fascism. No wonder that Bonhoeffer saw the supreme totalism of his day as a threat demanding no less than a renewed confession of faith, a historic moment of *status confessionis*.

But what would Bonhoeffer say today? I believe he would again denounce a totalism which endangers peace. Brushing aside the tactical, political, and moral arguments about the bomb, he would push decisively to the theological crux: an idolatry that befuddles minds and displaces Christ. Rather than fascism or even communism, today's totalism is *'nuclearism'* — which Lifton defines as 'the passionate embrace of nuclear weapons as a solution to death anxiety and a way of restoring a lost sense of immortality. Nuclearism is a secular religion, a total ideology...'[14]

The issue above all is a theological one: what (or better, who) is the final *reality*, in its wholeness and ultimacy? Elswhere I have argued that nuclearism today, a totalism spawned by the boundless effects of the bomb, is a thriving, functional religion, indeed a heresy.[15] Yet the church limits itself to piecemeal moral critiques; it has hardly come to grips with the Bomb on a theological level.

Bonhoeffer can help us, as a 'theologian of reality.'[16] He insisted the world has been restructured by the form of Jesus Christ within it, and so the Christian life is one of formation — responding to this new reality. Such a vision of 'the real' simply cannot be harmonized with that of the Cold War 'realists,' or with any totalism — whether Nazi or nuclearist.

Here then is Bonhoeffer's contribution. The peace movement is ineffective when it ignores the deeply religious fascinations and fears commanded by nuclearism. A resilient and demonic totalism can only be exorcised by a church renewed in its confession. From this theological vista we can view peace, not as a problem, but as God's command. 'We want to pray that this word may be given us today...'

NOTES

1. See Eberhard Bethge, *Dietrich Bonhoeffer: Theologian, Christian, Contemporary* (London: Collins, 1970), p. 155. For the best summary of the textual evidence on this subject, see Dale W. Brown, 'Bonhoeffer and Pacifism,' *Manchester College Bulletin of the Peace Studies Institute* 11:1 (June 1981): 32-43.

2. *Dietrich Bonhoeffer: Reality and Resistance* (Nashville: Abingdon, 1972); the quotation is on p. 15.

3. Rasmussen, p. 120; see pp. 120-124.

4. '11 April 1944,' *Letters and Papers from prison,* enlarged edition, ed. Eberhard Bethge (New York: Macmillan, 1972), p. 272.

5. Bethge, in *Newsletter* No. 12 (April 1978), International Bonhoeffer Society for Archive and Research, English Language Section, pp. 6-7.

6. 'Gandhi and Bonhoeffer,' *Manchester College Bulletin of the Peace Studies Institute* 11:1 (June 1981): 44-49.

7. Ibid., p. 46.

8. Bonhoeffer, *Ethics,* ed. Eberhard Bethge (New York: Macmillan, 1965), pp. 188, 194, 195.

9. Such themes include the critique of religion in a world come of age, cooperation with secular allies as a penultimate path to the ultimate, a compression of modern piety into prayer and righteous action, a social ontology that supports an ethic of being-for-others, a defense of human maturity against all dehumanizing dependencies and the deed of free responsibility which in extreme cases might involve complicity in violence. See G. Clarke Chapman, Jr., 'Bonhoeffer: resource for Liberation Theology,' *Union Seminary Quarterly Review* 36:4 (Summer 1981): 225-242, and Julio de Santa Ana, 'The Influence of Bonhoeffer on the Theology of Liberation,' *The Ecumenical Review* 28:2 (April 1976): 188-197.

10. See Brown, Davis, and Rasmussen, op. cit. Also see F. Burton Nelson, 'The Relationship of Jean Lasserre to Dietrich Bonhoeffer's Peace Concerns in the Struggle of the Church and Culture,' *Union Seminary Quarterly Review* 40:1-2 (1985): 71-84; Keith W. Clements, *A Patriotism for Today: Dialogue with Dietrich Bonhoeffer* (Bristol, U.K.: Bristol Baptist College, 1984), especially pp. 116-126.

11. Bonhoeffer, 'The Church and the peoples of the World,' *No Rusty Swords,* Fontana edition (London: Collins, 1970), pp. 286-287; see 'A Theological Basis for the World Alliance,' ibid., pp. 153-169; Bethge, *Dietrich Bonhoeffer*, pp. 158-160, 167.

12. See his correspondence with Barth, *No Rusty Swords* (Fontana ed.), pp. 226-228, and the declaration he and Martin Niemöller sent out, pp. 244f.

13. Lifton, *The Broken Connection: On Death and the Continuity of Life* (New York: Basic Books, Harper & Row, 1983), pp. 293-334, especially pp. 297-301.

14. Ibid., p. 369.

15. G. Clarke Chapman, *Facing the Nuclear Heresy: A Call for Reformation* (Elgin, IL: Brethren Press, 1986).

16. This is the subsitle of Andre Dumas' book, *Dietrich Bonhoeffer* (New York: Macmillan, 1971); see *Ethics*, pp. 188-213.

Acts 16:9, for 19 June, 1988, in Amsterdam

Eberhard Bethge

Last year, when Gerard Rothuizen asked me to give the sermon for this gathering, he also suggested the text:

> And a vision appeared to Paul in the night. There stood a man of Macedonia, and begged him, saying, 'Come over into Macedonia, and help us.' And after he had seen the vision, immediately we endeavored to go into Macedonia, assuredly gathering that the Lord had called us to preach the gospel unto them (Acts 16:9-10).

Because Europe is the topic of our International Bonhoeffer Conference, he proposed this verse under the theme: the first step of the Gospel into Europe.

Obviously, pointing to this as the beginning of Christian Europe might be overrating Luke's flowing narration. Yet, Luke might have had in mind an analogy which gives the verse some importance already in that first century. Indeed, in another dream story the High Priest of Jerusalem appears in the night to Alexander the Great of Macedonia and calls him the other way around: 'Come over and help us.' Alexander had in fact spared Jerusalem from destruction on his Asian campaign. Would that make Luke's narration an anti-story, such also being its intention?

This was, at any rate, a later discovery in my preparation for today's interpretation. My first thoughts after Gerard Rothuizen's call were two quite different recollections.

1

The Call of Europe

First, I recollected a breakfast in New York about twenty years ago. Maria von Wedemeyer, once Dietrich Bonhoeffer's fiancée, at that time Mrs. Weller, had invited me to their hotel to share breakfast with her and her husband. This breakfast lasted until midday. Maria and I were unable to end our sharing of the news of the family, old friends, and the recent events on the old continent. Rather late I realized how excluded Maria's husband had been from the world we both had been so absorbed in all the while. Then Mr. Weller made a remark: Is that still worthwhile? Hasn't the old continent gone, and gone out indeed? His remark troubled me. Didn't we still belong to that world — I certainly, and perhaps Maria as well? Did she after all really mean to be called to new shores? Who can stand and integrate fully that change of identity?

Dietrich Bonhoeffer, in that tricky situation of 1939, had himself been near the point of taking that final step to the new land of the U.S.A. Perhaps you remember the shaking notes of those days in the hot quadrangle at 120th Street; how he waited every day for the unequivocal call out of his daily reading of the *Herrenhuter Losungen* (Moravian daily scripture texts), 'assuredly gathering that the Lord had called him'

230

(Acts 16:10). This may have been, in concrete form, either the successful begging of Paul Lehmann — Come over and help us here in the U.S.A. — or the terribly longed for letter from Germany saying the opposite. Then, on the 20th of June he heard the definite voice. A few weeks later he boarded the boat back to Europe.

But Bonhoeffer's call had come from the opposite direction from Paul's. It was not the new shores which called him now, but the old ports: he was not setting out — so to speak — from Troas to Philippi, but from Philippi back to Troas. Returning for a moment to Paul the apostle in Acts, he listened to the call and undertook immediately to wed himself again to his lifetime task, namely, to spread the Gospel further and further to the West. That propelled him to those new shores which made his journey indeed a fateful step for us all to this day. It does not really matter much whether Paul, Luke and Silas already had in mind — by setting out for Europe — the consequences and dimensions which we today associate with their decision. For them it was probably the unknown beyond Roman civilization — forests, rocks, deserted horizons. For us it was once that continent of 'infinite riches in a little room' (as Christopher Marlow stated already four hundred years ago, in Canterbury), but at the same time, filled with infinite brutalities for us; now, it is that continent filled with its famous murderers and saviors, the Machiavellis and the Hammarskjölds, the Eichmanns and the Michael Kolbes, the Albert Schweitzers and the Stalins, the saints and bystanders and accomplices of today. And, of course, I am aware that I preach here as a German in the city of Anne Frank.

But getting back to Dietrich Bonhoeffer — the call he heard in 1939 in New York did wed him to his lifetime task which, in all its fragmentation, was fulfilled in an unprecedented fullness. The call propelled him not further to the West, but back into that old cursed Europe, albeit to unknown new shores; new shores of witnessing against the presence of those murderous new gods and idols in Europe and *for* the presence of Paul's gospel of the disgraced God on that continent, particularly in the Germany of those days. Berlin called New York, the Marienburger Allee called the Prophet's Chamber on Broadway: Come over and help us! And Bonhoeffer, after hearing the voice, 'immediately endeavoured to go. . . assuredly gathering that the Lord had called' him.

Yet he did not return as a normal missionary to the slums or to the posh quarters of Europe in its edition of the city of Berlin. He returned as someone who was prepared to pay the costly price for a terribly misused Christian message.

The content of that call was apparently saying something like this: Now, be who you are. Win your inescapable identity by crossing your special ecclesiastical and theological Bosporus, in identifying yourself with the victims of your homeland. Here in the U.S., theology alone waits for you, but not the living Christ. He waits for you in the midst of the disgraced and disfigured Jews of your homeland and in the company of your own guilt-stricken folk and friends.

2

The Text of Gland, 1932

My second reaction to Rothuizen's petition was of a different character, namely, to ask: Did Dietrich ever preach on Acts 16:9ff.? No, he did not.

But then I discovered that he had used our verse on a prominent, earlier occasion in 1932. Bishop Ammundsen of Denmark, who was to give the closing address at the Ecumenical Youth Conference of the World Alliance of Life and Work in Gland, Switzerland, was unexpectedly prevented from coming. Thus Bonhoeffer, one of the co-leaders of the gathering, was asked to substitute on the spot. Consequently we see him packing everything that concerned him in those days into his forceful speech: his critical questions, analysis, and answers about the new Christian governments in Europe (Von Papen had at that time just become the new German Chancellor) which were re-arming and heating up from the four motives of 'money, economy, the thirst for power and — so worldly — love of the fatherland' a new hunger and hate; about the ecumenical efforts of the churches which were better seen as 'funerals of the churches in Europe.' He preached that only the presence of the Cross may make the world tremble. The World Alliance should understand itself as 'the terrified, anxious Church of Christ' which calls for the presence of the Crucified, insisting that 'today there must be no more war — the cross will not have it, because war now annihilates the creation of God' (this was said before any knowledge of nuclear warfare — or did Dietrich know something through his brother Karl-Friedrich, the successful researcher of 'heavy water'?). Peace which damages righteousness and truth is not peace and the Church of Christ must protest against such peace.

It is here that the speech which began with the trumpet: 'The Church is dead', concludes with the quote from Acts 16:9ff.

> It was a turning point in world history when Paul had a vision in the night in which he saw a man of Macedonia, a European, who bade him 'come over and help us'. Paul was ready and went. The second time the call goes out to us, the Church. The second time Europe calls 'Come and help us'. Europe, the world is going to be conquered [should be conquered?] a second time by Christ. Are we ready?

'A second time' Dietrich says here. We know now how this 'second time' of 1932 created its 'third time' seven years later, and took quite another *Gestalt*, different from Gland, different from those still rather imperially formulated appeals in that beautiful Swiss village. Yet even there something is already present which does not sound like present evangelistic means and efforts to fill huge city halls.

There is already here that *Gestalt* of Christ into which one must be drawn — not the masses entertained by conversion shows, not the Christ as a shining imperial idol.

There is, as some of you may remember, a contemporary echo of Gland which shows that Bonhoeffer was already at a point at which his listeners had probably not yet arrived. The chairman of the conference, the Bishop of Ripon, had written in the *Yorkshire-Post* about that 'passionate proclamation of the Church' by the German co-chairman. He wrote in his article about Bonhoeffer's conclusion to his speech:

'Europe has to be conquered a second time by and for Christ.' But Bonhoeffer had not included 'for Christ.'

Is this an important difference? Is the result really important and discernible? I am rather sure that Bonhoeffer would not have added the 'for Christ', and that he, even here, did not speak the language of an optimistic ideology, of a 'crusade for Christ'.

Only a few years later I remember how he cautioned us in Finkenwalde against turning our attention for too long and too forcibly upon ourselves as crusaders for Christ. He argued that in so doing our strength would all too quickly fade, and we would no longer really listen and follow the call 'Are you ready?' This call was a call to follow the cross, not a crusade.

Or considers *Ethics,* in which Bonhoeffer turns our eyes not to our 'Gestaltgeben' — giving Christ our religious or pious forms of creativity — but to Christ's 'Gestaltwerden Christi mitten unter uns' — taking the form of the Crucified in our midst, or 'being drawn into the messianic suffering' which he then describes as *the* way to freedom!

This came, as you may remember, to an existential climax which he expressed in a letter written to me just a week after the failure of the plot of July 1944 — and which I rediscovered for myself only recently. There he turned my attention back again to the final stanza of the poem he had written the day after the failure: 'Come now, thou greatest of feasts on the journey to freedom... death... Freedom... dying, we now may behold thee revealed in the Lord.' In this letter of July 28, he explains once more how and why this failed conspiracy meant still, or even more so, a gain in freedom and not a loss, a new victory in the way of suffering and in this immanent death by the hangman. Bonhoeffer, in fact, referred to this impending event of a public disgracing death as a decisive step on his way to freedom 'now in the face of God himself.' And he concluded this paragraph by emphasizing that this idea was now for him and for all of his friends 'very important and very comforting.' Why this pointed evaluation — not only 'comforting', but 'very important' too?

The answer: this actual death is the final liberation from the longtime suction into being an accomplice (*Komplizentum*) to the German crime, ambiguously silent and a seeming bystander in the midst of the perpetrators, even cooperating with *Einsatzgruppen*-commanders (Nebe, Helldorf). It is a final liberation from the apparent continuous betrayal of the victims and now reveals the truth of their solidarity with them. This deception now ends with this death before the eyes of all and forever real — this death after the failure has broken the suffocating chains to pieces. Therefore, the idea of freedom through this death has, for Bonhoeffer, not only the pious meaning that going to heaven is 'very comforting', but even more the political significance of being 'very important.'

No, Bonhoeffer's existential answer in 1939 to his special call 'Come over and help us' does not have much to do with modern evangelism. And though his appeal in Gland in 1932 reveals some elements of the enthusiasm of a young ecumenist, it does not reveal an ardent, spiritual Europe-crusader, a skillful marketing officer for the gospel in old Europe, offering faith as the solution to all our problems. Bonhoeffer's question of Gland in 1932 'Are you ready?', and his much more silent approach on the new shores of old Europe — the crossing of his Bosporus in 1939 — meant self-delivery to the crossroad to freedom which made radiating the Gospel possible once more. It meant the transformation from a possible second *Gestalt* of Christ's conquest to that third conquest by Christ or by faith or by the costly grace of the Gospel.

3

What About Us?

But, what about us? Are we ready for the possible fourth conquest by Christ? Would I be better off finishing with a question mark 'Amen' and not attempting a solid exclamation point 'Amen'?

Let us first try to relieve the heavy burden which is placed upon us by the meditation on Bonhoeffer's call to cross his Bosporus. To be honest, we are not, nor would we want to become, Dietrich Bonhoeffers. Dietrich himself did not like copies! And he especially did not want to distribute unbearable duties — he wanted to expend, if possible, even more exhilarating gifts.

In fact, because he answered that call back to the damned centre of Europe in 1939, we now can enjoy those *Letters and Papers from Prison* with those 'infinite riches in that little room.' Through them he teaches us to rediscover a beautiful Europe, to experience it as sheer life again: the Art of the Fugue, Solveig's Song, the *hilaritas* of Raphael, Mozart, Walter van der Vogelweide, the Bamberg Horseman, Luther, Rubens, Hugo Wolf, Karl Barth (as he mentions them on the 9 March 1944). And I add to these: making poems, making friends, the 'good powers.' He speaks of the gifts which are *einfach irdisch* (just earthly) and rejects any poisoning of the *Mitte des Lebens* (the middle, center of life). Undiminished, those gifts build up in our souls fruits of the Gospel which shine out of the darkest period of its history. It is a foul and a bad Christian who shuts his eyes to them — and anti-Bonhoefferian as well!

At this point please permit me to insert a remark which was written to me in a recent letter by Gerard Rothuizen. It is an astonishing sign of Gerard's presence in all the misery of his cruel illness on the occasion of *his* conference – now without him. He tells me in this letter of May 25 that he had finished an article on Resurrection and the Hereafter just before the latest decline in his health, and that he called the meditation 'As Lake Geneva.' With this theme he refers to a short story which Jørgen Glenthøj had told us in *Mündige Welt* 2, page 198, namely that Dietrich, on his visit with Karl Barth in Basel in September, 1941, had spoken with his great friend about the 'Jüngste Tag' (The Day of Judgment). There Bonhoeffer asked: 'Do you believe that all things will come back? Will it then be – as Lake Geneva?' Karl Barth answered: 'Yes, like Lake Geneva.' And you may remember what the encounter with Lac Leman means for a North German, for Bonhoeffer as well as Gerard Rothuizen. Gerard continued in his letter: 'Will you please [he meant me] introduce me to Dietrich when we all enjoy there our "eschatological picnic"? Please do!'

But then, realizing those 'infinite riches', we must not use them as drugs for escaping the full participation in the existing blessed *and* cursed heritage of this continent. This is true even for our American friends who have their own ineradicable identity which I have come to know.

The call for us today asks that we cross our own Bosporus in various dimensions, in both individual and corporate forms, wherever that call reaches us. I mention just a few examples and hope that your particular call meets you not in desperate isolation but in the still promising 'communion of saints.' The call speaks to us as *citizens* of this old continent, as *church members*, as *teachers* of our continental theological framework, or as simple *believers* in 1988. There are many more levels, but some may be particularly challenging for the world of the Bonhoeffer Society. You will think it over, I am sure.

3.1 As a *citizen* I am troubled — not only by our responsibilities for disarmament and for anti-apartheid involvements, but also by that new human ability, developed in the last fifteen years, to form nature arbitrarily — and I am helpless, too, at my age. Does this ability mean hope for curing cancer or expectation of unthinkable horrors? Can our countries put on the brakes once we begin yet again on the road to self-destruction? What does it mean here when the Christian citizen hears his call: 'Come over and help us'?

3.2. As a *church member* in my tradition I am rather sure that the call means the painful exodus out of the inherited forms of our *Volkskirchen* particularly in the realm of Bonhoeffer's thought and witness: those forms in which our *Volkskirchen* have become accomplices to the re-armers or their theologians who took on the role of 'hairdressers for the theological wig of the emperor' (*Wiederkehr*); or in which our burdened and chained church governments behave as agents for ready reconciliation between the perpetrators and the victims and bystanders, without changing the status quo; those churches which make the Crucified a slaveholder who has ceased to call away believers from the false imperial gods who always make victims of others. In the context I feel that there is no more appropriate call for crossing our Bosporus than to write our own 'Kairos-documents' and act as our South African brothers and sisters, who have given us a great example.

3.3. As *teachers* of European Reformation theology, which means teachers of that always ready *sola gratia,* we must still listen to Bonhoeffer, who saw the point and is still far ahead of us, when he sees the poisoning separation of that central notion — grace alone — from the first commandment. Such a separation means that one can have grace without clearly renouncing other gods next to the one liberating God of Israel — Greek gods, Teutonic gods, American gods, Marxist and capitalist gods, even an imperial Christ-god. But *sola gratia* is the distinctive grace of a distinctive being, namely the God of Israel, to whom we belong through Jesus Christ. In Gland, Bonhoeffer articulated the realm of grace as obtainable in that 'terrified, anxious Church of the Crucified' and twelve years later, in Tegel-prison, as true and real in the crowd of the 'man for others'. This grace of that God is surely not the ever-ready guarantor of the status quo of Europe. It is still the judgement of the Europeans who do not stop to destroy, and it is still the comforter of those who still are destroyed while they hear sermons of the sola gratia for all.

3.4.   Finally as *believers* in present Europe. What are we called for? Are we called to spread the shallowness of optimism? Or called for the contagious pessimism which gives special joy to the Devil? The Devil has preferences for skeptical prophets and waits for turning his believers into cynics. I am inclined to still agree with Martin Luther who said that the Gospel, brought from Troas to Philippi is never fading away as such, but that it might fade away from our place as the pelting rain (Platzregen); there it was, but now it has gone, is past, over, given to other places and nations. Today I hear Irving Greenberg, the New York rabbi: 'In the light of the Holocaust, classical Christianity dies to be reborn to new life: or it lives unaffected to die to God and man' (Fleischner, *Auschwitz*, p. 36).

That means we may have to endure the truth of both: God's 'NO' and God's 'YES' in Christ. The No to our European crimes in history and today, its deathridden ways. The Yes to this Europe, still a part of his creation and conquered a second, a third, or even a fourth time by Christ. Before giving it up Bonhoeffer gave up himself for it. And he understood God's Yes *in* the No, and his No *in* the Yes and even making the Yes more contagious then the No!

On 21 September 1941, only a few days before he discovered the beginning of the final deportations taking place in Berlin (and reported this immediatley to some responsible generals), when he was still in Switzerland, he wrote to Erwin Sutz for his wedding:

> Now in the midst of demolition of the things – one wants to build up: in the midst of living just from hour to hour, from day to day – a future; in the midst of being driven out from the earth – a piece of earth; in the midst of common misery – a piece of happiness.
> And it is the overwhelming fact that God says Yes to such a strange desire; that – whilst usually it should be the other way round – God agrees here in our will (*Gesammelte Schriften* I, 50).

Additional Papers

The following 'papers' given at the Amsterdam Conference are available from the authors.

Jørgen Glenthøj, Dietrich Bonhoeffer and the Dassel Conference
Bernhard Marx, Dialogue as an Ethical Principle (Dialog als ethisches Prinzip)
Larry Rasmussen, Human Power and Divine Presence in a New Era — A Comparison of Dietrich Bonhoeffer and Irving Greenberg
Campbell Stamp, Bonhoeffer's Spirit-Christology
Charles Sensel, Who Are Wesley and Bonhoeffer Beyond 1984?
Michael Lapsley, Dietrich Bonhoeffer and the Struggle for Liberation in Southern Africa
Eleanor Neel, Bonhoeffer's Ethics and the Death Penalty in the USA
Charles Marsh Jr., A Quiet Revolution: Bonhoeffer's Reading of Heidegger
Irene Meijer, Bonhoeffer's View on the Position of Male and Female in Society
Ruth Zerner, Bonhoeffer's Godchildren: The Legacy of Dietrich Bonhoeffer
J. Patrick Kelley, Covenant and Ethics: Bonhoeffer and Political Rights in the Early Years of the Third Reich
James Burtness, Report on *Shaping the Future: The Ethics of Dietrich Bonhoeffer*
Werner Koch, The Acceptance of Guilt by Dietrich Bonhoeffer

Contributors

EBERHARD BETHGE, D.D., student, close friend and interpreter of the life and work of Dietrich Bonhoeffer, is the author of numerous essays and monographs, including *Dietrich Bonhoeffer: Man of Vision, Man of Courage,* the definitive Bonhoeffer biography, the editor of several volumes of the *Gesammelte Schriften,* a collaborator on the new *Dietrich Bonhoeffer Werke* and President of the International Bonhoeffer Society for Archive and Research. Address: Flachsgraben 9/D-5307 Wachtberg-Villiprott/B.R.D.

RENATE BETHGE (NÉE SCHLEICHER), co-editor with her husband, Eberhard, and co-editor of Bonhoeffer's *Fiction from Prison,* in the new D.B.-Werke, is the daughter of Ursula Bonhoeffer and Dietrich Bonhoeffer's fellow resister, Rüdiger Schleicher. Mrs. Bethge is an active lecturer as a living witness to the Hitler period and the Christian German experience in the face of the Holocaust. Address: Flachsgraben 9/D-5307 Wachtberg-Villiprott/B.R.D.

ALLAN A. BOESAK, (Cape Town), was President of the World Alliance of Reformed Churches and an active voice and leader in the struggle of the churches of Southern Africa against the institution and ideology of *apartheid.* Dr. Boesak studied at Kampen with Gerard Rothuizen and earned his doctorate with a dissertation on the theme, *Farewell to Innocence. A Social-Ethical Study on Black Theology and Black Power* (1976). Address: Hoekstraat 6/Glenhaven/Belleville Suid/7530 South Africa.

JAMES H. BURTNESS, TH.D. (Princeton Theological Seminary), a minister of the Evangelical Lutheran Church in America, did doctoral work in New Testament studies. He served as a parish pastor in Oregon (U.S.A.) and as Visiting Professor of New Testament, Madras Theological Seminary (India). Dr. Burtness is currently Professor of Systematic Theology and Ethics at Luther-Northwestern Theological Seminary in St. Paul, Minnesota (U.S.A.) and has served on the IBS English Language Section Board. Areas of interest in addition to Bonhoeffer studies include medical ethics and ethical methodology. Address: Luther-Northwestern Theological Seminary/248·1 Como Avenue S.W./Saint Paul/ MN 55108/ U.S.A.

GUY C. CARTER, PH.D. (Marquette University, Milwaukee), is a minister of the Evangelical Lutheran Church in America and is currently serving as an exchange pastor in the Evangelical Lutheran Church of Hannover, F.R.G.. Dr. Carter serves on the Board of the IBS English Language Section and since June 1988 as IBS General Secretary. His doctoral dissertation was written on the theme, *Confession at Bethel, August 1933 — Enduring Witness: The Formation, Revision and Significance of the*

First Full Theological Confession of the Evangelical Church Struggle in Nazi Germany (1987). Areas of interest include Bonhoeffer studies, German Church Struggle research and American religious history. Dr. Carter served as scientific Secretary and Supervisor for the 5th International Bonhoeffer Society Conference. Address: Heinrichstrasse 13/D-3250 Hameln/ B.R.D.

G. CLARKE CHAPMAN, PH.D. (Boston University), teaches in theology, culture and social ethics at Moravian College, Bethlehem, Pennsylvania (U.S.A.). Active in the peace movement, Dr. Chapman chairs the Interfaith Peace Resource Center. He has published articles on Bonhoeffer's relevance to contemporary issues such as the theologians of hope and liberation and is author of *Facing the Nuclear Heresy: A Call for Reformation* (1986). Dr. Chapman has co-chaired the Liberation Theology Working Group of the American Academy of Religion since the group's organization in 1974. Address: Moravian College/Bethlehem/PA 18018/ U.S.A.

KEITH W. CLEMENTS, author of *A Patriotism for Today. Dialogue with Dietrich Bonhoeffer* (1986), teaches at Bristol Baptist College, an affiliated college of Bristol University (United Kingdom). Address: Bristol Baptist College/Woodland Road/ Bristol/BS8 IUN England.

JOHN W. DE GRUCHY, D.TH., is Professor of Christian Studies at the University of Cape Town (South Africa). He has published widely on Christianity and the Church in South Africa, including studies on Dietrich Bonhoeffer. Dr. de Gruchy is general editor of the series *The Making of Modern Theology*, and editor of the *Journal of Theology for South Africa*. Address: Dept. of Religious Studies/University of Cape Town/Private Bag/Rondebosch 7700 South Africa.

FRITS DE LANGE, Dr. theol. (Theological Seminary of the Reformed Church, Kampen), served for four years as scientific assistant at Kampen and for the past three years as pastor of the Dutch Reformed Church of Paris. Dr. de Lange's 1985 doctoral dissertation, *Grond onder de voeten: Burgerlijkheid bij Dietrich Bonhoeffer*, has been published in summary form as *Een burger op zijn best: Dietrich Bonhoeffer* (1986). De Lange continues to investigate the social and cultural milieu of the Bonhoeffer family as related to prominent themes in Bonhoefferian theology such as 'wordly Christianity.' Address: 24, Rue Berlioz/F-92330 Sceaux/ France

ERNST FEIL, Dr. theol. (University of Münster), is professor in the Faculty of Catholic Theology, University of Munich, and is author of *Die Theologie Dietrich Bonhoeffers. Hermeneutik-Christologie-Weltverständnis* (4d ed. 1991; English translation by Martin Rumscheidt, 1985), Religio. Die Geschichte eines neuzeitlichen Grundbegriffs vom Frühchristentum bis zur Reformation (1986), Antithetik neuzeitlicher Vernunft. 'Autonomie - Heteronomie' und 'rational - irrational' (1987). He is editor of *Verspieltes Erbe? Dietrich Bonhoeffer und der deutsche Nachkriegsprotestantismus*, Internationales Bonhoeffer Forum, No. 2 (1979) and *Konsequenzen. Dietrich Bon-*

hoeffers Kirchenverständnis heute, Internationales Bonhoeffer Forum, No. 3 (1979, with Ilse Tödt). Professor Feil is co-editor of *Diskussion zur 'Theologie der Revolution'* (2d ed. 1970, with R. Weth), *Gesellschaft und Theologie* (1970-79), *Internationales Bonhoeffer Forum* (1976 -) and *Dietrich Bonhoeffer Werke* (1983 -), and has authored numerous articles in the areas of theology and philosophy. Address: Grubenweg 13/D-7031 Gilching/B.R.D..

ALBERT H. FRIEDLANDER, PH.D. (Columbia University, New York), is Rabbi of Westminster Synagogue, London, and Dean and Senior Lecturer in History and Theology at Leo Baeck College, London. A songwriter, lyricist and librettist, Dr. Friedlander's publications in religious history and theology include *Leo Baeck: Teacher of Theresienstadt* (1968), *Never Trust a God over 30: Religion on the Campus* (ed., 1968), Leo Baeck's *This People Israels* (trans., and ed., 1968), *Out of the Whirlwind: Literature of the Holocaust* (1969), *Meir Gertner: An Anthology* (ed., 1978), *Existenz nach Auschwitz* (1980), George Salzberger's *Leben und Werke* (ed., 1982), *The Five Scrolls* (ed., 1985 with H. Bronstein), *Versöhnung mit der Geschichte* (1985 with Richard von Weizsäcker and Helmut Kohl), *Jüdische Heilige* (in *Nahe der Nabe des Rades,* with Kämpchen and Sartory, 1985) and *The Death Camps and Theology* (1985). Address: Westminster Synagogue/Kent House/Rutland Gardens/ Knightsbridge/London/SW7 IBX England.

JØRGEN GLENTHØJ, Lic. theol., a minister of the Evangelical Lutheran Church of Denmark, in which he serves as a parish pastor in Jutland, has rendered indispensable assistance to Bonhoeffer studies through his documentary detective work published in the series, *Die Mündige Welt,* and in numerous monographs and periodical articles. Address: Borum Byvej 4/Borum/8471 Sabro/Denmark.

JOHN D. GODSEY is emeritus Professor of Systematic Theology at Wesley Theological Seminary, Washington, D.C. (U.S.A.). Professor Godsey is a pioneer in Anglo-American Bonhoeffer studies, author of the first English-language book in the field, *The Theology of Dietrich Bonhoeffer* (1960), co-founder of the IBS Language Section, and editor of the English Language Section Newsletter. Address: Wesley Theological Seminary/4500 Massachusetts Ave. NW/Washington/DC 20016/ U.S.A..

CLIFFORD J. GREEN, PH.D. (Union Theological Seminary, New York), President of the IBS English Language Section, has taught theology at Wellesley College and Goucher College. Since 1981, Dr. Green has served as Professor of Theology and Ethics and as Director of the Public Policy Center at Hartford Seminary, Hartford, Connecticut, U.S.A. His published doctoral dissertation, *Bonhoeffer: The Sociality of Christ and Humanity* (1972), and more recent contributions elucidate the relation between Bonhoeffer's Christology and soteriology and Bonhofferian social ethics. Professor Green is an editor of *Dietrich Bonhoeffer Werke* and a member of the editorial committee of the proposed *Dietrich Bonhoeffer's Works.* Address: Hartford Seminary/77 Sherman Street/Hartford/CT 06105/ U.S.A.

JAMES PATRICK KELLEY, PH.D. (Yale University), serves as Treasurer of the IBS English Language Section and as Managing Editor of the Section's newsletter. Dr. Kelley is Professor of Religious Studies at Lynchburg College, Lynchburg, Virginia (U.S.A.). In his doctoral dissertation, *Revelation and the Secular in the Theology of Dietrich Bonhoeffer* (1980), Professor Kelley traces the development and continuity in Bonhoeffer's thought and praxis as it relates to a Christian piety lived out solidly in the world and through secular engagement. Kelley is the redactor of an audio-visual documentary collection of memoirs of living witnesses and participants in the Church Struggle and anti-Nazi resistance. Address: Dept. of Religious Studies/Lynchburg College/Lynchburg/VA 24501/ U.S.A.

WERNER KOCH, Dr. theol., in 1935 was one of the students studying with Bonhoeffer in Finkenwalde. Later a 'foreign correspondent' for the Confessing Church, Dr. Koch was imprisoned in Sachsenhausen. Since the war, a lecturer on the Church Struggle and on political resistance, he and has been involved in the international peace movement. In 1972 he received the doctor's degree in Paris. Publications include *Kirche und Staat im Dritten Reich* (1971); *Sollen wir K. weiter beobachten? Ein Leben in Widerstand* (1982). Address: Hauptstrasse 33/D-4459 Emlichheim/ B.R.D.

MARTIN KUSKE, Dr. theol. (University of Rostock), is Secretary of the Bonhoeffer-Kommitee beim Bund der Evangelischen Kirchen in der D.D.R. (IBS G.D.R. Section) and was organizer of the 4th International Bonhoeffer Society Conference held at Hirschluch near Storkow, G.D.R., in June of 1984. Dr. Kuske has served as Director of Studies of the Preachers' Seminary, Gnadau, G.D.R., and is currently a parish pastor of the Evangelical Lutheran Church of Mecklenburg in Teterow, G.D.R. He is the author of *Das Alte Testament als Buch von Christus, Dietrich Bonhoeffers Wertung und Auslegung des Alten Testamtents* (1970); published in English translation as *The Old Testament as the Book of Christ, An Appraisal of Bonhoeffer's Interpretation* (1976), and *Weltliches Christsein, Dietrich Bonhoeffers Vision nimmt Gestalt an* (1984). Address: Schulzstrasse 2/DDR-2050 Teterow/ D.D.R.

MICHAEL LAPSLEY is an Anglican missionary priest currently serving the Lutheran World Federation's Program on Church and Liberation through the Zimbabwe National Committee of the LWF. Father Lapsley, a member of the African National Congress, was forced to leave South Africa for Lesotho following the Soweto Uprising of June 1976. As part of the exiled ANC community in Lesotho from 1976 to 1983, Father Lapsley reexamined his own attitude toward nonviolent and violent resistance to the *apartheid* regime of South Africa. It is out of that experience and his present work that he sustains theological reflection and dialogue with the work and witness of Dietrich Bonhoeffer as related to the need for concrete churchly and political praxis on Southern Africa today. Address: Box UA 541/Union Ave./Harare/ Zimbabwe.

JÁN LIGUŠ, Dr. theol., University Pastor and member of the Comenius Faculty, Prague (C.S.S.R.). is Secretary of the IBS Czechoslovak Section. Address: ul. Vrazova 4/ČSSR-150 00 Praha 5/Č.S.S.R.

ROBIN W. LOVIN, PH.D. (Harvard University), is Associate Professor of Ethics and Society at the Divinity School of the University of Chicago and was a John Simon Guggenheim Memorial Fellow in 1987-88. Author of *Christian Faith and Public Choices: The Social Ethics of Barth, Brunner, and Bonhoeffer,* Professor Lovin's research centers on religion and political thought. A member of the IBS English Language Section Board, Lovin heads the Bonhoeffer's Works Editorial Board for the proposed translation of *Dietrich Bonhoeffer Werke*. Address: Univ. of Chicago Divinity School/Swift Hall/Chicago/IL 606371 U.S.A.

CHARLES R. MARSH, JR., PH.D. (University of Virginia), holds degrees from Gordon College, Wenham, Massachusetts, U.S.A. (B.A.), and Harvard University (M.T.S.). Mr. Marsh recently completed a dissertation on early philosophical influences on Dietrich Bonhoeffer. Address: Loyola College/Baltimore, MD 2120/U.S.A.

BERNHARD MARX is a physicist in the Academy of Building in Berlin, G.D.R. Mr. Marx is a member of the working group, 'Theology and Natural Science' in the Theological Study Section of the League of Evangelical Churches in the G.D.R. In the past, Marx has studied Bonhoeffer's understanding of reality and the understanding of the relation between humanity and world according to Bonhoeffer and Buber. Address: Bruno-Leuschner-Strasse 56/DDR-1140 Berlin/ D.D.R.

A.A. IRENE MEIJER is a pastor of the Dutch Reformed Church and has been a member of the IBS Dutch Section since its organization in 1977 and currently serves as Section Secretary. In addition to her interest in the relation between Bonhoeffer's theology and the liberation of women, Pastor Meijer is interested in investigating the role and significance of music in Bonhoeffer's life and work. Address: Petruslaan 6/6564 AK H. Landstichting/ Nederland.

RAYMOND MENGUS, M.A. (political science, University of Strasbourg), (philosophy, Sorbonne), D.D. (Strasbourg) is a Catholic priest and Professor of Theological Ethics at the University of Strasbourg (France). Professor Mengus is author of *Théorie et Pratique chez Dietrich Bonhoeffer (1978)* and *Wirkungen. Gespräche über Dietrich Bonhoeffer* (1978). Address: 4, Rue du Jaubourg de Pierre/F-67000 Strasbourg/ France.

HIROSHI MURAKAMI, M.DIV. (Tokyo Union Theological Seminary), served two congregations in Japan and thereafter studied Christian Ethics at Berlin, Wuppertal and Bonn. From 1974 to 1978 Professor Murakami was Secretary for Studies of the Association of Churches and Missions in South-Western Germany. Since 1978, Professor Murakami has taught at Tokyo Christian Women's University. Address: 639 Ichinomiya/Tama-shi/Tokyo 206/ Nippon.

ELEANOR NEEL, M.M. (American Conservatory of Music, Chicago), studied at McCormick Theological Seminary, Chicago, U.S.A., and has served as a professional member of the Chicago Symphony Orchestra Chorus, as soloist for the Chicago Symphony and as staff soloist for a number of churches including the Rockefeller Chapel of the University of Chicago. In addition to her work in church music, Mrs. Neel is Regional Membership Co-ordinator of Amnesty International for the States of Arkansas and Oklahoma, U.S.A. She is a member of the IBS English Language Section. Theological interests include application of the Bonhoefferian themes of worldly Christianity to the struggle for justice of movements and organizations such as Amnesty International. Address: 735 Crest Drive/Fayetteville/AR 72701/ U.S.A.

WILLIAM J. PECK, PH.D., is Bowman Gray Associate Professor of Religion at the University of North Carolina, Chapel Hill, North Carolina, U.S.A. Professor Peck serves on the Board of the IBS English Language Section which he also serves as a member of the Section's Publications Committee. Interests and areas of research include Bonhoeffer's reading and use of Hegel and Nietzsche. Address: Religion Dept./University of North Carolina/Chapel Hill/NC 27514/ U.S.A.

GABRIELE PHIELER is a Lutheran parish pastor in the G.D.R. where she is responsible for three congregations. A participant in the 4th International Bonhoeffer Society Conference held at Hirschluch bei Storkow, G.D.R., in 1984, Pastor Phieler studies Bonhoeffer's theology especially in the context of pastoral care and the theology of hope Bonhoeffer offers within the milieu of Christianity in the G.D.R. and Eastern Europe. Address: August-Bebel-Strasse 46/DDR-6706 Unterwellenborn/ D.D.R.

POULOSE MAR POULOSE, TH.D. (Graduate Theological Union, Berkeley), is the Bishop of the (Nestorian) Church of the East in India. Bishop Poulose's graduate studies in the area of systematic and philosophical theology culminated in a doctoral dissertation on the theme, 'A Bonhoefferian Corrective of Karl Marx's Critique of Religion.' Bishop Poulose currently serves as Chair of the World Student Christian Federation based in Geneva. Address: Metropolitan House/Drichur 67001/Kerala/ India.

LARRY L. RASMUSSEN, PH.D. (Union Theological Seminary, New York), taught in the Department of Religion, St. Olaf College, Northfield, Minnesota (U.S.A.), served as Professor of Christian Social Ethics at Wesley Theological Seminary, Washington, D.C. (U.S.A.) and is currently Reinhold Niebuhr Professor of Social Ethics at Union Theological Seminary, New York. Dr. Rasmussen has served on the IBS Language Section Board. Address: Union Theologic Seminary/3041 Broadway at Reinhold Niebuhr Place/New York/NY 10027.

EDWIN H. ROBERTSON, M.A. (theol., Oxford University), B.Sc. (physics, London University), is a writer, broadcaster and Baptist minister, with present pastoral charge in Hamstead, London. Translator of Bonhoeffer's *Gesammelte Schriften* in selection into four volumes, editor and presiding translator of Eberhard Bethge's biography, *Dietrich Bonhoeffer*, author of several books about Bonhoeffer's theology, including *The Shame and the Sacrifice* (1987), he has just completed writing the book for which

Bonhoeffer provided the 'outline.' Address: 33 Briarsdale Gardens/Hampstead/London/NW3 England.

GERARD ROTHUIZEN, Dr. theol., in whose memory this volume is dedicated, was Professor of Encyclopedia and Ethics at the Theological Seminary of the Reformed Churches of the Netherlands, Kampen. Author of *Aristocratisch Christendom* (1969), a study of Bonhoeffer's idea of the *disciplina arcani* and how this was manifested in Bonhoeffer's life, *Wat is theologie? Bonhoeffers laatste woord tot zijn studenten* (1970), a study of Bonhoeffer's approach to the discipline of theology, and *Een spaak in het wiel: Dietrich Bonhoeffer over de vrede* (1985), an investigation of Bonhoeffer's resistance activity for the sake of peace. Professor Rothuizen formulated the general theme of this 5th International Bonhoeffer Society Conference on *Bonhoeffer's Ethics and Europe*.

CHARLES WERNER SENSEL, an ordained minister of the United Methodist Church, holds degrees from Kentucky Wesleyan College (A.B. cum laude) and Garrett-Evangelical Theological Seminary (B.D.), with continuing education at the Chicago Ecumenical Institute. Currently serving First United Methodist Church in Chillicothe, Illinois (U.S.A.), Pastor Sensel is exploring methods and uses of non-religious language at the local and denominational levels. Address: First United Methodist Church/1023 N. Sixth Street/Chillicothe/IL 6.1523/ U.S.A.

CAMPBELL STAMP, B.A., former insurance broker and city magistrate, was ordained an Anglican priest and served as the first City Centre Chaplain, Newcastle-upon Tyne, England, 1976-1981. Father Stamp's paper for this conference was based on his thesis, *'Christology in the Later Thought of Dietrich Bonhoeffer.'* Address: 100 Osborne Road/Newcastle-upon-Tyne/ NEZ 2TD England.

HEINZ EDUARD TÖDT, Dr. theol., wrote his doctoral dissertation on the theme, 'The Son of Man in the Synoptic Tradition,' and is emeritus Professor of Systematic Theology and Ethics at the University of Heidelberg. A member of FEST (Forschungsstätte der Evangelischen Studiengemeinschaft / Protestant Institute for Interdisciplinary Research), Professor Tödt is co-director of the 'Bonhoeffer-Dohnanyi Project' at the University of Heidelberg with Dr. theol. Ernst Albert Scharffenorth. Professor Tödt's fields of research include the German Church Struggle, the persecution of the Jews, the anti-Nazi resistance, human rights, history of church and theology. Professor Tödt is chair of the editorial committee of *Dietrich Bonhoeffer Werke*. His latest publication is entitled *Perspektiven theologischer Ethik* (1988). Address: Schlosswolfsbrunnenweg 20/D-6900 Heidelberg/ F.R.G.

ILSE TÖDT (NÉE LOGES), PH.D. (University of Göttingen), wrote her doctoral dissertation on the theme, *North American Woodland Indians and the Moravian Mission*. A member of FEST, Dr. Tödt has contributed to several theological interdisciplinary publications. She is co-editor of *Schöpfung und Fall*, *Nachfolge* and *Ethik* in *Dietrich*

Bonhoeffer Werke, and of Ferenc Lehel's notes taken on Bonhoeffer's seminar on Hegel's philosophy of religion, *Dietrich Bonhoeffers Hegel-Seminar 1933, nach den Aufzeichnungen von Ferenc Lehel* (1988). Address: Schlosswolfsbrunnenweg 20/ D-6900 Heidelberg/ B.R.D.

RENÉ VAN EYDEN, Dr. theol., is Lecturer in Systematic and Practical Theology at the Catholic Theological University Utrecht (Netherlands), where he is in charge of women's studies. He has written articles on the life and theology of Dietrich Bonhoeffer and in the field of theological women's studies. Special interests include Bonhoeffer's theme 'religionless Christianity.' Dr. van Eyden serves on the board of the IBS Dutch Section. Address: Laan van Vollenhove 2263/3706 HB Zeist/ Nederland.

HANS-DIRK VAN HOOGSTRATEN, Dr. theol., Protestant member of the Faculty of Catholic Theology, University of Nijmegen (Netherlands) in which he serves as Professor of Social Ethics, is Chair of the IBS Dutch Section. Professor van Hoogstraten's doctoral dissertation, *Interpretatie. Een onderzoek naar de veranderingen in het denken van Dietrich Bonhoeffer en naar de consequenties daarvan voor de vertolking van de Bijbel*, is an investigation of Bonhoeffer's Biblical hermeneutics. In his monograph *Het Gevangen Denken* (1986) he elaborates Bonhoeffer's program of non-religious interpretation of biblical and theological concepts. Address: Berg en Dalseweg 126/6522 BX Nijmegen/ Nederland.

CHARLES C. WEST, PH.D. (Yale University), is Stephen Colwell Professor of Christian Ethics at Princeton Theological Seminary, New Jersey (U.S.A.). He has served as Associate Director of the Ecumenical Institute (Bossey) of the World Council of Churches and as an American fraternal worker with the Evangelical Church in Berlin. Professor West has specialized in Marxist-Christian relations. In the 1950s, he was one of the early English-language interpreters of Bonhoeffer through articles and his book, *Communism and the Theologians*. Professor West has served on the IBS English Language Section Board. Address: Princeton Theological Seminary/C.N. 721/Princeton/NJ 07542/ U.S.A.

JURJEN WIERSMA, Dr. theol. (University of Amsterdam), studied theology at Amsterdam, at the Chicago Theological Seminary and at the Divinity School of the University of Chicago (U.S.A.). Professor of Ethics and Philosophy at the Divinity School of Protestant Theology in Brussels (Belgium). Areas of interest concern 'Europe 1992' as an ethico-theological challenge, Polemology and theological journalism. A member of the IBS Dutch Section, Professor Wiersma served as Special Secretary for the 5th International Bonhoeffer Society Conference. Author of *Inclusief Handelen, met Bonhoeffer en Gandhi op weg naar sociale verdediging* (1988). Address: Universitaire Faculteit voor Protestantse Godgeleerdheid/Bollandistenstraat 40/1040 Brussel/ Belgie.

RUTH ZERNER, PH.D. is Professor of History in the Herbert H. Lehman College, City University of New York (U.S.A.). Professor Zerner has published articles on Bonhoeffer and the Jews and Bonhoeffer's understanding of the state and history. She has served on the IBS English Language Section Board. Address: 3333 Henry Hudson Parkway/20 a/Bronx/NY 10463/ U.S.A.